SPURGEON COMMENTARY

SONG OF SOLOMON & JONAH

"Charles Haddon Spurgeon is aptly titled the 'Prince of Preachers.' He remains one of the greatest and most influential communicators of the word of God in history. To see his thoughts on a particular text during my sermon preparation is both immensely valuable and a profound privilege. I utilize the Spurgeon Commentary series every time I tackle a passage that Spurgeon has covered. Pastors and aspiring preachers, small group leaders and Sunday school teachers, anyone seeking to deepen their faith and grow in their intimacy with the Lord—use this gift."

R. G. COLPITTS,
lead pastor, Swift Creek Baptist Church,
Colonial Heights, Virginia

"The Spurgeon Commentary series helps you swim through the vast sea of Spurgeon's sermons by compiling and organizing his brilliant sermons into a commentary. I hope more preachers, teachers, and students of God's word will read and reap from the spiritual treasures overflowing in these Spurgeon commentaries. If you want more Christ-exalting, joy-inducing, text-illuminating comments on the Scriptures—stock up on Spurgeon."

J. A. MEDDERS,
author and preacher of Christ

"I am thrilled with the Spurgeon Commentary series by Lexham Press. The late Charles Spurgeon was perhaps one of the finest nineteenth-century preachers of the biblical text and his insights are pure gold. Elliot Ritzema has done a service to the church in compiling the best of what Spurgeon has to offer today's student and expositor."

NATE PICKOWICZ,
teaching pastor, Harvest Bible Church,
Gilmanton Iron Works, New Hampshire;
author of *How to Eat Your Bible*

SPURGEON COMMENTARY

SONG OF SOLOMON & JONAH

Charles H. Spurgeon

Elliot Ritzema & Lynsey M. Stepan

Editors

LEXHAM PRESS

Spurgeon Commentary: Song of Solomon and Jonah

Lexham Press, 1313 Bay St., Bellingham, WA 98225
LexhamPress.com

Print ISBN 9781683598923
Library of Congress Control Number 2024949393

First edition published 2026 as individual digital Logos editions and as collected print volume.

Lexham Editorial: Elliot Ritzema, Lynsey M. Stepan, Katrina Smith, Mandi Newell, Abigail Stocker, Samuel Leon
Cover Design: Joshua Hunt
Typesetting Design: ProjectLuz.com

25 26 27 28 29 30 31 / US / 12 11 10 9 8 7 6 5 4 3 2 1

If I must prefer one book above another, I would prefer some books of the Bible for doctrine, some for experience, some for example, some for teaching, but let me prefer this book above all others for fellowship and communion. When the Christian is nearest to heaven, this is the book he takes with him. There are times when he would leave even the Psalms behind, when standing on the borders of Canaan, when he is in the land of Beulah, and he is just crossing the stream, and can almost see his Beloved through the rifts of the storm-cloud, then it is he can begin to sing Solomon's Song.

—Charles Spurgeon, "Christ's Estimate of His People"

One of the most powerful preachers who ever lived was the prophet Jonah, and I believe that Jonah learned to preach by going, in the whale's belly, to the bottom of the Mediterranean. That voyage was better than a university education for him, and he became a good sound Calvinist before he was cast up again upon the land. He said, "Salvation is of the Lord," before the Lord told the fish to give him up, and I have no doubt that he often preached that doctrine afterwards; and if some preachers whom I know, instead of having lessons in elocution, were sent for a little while down into the depths of soul-despair, if they were tried, and plagued, and vexed, and chastened every morning, they would learn a way of speaking which would reach the people's hearts far better than any that can be learned by human teaching.

—Charles Spurgeon, "Gratitude for Great Deliverances"

Contents

Foreword

Charles Haddon Spurgeon (1834–1892) was known in his day as the Prince of Preachers, and his preaching remains legendary among evangelicals today. But how was Spurgeon as an expositor of Scripture? Modern readers have sometimes wondered. Perhaps in reading one of his devotional works or in examining his "road to Christ" in a sermon, some have found Spurgeon too loose in his handling of Scripture. For these careful exegetes, their conclusion might be that he should be admired more as a homiletician than a Bible teacher. Can Spurgeon be a faithful guide for us as an expositor of Scripture?

Indeed, every preacher should be open to critique, and Spurgeon is no different. We should not be surprised to find areas of improvement for any one of his sermons. At the same time, my contention is that Spurgeon had an unwavering commitment to the faithful exposition of Scripture. This can be seen in three commitments he held: a commitment to study, accurate exposition, and preaching Christ.

1: A COMMITMENT TO STUDY

Spurgeon was adamant about the importance of study in the ministry. Speaking to his students, he warned them against those who relied on oratory skills to the exclusion of study. Some denominations, like the Quakers or Plymouth Brethren, would take pride in their pastors not preparing sermons and receiving a word directly from the Spirit. But Spurgeon believed that "churches are not to be held together except by an instructive ministry; a mere filling up of time with oratory will not suffice."[1] The only alternative, then, was for the preacher to be committed to the work of study. Spurgeon's ministry was steeped in his study of God's word, works of theology, biblical commentaries, devotional writings, edifying sermons, religious poetry and hymns, and much more.[2]

To be sure, this commitment to study will look different for every pastor. Spurgeon would have said that his sermon preparation was constant. Everywhere he went, he was always thinking about his sermons, meditating on Scripture, reading books, looking for sermon illustrations, and mulling over sermon outlines ("skeletons," he called them). But more specifically, Spurgeon's sermon preparation formally began on Saturday evenings, probably around 6 p.m., and it could run late into the night. During this time, he would select a sermon text (after much prayer) and devote most of his time to personal, intense study of each text. Only after that personal study would he consult other sources. He would lay out commentaries and sermon volumes from his favorite preachers and move among his books, gathering insights like a bee among flowers. All this prayer and study would culminate in a half-sheet outline he would bring into the pulpit. Spurgeon's notes were sparse, but they represented a life devoted to study. As he would say to his students, "All sermons ought to be well considered and prepared by the preacher; and, as much as possible, every minister should, with much prayer for heavenly guidance, enter fully into his subject, exert all his mental faculties in original thinking, and gather together all the information within his reach."[3]

More evidence for Spurgeon's laborious study can be found in his writings. In *The Treasury of David*, a commentary on the Psalms, Spurgeon not only provides a robust commentary on all 150 psalms, but he shares his collection of all the best quotes that he could find from what others have written about the Psalms. These quotes show

---

1. C. H. Spurgeon, *Lectures to My Students: A Selection from Addresses Delivered to the Students of the Pastors' College, Metropolitan Tabernacle*, First Series (London: Passmore & Alabaster, 1875), 151.
2. This commitment can be seen in his pastoral library, which remains today at The Spurgeon Library on the campus of Midwestern Baptist Theological Seminary in Kansas City, MO.
3. Spurgeon, *Lectures*, 152.

Spurgeon's reading to range far and wide from every theological tradition across the centuries of church history. It truly is remarkable. The other work highlighting Spurgeon's commitment to study is *Commenting and Commentaries*. In it, Spurgeon provides brief, personal comments on the value and usefulness of 1,437 commentaries for every book of the Bible. Many scholars and preachers, both Victorian and modern, have remarked on how accurate and insightful Spurgeon was in his comments. He was a preacher committed to the diligent study of God's word.

2: A COMMITMENT TO ACCURATE EXPOSITION

Additionally, Spurgeon believed in the importance of faithful exposition. As creative and original a preacher as he was, Spurgeon taught his students to be constrained by the text in their preaching. He warned against the dangers of over-spiritualizing the biblical text. "Do not violently strain a text by illegitimate spiritualizing. ... How dreadfully the word of God has been mauled and mangled by a certain band of preachers who have laid texts on the rack to make them reveal what they never would have otherwise spoken."[4] Such preaching would either harm the hearers as they lost confidence in their ability to understand the word of God or discredit the preacher's ministry as their pride and vanity were exposed. When it came to parables, metaphors, prophecies, and other illustrative texts, Spurgeon urged his students to be discreet and exercise good judgment in their interpretation. Some allegorizing or spiritualizing may be appropriate, but never while ignoring the text in its original context.

The importance of reading Scripture in its context is why Spurgeon was also committed to Scripture reading in every church gathering. Spurgeon's sermons were often based on a single verse of Scripture. But he always included a Scripture reading in every service to complement the sermon text. This would usually be a reading of the surrounding context of the sermon text. Or there could be multiple readings, with the other reading being from a related text in the opposite Testament.

In these Scripture readings, Spurgeon did not merely read the text but commented on them. He provided brief "expositions,"

4. Spurgeon, *Lectures*, 103.

going verse-by-verse, explaining what each verse meant, and even making brief applications. The reason for all this was to equip his people to read their Bibles for themselves.

> We cannot expect to deliver much of the teaching of Holy Scripture by picking out verse by verse, and holding these up at random. The process resembles that of showing a house by exhibiting separate bricks. It would be an astounding absurdity if our friends used our private letters in this fashion, and interpreted them by short sentences disconnected and taken away from the context.[5]

In other words, a proper understanding of individual verses can only happen in the context of each chapter, which is to be understood in the context of the entire book and ultimately in the context of the whole Bible. Of course, to do this well, Spurgeon once again emphasized the importance of study to his students. In his own experience, he found himself preparing for these expositions as much, if not more, than for his sermons. "For the exposition, you must keep to the text, you must face the difficult points, and must search into the mind of the Spirit rather than your own. You will soon reveal your ignorance as an expositor if you do not study; therefore diligent reading will be forced upon you."[6]

Spurgeon found the discipline of expositing Scripture personally helpful in binding him to the word of God and not allowing him to rest on his rhetorical abilities. Having set up the sermon with a reading of the biblical context, it would have been wrong for him to preach the text in a totally unrelated direction. Instead, he always sought to have the sermon flow from the text in a way that was obvious to the listener. "The discourse should spring out of the text as a rule, and the more evidently it does so the better; but at all times, to say the least, it should have a very close relationship thereto."[7]

---

5. C. H. Spurgeon, *Commenting and Commentaries: Two Lectures Addressed to the Students of the Pastors' College, Metropolitan Tabernacle, Together with a Catalogue of Biblical Commentaries and Expositions* (London: Passmore & Alabaster, 1876), 22.
6. Spurgeon, *Commenting*, 24.
7. Spurgeon, *Lectures*, 74.

Spurgeon allowed some latitude in spiritualizing, "but liberty must not degenerate into license, and there must always be a connection, and something more than a remote connection—a real relationship between the sermon and its text."[8] As a preacher, Spurgeon was committed to disciplined and faithful exposition.

3: A COMMITMENT TO PREACHING CHRIST

Finally, Spurgeon was committed to preaching Christ in every sermon. As he famously declared in his first sermon in the newly built Metropolitan Tabernacle, "I would propose that the subject of the ministry of this house, as long as this platform shall stand, and as long as this house shall be frequented by worshipers, shall be the person of Jesus Christ."[9] Notice that Spurgeon's commitment was not so much to a message or a set of ideas. Instead, the good news of Christianity is found in the person of Christ. The gospel was intensely personal for Spurgeon, revealing a *Savior*. This commitment flowed from Spurgeon's understanding of Scripture.

The Bible culminates with the revelation of Jesus Christ, the Son of God. Therefore, when read in its proper, biblical-theological context, every text of Scripture points to Jesus. This was the tradition of English Puritanism in which Spurgeon was discipled. The Old Testament, in its narratives, poetry, laws, and prophecies, pointed forward to the coming Messiah. And the New Testament, in the Gospels and Epistles, revealed Jesus as the Messiah, the fulfillment of God's promises. Therefore, quoting a Welsh preacher, Spurgeon could say to his hearers,

> Don't you know young man that from every town, and every village, and every little hamlet in England, wherever it may be, there is a road to London? ... And so from every text in Scripture, there is a road to the metropolis of the Scriptures, that is Christ. And my dear brother, your business is when you get to a text, to say, "Now what is the road to Christ?" and then preach a sermon, running along the road towards

---

8. Spurgeon, *Lectures*, 74.
9. C. H. Spurgeon, "The First Sermon in the Tabernacle," in *The Metropolitan Tabernacle Pulpit Sermons*, vol. 7 (London: Passmore & Alabaster, 1861), 169.

> the great metropolis—Christ. ... I have never yet found a text that had not got a road to Christ in it, and if I ever do find one that has not a road to Christ in it, I will make one. I will go over hedge and ditch but I would get at my Master, for the sermon cannot do any good unless there is a savor of Christ in it.[10]

Spurgeon's commitment to preaching Christ was not homiletical but theological. Christ is the central meaning of the Scriptures. Therefore, in one way or another, the preacher should either find a road to Christ or make one. There may very well be worse and better roads to Christ in a text. But if the Scriptures exist to reveal Christ, this commitment to preaching Christ in every sermon is exactly right. This commitment makes Spurgeon a more trustworthy expositor of Scripture, not less.

CONCLUSION

Spurgeon's legacy is not of an entertainer or rhetorical performer. Rather, it is of a preacher committed to the accurate exposition of Scripture. Over forty years of ministry, he preached, taught, and wrote on virtually every book of the Bible, and he sought to do so faithfully. It is this teaching that continues to bear fruit. The Spurgeon Commentary series, then, seeks to compile the best of Spurgeon's biblical insights as a resource for Bible teachers today. Given his love of God's word and training preachers, he would have been pleased to see these books in the hands of pastors and church leaders. Being dead, Spurgeon still speaks, and I'm grateful for this series that gives voice to the Prince of Preachers in our day.

Geoff Chang

Kansas City, Missouri

January 30, 2024

10. C. H. Spurgeon, "Christ Precious to Believers," in *The New Park Street Pulpit Sermons*, vol. 5 (London: Passmore & Alabaster, 1859), 140.

Introduction

The great nineteenth-century Baptist preacher Charles Spurgeon crammed a remarkable amount of writing and speaking into his fifty-seven years. His words fill more than a hundred volumes. Although his sermons and writings touch on every book of the Bible at some point, he wrote commentaries only on Psalms (the multi-volume *Treasury of David*) and Matthew (*The Gospel of the Kingdom*). It can be difficult to find his teachings on other biblical books within his massive body of work.

That's why we created the Spurgeon Commentary series. The idea behind this series is simple: Take material from Spurgeon's sermons and writings and organize it into commentary format. This format includes several features I believe will be particularly helpful for both the devotional reader and the preacher preparing for a sermon.

Each section of the commentary includes three kinds of comments from Spurgeon: exposition, illustration, and application. The exposition sections do not simply deal with a block of biblical text as a whole; they are organized by *verse* as well as the *words within that verse*. This means that you can easily find what Spurgeon says about a particular verse or phrase. The individual phrases Spurgeon comments on within a verse are set in bold text. Some verses have long paragraphs of exposition, while others have a little or none at all. This reflects how much Spurgeon wrote on each verse. We have tried to include as much content as possible in places where Spurgeon wrote a lot, but unfortunately we have had to be selective at times.

When preachers are studying a text in preparation for a sermon, they often watch for good illustrations they can use to drive their point into the hearts of their listeners. To aid in this task, whenever Spurgeon used a story or a comparison to illustrate a truth found in a verse, we have set that illustration apart for easy reference. Some sections of the commentary will have more illustrations than others, depending on how many Spurgeon used.

The application content at the end of each section contains Spurgeon's exhortations to his hearers to act on the truths he was drawing out from the text. We've often drawn the application content from a few different sermons on a passage. Each section of the commentary includes between one and four applications, depending on how much Spurgeon wrote and preached on that passage.

How much of this commentary is truly Spurgeon, and how much is from the editors? Hopefully, there is as much Spurgeon as possible, and the editors fade into the background. Section titles, including those for illustrations and applications, come from the editors. All other words are Spurgeon's, although we have updated his language in some places for greater readability. For example, we have changed "thee" and "thou" to "you." Additionally, we have supplied modern equivalents to archaic words that may be unfamiliar to today's reader. However, Bible quotations are taken from the King James Version (KJV), which Spurgeon used. It is often the case that when a word or phrase in the KJV is unfamiliar or misleading to us, it was to Spurgeon's audience as well, and he took the time to explain it.

In an effort to highlight Spurgeon's relevance to a present-day audience, we have left out discussions that were only applicable to the issues and controversies Spurgeon was speaking to in his own day. Instead, we've focused on the content that a present-day audience can relate to. Thankfully, much of what Spurgeon said and wrote is truly timeless. Although we have often gathered content from multiple sources in the same paragraph, we have not used ellipses, which would be more of a distraction than a help. Instead, we have included sources in a list at the end of each section of the commentary.

It is my hope that this commentary series will make Spurgeon's writings more accessible to today's readers, and perhaps even introduce him to people who have not had the pleasure of reading him before now. Through this series may it be, as it is written on the last page of his *Autobiography*, that Spurgeon "continues to preach the gospel he loved to proclaim while here—the gospel of salvation by grace, through faith in the precious blood of Jesus."[1]

Elliot Ritzema

Easter, 2024

1. C. H. Spurgeon, *C. H. Spurgeon's Autobiography, Compiled from His Diary, Letters, and Records, by His Wife and His Private Secretary: Volume 4, 1878–1892* (Chicago; New York; Toronto: Fleming H. Revell Company, 1900), 378.

SONG OF SOLOMON 1

SONG OF SOLOMON 1:1–7

1 The song of songs, which is Solomon's.
2 Let him kiss me with the kisses of his mouth:
For thy love is better than wine.
3 Because of the savour of thy good ointments
Thy name is as ointment poured forth,
Therefore do the virgins love thee.
4 Draw me, we will run after thee:
The king hath brought me into his chambers:
We will be glad and rejoice in thee,
We will remember thy love more than wine:
The upright love thee.
5 I am black, but comely, O ye daughters of Jerusalem,
As the tents of Kedar, as the curtains of Solomon.
6 Look not upon me, because I am black,
Because the sun hath looked upon me:
My mother's children were angry with me;
They made me the keeper of the vineyards;
But mine own vineyard have I not kept.
7 Tell me, O thou whom my soul loveth,
Where thou feedest, where thou makest thy flock to rest at noon:
For why should I be as one that turneth aside by the flocks of thy companions?

EXPOSITION

1 **The song of songs, which is Solomon's** I shall not attempt to prove that the Song of Solomon has a spiritual meaning. I am sure it has. It has been frequently said, and, I believe,

has commonly been thought, that this song was originally written by Solomon upon his marriage with Pharoah's daughter. Now I am as sure as I am of my own existence that this is one of the grossest mistakes that ever was committed. There is nothing about Pharoah's daughter in it. It is, first of all, improbable that it was written of her; and in the next place, I will go further and affirm that it is impossible that it could have been written by Solomon in honor of her.

If you look all through the song you will find that this is so. In the first beginning, she is compared to a shepherdess. Now, all shepherds are abominations to the Egyptians. Do you think, therefore, that Solomon would compare an Egyptian princess to the very thing which she abominated? In the next place, all the scenery is in the land of Canaan, none of it in Egypt; and besides that, all the places that Solomon speaks of, such as Engedi, Lebanon, Amana, and Damascus, were all out of the way. Not one of them would have been passed in coming out of Egypt into Jerusalem, and very probably the Egyptian princess did not even know there were such places at all, so that if Solomon had wished to praise her he would not have compared her eyes to the fish ponds of Heshbon, but would have spoken of the sweet waters of the Nile. Besides, it could not have been Pharoah's daughter. Did Pharoah's daughter ever keep sheep? And yet the person who is represented here did. Did the watchman ever follow her about the streets, and try to take away her veil from her? Solomon would have shown them something if they had; therefore, that is impossible.

In one place, Solomon compares her to a company of horses in Pharoah's chariot. Now, horses were, among the Israelites, common things. What would Pharoah's daughter have said if Solomon had compared her to a company of horses? She might have well looked him in the face and said, "Have you not some better comparison for me than my father's horses?" It is very unlikely that Solomon perpetrated that folly. It is improbable, therefore, and we may almost say impossible, that it could be Pharoah's daughter. She never came from Lebanon and from the top of Amana. Most probably she never heard of those places, or, if she heard of them, she could not have come from them, for she came from Egypt.

2 **Let him kiss me with the kisses of his mouth** The person here alluded to is not named. This omission is very common and usual to all-absorbing love. The spouse is thinking so much of Christ Jesus her Lord that it is not necessary for her to name him. She cannot make a mistake, and she is so oblivious of all besides, that she does not think of them, nor of those who would ask, "Who is this of whom you speak?" The communion is so close between herself and her Lord that his name is left out: "Let *him* kiss me."

By the kiss is to be understood that strange and blessed manifestation of love which Christ gives from himself to his children. Inasmuch as the word "kisses" is in the plural, the spouse asks that she may have the favor multiplied. Inasmuch as she mentions the "mouth" of her Bridegroom, it is because she wishes to receive the kisses fresh and warm from his sacred person.

For thy love is better than wine It is better in itself, for it is more costly. Did it not flow out in streams of blood from a better winepress than earth's best wine has ever known? It is better, too, in its effects: more exhilarating, more strengthening, and it leaves no ill results.

Many a man has beggared himself, and squandered his estate, through his love of worldly pleasure, and especially through his fondness for wine, but the love of Christ is to be had without money. What does the Scripture say? "Come, buy wine and milk without money and without price" (Isa 55:1). The love of Christ is unpurchased, and I may add that it is unpurchasable. Solomon says, in the eighth chapter of this book, "If a man would give all the substance of his house for love, it would utterly be contemned" (Song 8:7), and we may as truly say, "If a man would give all the substance of his house for the love of Christ, it would be utterly contemned." The love of Jesus comes to his people freely; not because they deserve it, or ever will deserve it; not because, by any merits of their own, they have won it, or by any prayers of their own, they have secured it. It is spontaneous love; it flows from the heart of Christ because it must come, like the stream that leaps from an ever-flowing fountain. If you ask why Jesus loves his people, we can give no other reason than this: "Because it seemed good in his sight."

Christ's love is the freest thing in the world—free as the sunbeam, free as the mountain torrent, free as the air. It comes to the child of God without purchase and without merit, and in this respect, it is better than wine.

3 **Because of the savour of thy good ointments Thy name is as ointment poured forth** There is such a sweetness in the name. It is not like a box of ointment shut up, but like a sweet perfume that fills the room. For the merits of Jesus are so sweet that they perfume heaven itself. It was not on Calvary alone that that sweet ointment was known; it was known in the seventh heaven.

The spouse surveys all the attributes of Christ, and she compares them to separate and precious ointments. Christ is anointed as Prophet, Priest, and King, and in each of these anointings he is a source of sweetness and fragrance to his people. But as if jealous of herself for having talked of the "ointments" when she should have spoken of him, she seems to say, "Your very name is as an alabaster box when it is opened, and the odor of the precious spikenard fills the room."

Therefore do the virgins love thee The way to make us love God is for the love of God to be shed abroad in our hearts by the Holy Ghost.

4 **Draw me** We do not need to be born again; we who are believers in Christ have had that miracle wrought upon us already. We are not asking now for pardon and justification; as believers in Christ, we have these priceless boons already. What we want is the gentle influence of the Holy Spirit to attract us nearer to Christ, so each one cries to the Lord, "Draw me." We are not dead; we are quickened and made alive. Our

very pain and anguish, because we are not able to come to Christ as we would, prove that we are alive. I commend this prayer to you: "Lord, draw me; draw me." It is the work of Christ to draw. "I, if I be lifted up from the earth, will draw all men unto me" (John 12:32). It is the work of the Father. "No man can come to me," said Christ, "except the Father which hath sent me draw him" (John 6:44). It is the work of the Spirit of God to draw a soul toward Christ.

we will run after thee The spouse feels, perhaps, as you do now: heavy of heart. She cannot fly, nor go to reach her Lord; but her heart longs after him, so she cries, "Draw me, we will run after thee." While she prays the prayer, others feel it suitable to them also, so they join with her. When Christ draws us, we do not walk, but "run" after him; there is no heavy going then. When Christ draws us, how swiftly do we fly, as the dove to the dovecote, when Jesus's grace entices us.

The king hath brought me into his chambers: The King has brought me into his chambers; and now I see how truly royal he is. The King has done it. *The* King—not *a* king, but that King who is King of all kings, the most royal of all monarchs, "the prince of the kings of the earth" (Rev 1:5), even my Lord Jesus, "hath brought me into his chambers."

We will be glad and rejoice in thee The text does not merely speak about Christ's love, and Christ's love to me, but it talks about *Christ himself*. "We will be glad and rejoice in thee"—not only in his love, but in himself. Do try to let your thoughts dwell upon Christ, his complex person, God and man, and all the wonders which lie wrapped up in Immanuel, God with us. Your work, Lord, is fair; but the hand that wrought the work is fairer still. All your designs of love are full of splendor, but what shall we say of the mind that first gave creation to those designs? The glance, the look of love which you have given me, is blessed; but oh, those eyes of yours, those eyes which are brighter than the stars of the morning! The Lord Jesus is better than everything that comes from him. His gifts are infinitely precious; then what must he himself be? Come, then, and let us be glad and rejoice in him, and let us remember his love more than wine.

We will remember thy love more than wine The Hebrew word for "love" here is in the plural: "We will remember thy *loves*." Do not think, however, that the love of Jesus is divided, but know that it has different channels of manifestation. All the affections that Christ has, he bestows upon his church, and these are so varied that they may well be called "loves" rather than "love." The Septuagint translation is, "We will remember thy *breasts*." Bossuet, and many of the Romanist expositors who have brought much sanctity of thought and fervent appreciation of heart to bear upon this superlative Song, dilates very sweetly upon the word "breasts" as it appears in the Latin Vulgate. I am disposed to be content with our own Version, with the alteration of one letter: "We will remember thy *loves* more than wine."

By this expression we must understand, of course, all the love of Jesus, from the beginning even to the end; or, rather, to that eternity which has no end. We will remember those acts of love of which we have heard with our ears, and our fathers have declared unto us. It has been told us by inspired prophets, and God has revealed it to us in his Word, by his Spirit, that Jesus Christ loved us from before the foundation of the world. We believe that his love is no passion of modern date—no mere spasm of pity. It is ancient as his glory which he had with the Father before the world was; it is one of the things of eternity. This love divine is not a spring that welled up only a few days ago, but it is an everlasting fountain which has never ceased to flow.

ILLUSTRATION

We Remember Extraordinary Things

Preaching Themes: Love of God

If we were asked whether we recollected that the sun had risen, we might say, "It is not a matter of memory at all. I feel certain that it did, though I did not see it." But if we are asked if we ever saw an eclipse, "Oh, yes!" we reply, "we recollect that; we remember watching it, and how disappointed we were because it was not so dark as we expected it to be." Many people do not notice the stars much, but who forgets the comet? Everybody recollects that phenomenon of nature because it is unusual. When we see something strange, uncommon, out of the ordinary way, the memory at once fixes upon it, and holds it fast.

So is it with the love of Christ. It is such an extraordinary thing, such a marvelous thing, that the like was never known. Ransack history, and you cannot find its parallel. There is but one love that is like it, that is the love of the Father to his only begotten Son. Besides this, there is nothing to which we can compare the love of Christ to his people.

The upright love thee So it seems, then, that if we remember Christ, *we shall have a respect for his people.* His people are the upright; and she, who speaks in the sacred Canticle, here looks around upon them and says, "The upright love thee." "That commends thee to me; for if they who are of a chaste spirit love thee, much more should I." I think, if you feel as I do sometimes, you would be glad to be sure that you were even the least in God's house. We know the upright love Christ, and we love the upright because they do so; and we esteem Christ because the better men are, the more they think of him.

5 **I am black, but comely** This Canticle is a marriage song—it therefore speaks less of the battlefield than some other portions of Scripture, for at the marriage feast allusions to

trial and to warfare ought to be but few. Yet that the church is not altogether sanctified is clear if you note such passages as this. "I am black," says she, "but comely, O ye daughters of Jerusalem, as the tents of Kedar, as the curtains of Solomon." She is black; here is her natural state. Here we have the manifestation of her continued depravity of heart. "I am black, but comely"; here is her spiritual condition. The Spirit of God has clothed her with beauteous graces; Christ has washed her and made her fair in his sight.

As the tents of Kedar, as the curtains of Solomon A strange contrast is a believer. He is black in himself, but he is comely in Christ. In himself he is foul as the smoke-dried tents of Kedar; but in his Lord he is as comely and rich as the curtains of Solomon.

6 **Look not upon me, because I am black** The person who says, "Look not upon me, because I am black," is described by someone else in the eighth verse as the "fairest among women." Others, who thought her the fairest of the fair, spoke no less than the truth when they affirmed it; but in her own esteem she felt herself to be so little fair, and so much uncomely, that she implored them not even to look upon her.

Because the sun hath looked upon me She had been made a keeper of the vineyards, and having to trim the vines, the sun had shone upon her; and she says, "Look not upon me, because I am black, because the sun hath looked upon me." The blackness that she confessed was a blackness occasioned by her having to bear the burden and heat of the day.

My mother's children were angry with me The text is the language of complaint. We are all pretty ready at complaining, especially of other people. Not much good comes of picking holes in other men's characters, and yet many spend hours in that unprofitable occupation. It will be well for us, at this time, to let our complaint, like that of the text, deal with ourselves.

They made me the keeper of the vineyards It would appear that the bride was in trouble about a certain charge which had been given to her, which burdened her, and in the discharge of which she had become negligent of herself. She says, "They made me the keeper of the vineyards," and she would wish to have kept them well, but she felt she had not done so, and that, moreover, she had failed in a more immediate duty: "Mine own vineyard have I not kept."

But mine own vineyard have I not kept To the Christian there must always be a far higher, deeper, purer, truer motive than self in its widest sense; or else the day must come when he will look back upon his life, and say, "They made me the keeper of the vineyards; but mine own vineyard"—that is, the service of Christ, the glory of him that bought me with his blood—"have I not kept."

There is a vineyard that a great many neglect, and that is *their own heart*. It is well to have talent; it is well to have influence; but it is better to be right within yourself. It is well for a man to see to his cattle, and look well to his flocks and to his herds; but let him not forget to cultivate that little patch of ground that lies in the center of his being. Let him educate his head, and intermeddle with all knowledge; but let him not forget that there is another plot of ground called the heart, the character, which is more important still. Right principles are spiritual gold, and he who has them, and is ruled by them, is the man who truly lives. He has not life, whatever else he has, who has not his heart cultivated, and made right and pure.

ILLUSTRATION

Hating the Smell of Violets

Preaching Themes: Complaining, Hypocrisy

It is very possible for a man to get to dislike the very religion which he feels bound still by force of custom to go on teaching to others. "Is that possible?" says one. Alas! That it is.

Have you never heard of the flower girl in the streets? What is her occupation? I dare say some girls like her have passed by and seen her with a great basket full of violets, and said: "What a delightful occupation, to have that fragrant smell forever near to one!" Yes, but there was one girl who sold them, and said she hated the smell of violets. She had got to loathe them, and to think that there was no smell in the world so offensive, because they were always under her nostrils all day, and taken home to her little scanty room at night, and having nothing but violets around her, she hated them altogether.

And I do believe that there are persons without the grace of Christ in their hearts who keep on talking about grace, and mercy, and practicing prayer, and yet in their heart of hearts they hate the very fragrance of the name of Jesus, and need for there to come on them an awakening out of their sleep of presumption and hypocrisy, to make them know that though they thought they were the friends of God, they were, after all, his enemies. They were mere keepers of other men's vineyards, but their own vineyards had gone to ruin.

---

7 **Tell me, O thou whom my soul loveth** Every word of the inquiry is worthy of our careful meditation. You will observe, first, concerning it, that it is *asked in love.* She calls him to whom she speaks by the endearing title, "O thou whom my soul loveth." Whatever she may feel herself to be, she knows that she loves *him.* She is black, and ashamed to have her face gazed upon, but still she loves her Bridegroom. She has not kept her own vineyard as she ought to have done, but still she loves him; that she is sure of, and therefore boldly declares it. She loves him as she loves none other in all the world. He only can be called "him whom my soul loveth." She knows none at

all worthy to be compared with him, none who can rival him. He is her bosom's Lord, sole prince and monarch of all her affections. She feels also that she loves him intensely—from her inmost *soul* she loves him. The life of her existence is bound up with him: if there be any force and power and vitality in her, it is but as fuel to the great flame of her love, which burns alone for him.

Mark well that it is not "O thou whom my soul believes in." That would be true, but she has passed further. It is not "O thou whom my soul honors." That is true too, but she has passed beyond that stage. Nor is it merely "O thou whom my soul trusts and obeys." She is doing that, but she has reached something warmer, more tender, more full of fire and enthusiasm, and it is "O thou whom my soul *loveth*."

ILLUSTRATION

A Love That Forgets All Others

Preaching Themes: Beauty, Love, Love of God

When Tigranes and his wife were both taken prisoner by Cyrus, Cyrus turning to Tigranes said, "What will you give for the liberation of your wife?" And the king answered, "I love my wife so that I would cheerfully give up my life if she might be delivered from servitude." Whereupon Cyrus said, "If there was such love as that between them, they might both go free." So when they were away and many were talking about the beauty and generosity of Cyrus, and especially about the beauty of his person, Tigranes, turning to his wife, asked her what she thought of Cyrus, and she answered that she saw nothing anywhere but in the face of the man who had said that he would die if she might only be released from servitude. "The beauty of that man," she said, "makes me forget all others."

And truly we would say the same of Jesus. We would not decry the angels, nor think ill of the saints, but the beauties of that man who gave his life for us are so great that they have eclipsed all others, and our soul only wishes to see him and not another; for, as the stars hide their heads in the presence of the sun, so may you all be gone, you delights, you excellencies, when Christ Jesus, the chief delight, the chief excellency, makes his appearance.

Where thou feedest She asked him to tell her, as if she feared that none but himself would give her the correct answer; others might be mistaken, but he could not be. She asked of him because she was quite sure that he would give her the kindest answer. Others might be indifferent and might scarcely take the trouble to reply; but if Jesus would tell her himself, with his own lips, he would mingle love with every word, and so console as well as instruct her. Perhaps she felt that nobody else could tell her as he could, for others speak to the ear, but he speaks to the heart: others speak with lower degrees of influence, we hear their speech but are not moved thereby; but Jesus speaks, and the Spirit goes with every word he utters, and therefore we hear to profit when he converses with us.

where thou makest thy flock to rest at noon She wishes to know how Jesus does his work, and where he does it. It appears, from the eighth verse, that she herself has a flock of kids to tend. She is a shepherdess and wants to feed her flock; hence her question, "Tell me where thou feedest?" She desires those little ones of hers to obtain rest as well as food, and she is troubled about them; therefore she says, "Tell me where thou makest thy flock to rest," for if she can see how Jesus does his work, and where he does it, and in what way, then she will be satisfied that she is doing it in the right way, if she closely imitates him and abides in fellowship with him. The question seems to be just this: "Lord, tell me what are the truths with which you feed your people's souls; tell me what are the doctrines which make the strong ones weak and the sad ones glad; tell me what is that precious meat which you are wont to give to hungry and fainting spirits, to revive them and keep them alive; for if you tell me, then I will give my flock the same food. Tell me where the pasture is where you feed your sheep, and straightway I will lead mine to the self-same happy fields. Then tell me how you make your people to rest. What are those promises that you apply to the consolation of their spirit, so that their cares and doubts and fears and agitations all subside? You have sweet meadows where you make your beloved flock to lie calmly down and slumber; tell me where those meadows are that I may go and fetch the flock committed to my charge, the mourners whom I ought to comfort, the distressed ones whom I am bound to relieve, the desponding whom I have endeavored to encourage; tell me, Lord, where you make your flock to lie down, for then, under your help, I will go and make my flock to lie down too. It is for myself, but yet far more for others, that I ask the question, 'Tell me where thou feedest, where thou makest them to rest at noon.' "

I have no doubt that the spouse did desire information for herself and for her own good, and I believe Dr. Watts had caught some of the spirit of the passage when he sang,

> Fain would I feed among thy sheep,
> Among them rest, among them sleep.[1]

But it does not strike me that this is all the meaning of the passage by a very long way. The bride says, "Tell me where thou feedest thy flock," as if she would wish to feed with the flock; "where thou makest thy flock to rest," as if she wanted to rest there too. But it strikes me the very gist of the thing is this: that she wished to bring her flock to feed where Christ's flock feeds, and to lead her kids to lie down where Christ's little lambs were reposing. She desired, in fact, to do her work in his company; she wanted to mix up her flock with the Lord's flock, her work with his work, and to feel that what she was doing she was doing for him, and with him, and through him.

1. A quotation from the Isaac Watts hymn "Thou Whom My Soul Admires Above." —ed.

She had evidently met with a great many difficulties in what she had tried to do. She wished to feed her flock of kids but could not find them pasture. Perhaps when she began her work as a shepherdess she thought herself quite equal to the task, but now the same sun which had bronzed her face had dried up the pasture, and so she says, "O thou that knowest all the pastures, tell me where thou feedest, for I cannot find grass for my flock." Suffering herself from the noontide heat, she finds her little flock suffering too; and she inquires, "Where do you make your flock to rest at noon? Where are cool shadows of great rocks which screen off the sultry rays when the sun is in its zenith and pours down torrents of heat? For I cannot shade my poor flock and give them comfort in their many trials and troubles. I wish I could. O Lord, tell me the secret art of consolation; then will I try to console my own charge by the self-same means."

We would know the groves of promise and the cool streams of peace, that we may lead others into rest. If we can follow Jesus we can guide others, and so both we and they will find comfort and peace. That is the meaning of the request before us.

For why should I be as one that turneth aside by the flocks of thy companions? If she should lead her flock into distant meadows, far away from the place where Jesus is feeding his flock, it would not be well. As a shepherdess would naturally be rather dependent, and would need to associate herself for protection with others, suppose she should turn aside with other shepherds, and leave her Bridegroom, would it be right? She speaks of it as a thing most abhorrent to her mind, and well might it be. For, first, would it not look very unseemly that the bride should be associating with others than the Bridegroom? They have each a flock: there is he with his great flock, and here is she with her little one. Shall they seek pastures far off from one another? Will there not be talk about this? Will not onlookers say, "This is not seemly: there must be some lack of love here, or else these two would not be so divided"?

Stress may be put, if you like, upon that little word "I." Why should *I*, your blood-bought spouse; I, betrothed to you, before ever the earth was; I, whom you have loved—why should I turn after others and forget you?

Beloved, you had better put the emphasis in your own reading of it just there. Why should *I*, whom the Lord has pardoned, whom the Lord has loved, whom the Lord has favored so much—I, who have enjoyed fellowship with him for many years—I, who know that his love is better than wine—I, who have in times past been inebriated with his sweetness—why should I turn aside? Let others do so if they will, but it would be uncomely and unseemly for me. Try to feel that—that for you to work apart from Christ would have a bad look about it; that for your work to take you away from fellowship with Jesus would have a very ugly appearance. It would not be among the things that are honest and of good repute, for the bride to feed her flock in other company would look like unfaithfulness to her husband. What, shall the bride of Christ forsake her Beloved? Shall she be unchaste towards her Lord? Yet it would seem so if she makes companions of others and forgets her Beloved.

APPLICATION

Remember His Love to You

Let each one of us say to Christ, "I will remember your love *to me*." Brothers and sisters, I can believe in Christ's loving you, but there are times when it seems a great mystery that he should ever have loved me. I can truly say that, often, I have felt that if I might sit at the feet of the poorest, meanest, least of God's servants, and serve them, I would count it a heaven to do it if I did only feel sure of Christ's love to my own soul. I see so many beauties in my brothers and my sisters that I can admire the grace of God in them; but, often, I do see and feel so many imperfections in myself that I can only wonder that ever Christ should have loved me. I suppose that each of you feels the same; I am sure that you do if you are in a right state of heart, for, truth to tell, there is no beauty in any of us that he should desire us, and there is no excellence in any of us that could have made it worth his while to die for us. "God commendeth his love toward us, in that, while we were yet sinners, Christ died for us" (Rom 5:8). "When we were yet without strength, in due time Christ died for the ungodly" (Rom 5:6), and died for us as ungodly.

Come, then, will you not be glad and rejoice that ever Christ should have loved you? Will you not be glad and rejoice, and yet wonder all the while that ever it should have been possible for him to draw you "with cords of a man, with bands of love" (Hos 11:4), and bring you into living, loving, everlasting union with himself?

Take Your Distress to Jesus

Never let sin part you from Jesus. Under a sense of sin do not fly from him; that would be foolishness. Sin may drive you *from* Sinai; it ought to draw you *to* Calvary. To the fountain we should fly with all the greater alacrity when we feel that we are foul. And to the dear wounds of Jesus, from which all our life and healing must come, we should resort with the greater earnestness when we feel our soul to be sick, even though we fear that sickness to be unto death.

The bride, in the present case, takes to Jesus her troubles, her distress about herself, and her confession concerning her work. She brings before him her double charge, the keeping of her own vineyard, and the keeping of the vineyards of others. I know that I am speaking to many who are busy in serving their Lord. It may be that they feel great anxiety because they cannot keep their own hearts near to Jesus. They do not feel themselves warm and lively in the divine service; they plod on, but they are very much in the condition of those who are described as "faint, yet pursuing" (Judg 8:4). When Jesus is present, labor for him is joy, but in his absence his servants feel like workers underground, bereft of the light of the sun. They cannot give up working for Jesus—they love him too well for that—but they pine to have his company while they are working for him. Like the young prophets who went to the wood to cut down every man a beam for their new house, they say to their master, "Be content, we pray thee, and go with thy servants" (2 Kgs 6:3). Our most earnest desire is that we may enjoy sweet communion with Jesus while we are actively engaged in his cause. Indeed, this is most important to all of us. I do not know of any point which Christian workers need more often to think upon than the subject of keeping their work and themselves near to the Master's hand.

Cultivate the Vineyard of Your Heart

Have you ever thought about your heart yet? Oh, I do not mean whether you have palpitations! I am no doctor. I am speaking now about the heart in its moral and spiritual aspect. What is your character, and do you seek to cultivate it? Do you ever use the hoe upon those weeds which are so plentiful in us all? Do you water those tiny plants of goodness which have begun to grow? Do you watch them to keep away the little foxes which would destroy them? Are you hopeful that yet there may be a harvest in your character which God may look upon with approval? I pray that we may all look to our hearts. "Keep your heart with all diligence; for out of it are the issues of life" (Prov 4:23). Pray daily, "Create in me a clean heart, O God; and renew a right spirit within me" (Ps 51:10); for if not, you will go up and down in the world, and do a great deal, and when it comes to the end you will have neglected your noblest nature, and your poor starved soul will die that second death, which is the more dreadful because it is everlasting death.

How terrible for a soul to die of neglect! How can we escape who neglect this great salvation? If we pay every attention to our bodies, but none to our immortal souls, how shall we justify our folly? God save us from suicide by neglect! May we not have to moan out eternally, "They made me the keeper of the vineyards; but mine own vineyard have I not kept!"

SONG OF SOLOMON 1:8–17

8 If thou know not, O thou fairest among women,
Go thy way forth by the footsteps of the flock,
And feed thy kids beside the shepherds' tents.
9 I have compared thee, O my love,
To a company of horses in Pharaoh's chariots.
10 Thy cheeks are comely with rows *of jewels*,
Thy neck with chains *of gold*.
11 We will make thee borders of gold
With studs of silver.
12 While the king *sitteth* at his table,
My spikenard sendeth forth the smell thereof.
13 A bundle of myrrh *is* my wellbeloved unto me;
He shall lie all night betwixt my breasts.
14 My beloved *is* unto me *as* a cluster of camphire
In the vineyards of En-gedi.
15 Behold, thou *art* fair, my love; behold, thou *art* fair;
Thou *hast* doves' eyes.
16 Behold, thou *art* fair, my beloved, yea, pleasant:
Also our bed *is* green.
17 The beams of our house *are* cedar,
And our rafters of fir.

EXPOSITION

8 **If thou know not, O thou fairest among women** We have here an answer given by the Bridegroom to his beloved. She asked him where he fed, where he made his flock to rest, and he answered her. Observe carefully that this answer is *given in tenderness to her infirmity*, not ignoring her ignorance but dealing very gently with it. "If thou know not" is a hint that

she ought to have known, but such a hint as kind lovers give when they are inclined to hold themselves back from chiding.

Note next that the answer is *given in great love*. He says, "O thou fairest among women." That is a blessed cordial for her distress. She said, "I am black," but he says, "O thou fairest among women." I would rather trust Christ's eyes than mine.

ILLUSTRATION

What a Sculptor Sees in the Marble

Preaching Themes: Image of God, Sin

As the artist, looking on the block of marble, sees in the stone the statue which he means to fetch out of it with matchless skill, so the Lord Jesus sees the perfect image of himself in us, from which he means to chip away the imperfections and the sins until it stands out in all its splendor. But still it is gracious condescension which makes him say, "Thou art fairest among women," to one who mourned her own sunburnt countenance.

Go thy way forth by the footsteps of the flock The answer contains much sacred wisdom. The bride is directed where to go that she may find her beloved and lead her flock to him. If you would find Jesus, you will find him in the way the holy prophets went, in the way of the patriarchs and the way of the apostles. And if you desire to find your flock, and to make them lie down, very well, go and feed them as other shepherds have done—Christ's own shepherds whom he has sent in other days to feed his chosen.

I feel very glad, in speaking from this text, that the Lord does not give to his bride in answer to her question some singular directions of great difficulty, some novel prescriptions singular and remarkable. Just as the gospel itself is simple and homely, so is this exhortation and direction for the renewal of communion.

And feed thy kids beside the shepherds' tents Now, who are these shepherds? There be many in these days who set up for shepherds, who feed their sheep in poisonous pastures. Keep away from them; but there are others whom it is safe to follow. Let me take you to the twelve principal shepherds who came after the great Shepherd of all. You want to bless your children, to save their souls, and have fellowship with Christ in the doing of it; then teach them the truths which the apostles taught. And what were they? Take Paul as an example. "I determined not to know anything among you save Jesus Christ, and him crucified" (1 Cor 2:2). That is feeding the kids beside the shepherds' tents, when you teach your children Christ, much of Christ, all of Christ, and nothing else but Christ.

9 **I have compared thee, O my love, To a company of horses in Pharaoh's chariots** True believers are as strong, as noble, as beautiful as the horses in Pharaoh's chariot, which were renowned throughout all the world. Let us be like those horses. Let us all pull together; let us draw the great chariot of our King behind us; let us be content to wear his harness that we may be partakers of his splendid triumph.

10 **Thy cheeks are comely with rows of jewels, Thy neck with chains of gold** Christ here praises his church. Orientals were in the habit of wearing jewels in such abundance that their cheeks were covered with them. Then they multiplied the chains of gold upon their necks. The graces which Christ gives to his people, and especially the various parts of his own finished work, become to them like rows of jewels and chains of gold.

11 **We will make thee borders of gold With studs of silver** As if Father, Son, and Holy Ghost would all work together to make the believer perfectly beautiful.

12 **While the king sitteth at his table** This passage may be read in several ways. Literally, when Christ tabled among men,

when he did eat and drink with them, being found in fashion as a man, the loving spirit broke the alabaster box of precious ointment on his head while the king was sitting at his table. Three times did the church thus anoint her Lord, once his head and twice his feet, as if she remembered his threefold office, and the threefold anointing which he had received from God the Father to confirm and strengthen him. So she rendered him the threefold anointing of her grateful love, breaking the alabaster box, and pouring the precious ointment upon his head and upon his feet.

But the King is gone from earth. He is seated at his table in heaven, eating bread in the kingdom of God. Surrounded now not by publicans and harlots but by cherubim and seraphim, not by mocking crowds but by adoring hosts, the King sits at his table and entertains the glorious company of the faithful, the church of the firstborn whose names are written in heaven. He fought before he could rest. On earth he struggled with his enemies, and it was not till he had triumphed over all that he sat down at the table on high. There sit, you King of kings—there sit until your last enemy shall be made your footstool.

He is called "the King." I am told that the Hebrew word is very emphatic, as if it said, "*The* King"—the King of kings, the greatest of all kings. He must be such to us—absolute Master of our hearts, Lord of our soul's domain, the unrivaled One in our estimation, to whom we render obedience with alacrity. We must have him as King, or we shall not have his presence to revive our graces. And when the King communes with his people, it is said to be at "*his* table," not at ours. Especially may this apply to the table of communion. It is not the Baptists' table; it is not my table; it is his table, because if there is anything good on it, remember, he spread it. No, there is nothing on the table unless he himself be there. There is no food to the child of God unless Christ's body be the flesh, and Christ's blood the wine. We must have Christ. It must be emphatically his table by his being present, by his spreading it, his presiding at it, or else we have not his presence at all.

I find the Hebrew word here signifies a "round table." I do not know whether is intended what I understand by it—perhaps it is. It suggests to me a blessed equality with all his disciples; sitting at his round table, as if there were scarce a head, but he was one of themselves, so close the communion he holds with them sitting at the table; so dear his fellowship, sitting like one of themselves, made like unto his brothers in all things at his round table.

my spikenard sendeth forth the smell thereof The text implies that when the King is not present the spikenard yields no smell, but the spikenard is there for all that. The spouse speaks of her spikenard as though she had it, and only wanted to have the King come and sit at the table to make its presence known and felt.

ILLUSTRATION

A Wintering Oak Tree

Preaching Theme: Eternity

When the old oak has lost its last leaf by the howling blasts of winter, when the sap is frozen up in the veins, and you cannot, though you search to the uttermost bough, find so much as the slightest sign of verdant existence, still even then the substance is in the tree when it has lost its leaves.

And so, with every believer, though his sap seems frozen, and his life almost dead, yet if once planted, it is there; the eternal life is there when he cannot discover it himself.

---

13 **A bundle of myrrh is my well-beloved unto me** Christ Jesus is unutterably precious to believers. The words manifestly imply this: "A bundle of myrrh is *my well-beloved* unto me." She calls him her "well-beloved," and so expresses her love

most emphatically; it is not merely *beloved*, but well-beloved. Then she looks abroad about her, to find a substance which shall be at once valuable in itself, and useful in its properties; and lighting upon myrrh, she says, "A bundle of myrrh is my well-beloved unto me."

Jesus Christ is like myrrh. Myrrh may be well the type of Christ for its *preciousness*. It was an exceedingly expensive drug. We know that Jacob sent some of it down into Egypt as being one of the choice products of the land. It is always spoken of in Scripture as being a rich, rare, and costly substance. But no myrrh could ever compare with him, for Jesus Christ is so precious that if heaven and earth were put together they could not buy another Savior. When God gave to the world his Son, he gave the best that heaven had. Take Christ out of heaven, and there is nothing for God to give. Christ was God's all, for is it not written, "In him dwelleth all the fulness of the Godhead bodily" (Col 2:9)?

Myrrh, again, was *pleasant*. It was a pleasant thing to be in a chamber perfumed with myrrh. Through the nostrils myrrh conveys delight to the human mind; but Christ gives delight to his people, not through one channel, but through every avenue. It is true that all his garments smell of myrrh, and aloes, and cassia, but he does not have spiritual smell alone; the taste shall be gratified too, for we eat his flesh and drink his blood. Nay, our feeling is ravished, when his left hand is under us and his right hand embraces us. As for his voice, it is most sweet, and our soul's ear is charmed with its melody. Let God give him to our sight, and what can our eyes want more? Yes, he is altogether lovely. Thus every gate of the soul has commerce with Christ Jesus in the richest and rarest commodities.

Moreover, myrrh is *perfuming*. It is used to give a sweet smell to other things. It was mingled with the sacrifice, so that it was not only the smoke of the fat of kidneys of rams, and the flesh of fat beasts, but there was a sweet fragrance of myrrh, which went up with the sacrifice to heaven. And surely, beloved, Jesus Christ is very perfuming to his people. Does not he perfume their prayers, so that the Lord smells a sweet savor? Does he not perfume their songs, so that they become like vials full of odor sweet? Does he not perfume our ministry, for is it not written, he "causeth us to triumph in Christ, and maketh manifest the savour of his knowledge by us in every place. For we are unto God a sweet savour of Christ, in them that are saved, and in them that perish" (2 Cor 2:14–15). Our persons are perfumed with Christ. From where do we get our spikenard but from him? To where shall we go to gather camphire, which shall make our persons and presence acceptable before God, but to him? For we are "accepted in the beloved" (Eph 1:6). "Ye are complete in him" (Col 2:10), "perfect in Christ Jesus" (Col 1:28), for he "hath made us kings and priests unto our God, and we shall reign for ever and ever" (Rev 1:6).

Myrrh has *preserving* qualities. The Egyptians used it in embalming the dead: and we find Nicodemus and the holy women bringing myrrh and aloes in which to wrap the dead body of the Savior. It was used to prevent corruption. What is there which can preserve the soul but Christ Jesus? What is the myrrh which keeps our works, which in themselves are dead, and corrupt, and rotten—what, I say, keeps them from becoming a foul stench in the nostrils of God, but that Christ is in them? What we have done out of love to Christ, what we have offered through his mediation, what has been perfumed by faith in his person, becomes acceptable. God looks upon anything we say, or anything we do, and if he sees Christ in it, he accepts it; but if there is no Christ, he puts it away as a foul thing.

And I must not close this point without saying that myrrh might well be used as an emblem of our Lord from *its connection with sacrifice*. It was one of the precious drugs used in making the holy oil with which the priests were anointed and the frankincense which burned perpetually before God. It is this, the sacrificial character of Christ, which is at the root and bottom of all that Christ is most precious to his people.

But why is it said, "a *bundle* of myrrh?" First, for *the plenty of it*. He is not a drop of it, he is a casket full. He is not a sprig or flower of it, but a whole bundle full. There is enough in Christ for my necessities. There is more in Christ than I shall ever know—perhaps more than I shall understand even in heaven.

A bundle again, for *variety;* for there is in Christ not only the one thing needful, but "ye are complete in him" (Col 2:10); there is everything needful. Take Christ in his different characters, and you will see a marvelous variety—prophet, priest, king, husband, friend, shepherd. Take him in his life, death, resurrection, ascension, second advent; take him in his virtue, gentleness, courage, self-denial, love, faithfulness, truth, righteousness—everywhere it is a bundle. Some of God's judgments are manifold, but *all* God's mercies are manifold, and Christ being the sum of God's mercies, has fold upon fold of goodness. He is "a bundle of myrrh" for variety.

He is a bundle of myrrh, again, for *preservation*—not loose myrrh to be dropped on the floor or trodden on, but myrrh tied up, as though God bound up all virtues and excellencies in his Son: not myrrh spilled on the ground, but myrrh in a box—myrrh kept in a casket. Such is Christ. The virtue and excellence which goes out of Christ is quite as strong today as in the day when the woman touched the hem of his garment and was healed. "Able also to save them to the uttermost that come unto God by him" (Heb 7:25) is he still unto this hour.

A bundle of myrrh again, to show *how diligently we should take care of it*. We must bind him up, we must keep our thoughts of him and knowledge of him as under lock and key, lest the devil should steal anything from us. We must treasure up his words, prize his ordinances, obey his precepts, tie him up, and keep him ever with us as a precious bundle of myrrh.

And yet again, a bundle of myrrh *for speciality*, as if he were not common myrrh for everybody. No, no, no; there is distinguishing, discriminating grace—a bundle tied up for his people and labeled with their names from before the foundation of the world. No doubt there is an allusion here to the scent bottle used in every land. Jesus Christ is a bottle of myrrh, and he does not give forth his smell to everybody but to those who know how to draw forth the stopper, who understand how to get into communion with him, to have close dealings with him. He is not myrrh for all who are in the house but for those who know how to put the bottle to their nostrils and receive the sweet perfume.

He shall lie all night betwixt my breasts The church does not say, "I will put this bundle of myrrh on my shoulders"—Christ is no burden to a Christian. She does not say, "I will put this bundle of myrrh on my back"—the church does not want to have Christ concealed from her face. She desires to have him where she can see him, and near to her heart. The bundle of myrrh shall lie all night upon my heart. The words "all night" are not in the original; I do not know how they got into the translation. He is to be always there, not only all night but all day. It would be always night if he were not there, and it cannot be night when he is there, for "Midst darkest shade, if he appear, My dawning has begun."[1]

He shall always be upon our heart. I think that expression just means these three things. It is an expression of *desire*—her desire that she may have the consciousness of Christ's love continually. But then, it is not only her desire, but it is also her *confidence*. She seems to say, "He will be with me thus." To conclude, this is also *a resolve*. She desires, she believes, and she resolves it. "Lord, thou shalt be with me, thou shalt be with me always."

14 **My beloved is unto me as a cluster of camphire in the vineyards of En-gedi** He is not one sprig or spray of camphire, but a cluster of it. The spouse, you see, multiplies figures to describe her Bridegroom, and even when she has done so, she cannot reach the height of his glory.

> Nor earth, nor seas, nor sun, nor stars,
> Nor heaven, his full resemblance bears;
> His beauties we can never trace,
> Till we behold him face to face.[2]

1. A quotation from the Isaac Watts hymn "My God, the Spring of All My Joys." —ed.
2. A quotation from the Isaac Watts hymn "Go, Worship at Emmanuel's Feet." —ed.

15 **Behold, thou art fair, my love; behold, thou art fair; Thou hast doves' eyes** So Christ speaks of his church—she has the soft, mild, tender eyes of a dove. Besides, she has the discerning eye by which the dove can distinguish between carrion and fit food; and then she has a clear eye like that of the dove. You know that the dove, or pigeon, when it is taken far away from home, and wants to reach its cote, flies round and round till it gets up high. Then it looks for miles, perhaps for hundreds of miles, till it tracks with unerring eye its own resting place, or some familiar landmark, and then, with cutting wing, it flies through the ether till it reaches its home. So, every believer should have doves' eyes—eyes that can see from earth to heaven, and see Christ in his glory, even when his cause is disowned by men.

16 **Behold, thou art fair, my beloved, yea, pleasant: Also our bed is green** The "bed" expresses the near fellowship which Christ has with his people.

17 **The beams of our house are cedar, and our rafters of fir** We have the word "rafters" here, but it should be "galleries." The "house" perhaps denotes the whole church. The "galleries" signify the ordinances of grace. You notice that these are made of unrotting wood, the one of cedar and the other of fir.

APPLICATION

Christians Should Be Easily Discerned

If I understand a Christian rightly, he should be a man readily discerned. You do not need to write upon a box that contains spikenard, with the lid open, the word "spikenard." You will know it is there; your nostrils would tell you. If a man should fill his pockets with dust, he might walk where he would, and though he should scatter it in the air, few would notice it. But let him go into a room with his pockets full of musk, and let him drop a particle about, he is soon discovered, because the musk speaks for itself.

Now true grace, like spikenard or any other perfume, should speak for itself. You know our Savior compares Christians to lights. There is a crowd of people standing over there. I cannot see those who are in the shadow, but there is one man whose face I can see well, and that is the man who holds the torch. Its flames light up his face, so that we can catch every feature readily. So, whoever is not discovered, the Christian should be obvious at once. "Thou also art one of them; for thy speech bewrayeth thee" (Matt 26:73). Not only should the Christian be perceptible, but grace has been given to him that it might be in exercise. What is faith, unless it is believing? What is love, unless it is embracing? What is patience, unless it is enduring? To what purpose is knowledge, unless it is revealing truth? What are any of those sweet graces which the Master gives us, unless they yield their perfume? I fear we do not enough gaze upon that face covered with the bloody sweat, for if we did, as sure as the King was thus in our thoughts sitting at his table, we should be more like him. We should love him better, we should live more passionately for him, and should spend and be spent, that we might promote his glory. I just note this point, and then pass on, that believers' graces, like spikenard, are meant to give forth their smell.

Christ's Presence Changes Everything

We may plainly see that Christ is very precious to the believer, because *to him there is nothing good without Christ*. Believer, have you not found in the midst of plenty a dire and sore famine if your Lord has been absent? The sun was shining, but Christ had hidden himself, and all the world was black to you. Or it was a night of tempest, and there were many stars, but since the bright and morning star was gone on that dreary main, where you were tossed with doubts and fears, no other star could shed so much as a ray of light. O, what a howling wilderness is this world without my Lord! If once he grows angry and, though it be for a moment, hide himself from me, withered are the flowers of my garden; my pleasant fruits decay; the birds suspend their songs, and black night lowers over all my hopes. Nothing can compensate for the company of the Savior. All earth's candles cannot make daylight if the Sun of Righteousness be gone.

On the other hand, *when all earthly comforts have failed you, have you not found quite enough in your Lord?* Your very worst times have been your best times? You must almost cry to go back to your bed of sickness, for Jesus made it like a royal throne on which you reigned with him. Those dark nights were not dark; your bright days since then have been darker far. Do you remember when you were poor? How near Christ was to you, and how rich he made you! You were despised and rejected of men, and no man gave you a good word! Sweet was his fellowship then, and how delightful to hear him say, "Fear thou not; for I am with thee: be not dismayed; for I am thy God!" (Isa 41:10). As afflictions abound, even so do consolations abound by Christ Jesus. The devil, like Nebuchadnezzar, heated the furnace seven times hotter, but who would have it less furiously blazing? No wise believer. For the more terrible the heat, the greater the glory in the fact that we were made to tread those glowing coals, and not a hair of our head was singed, nor so much as the smell of fire passed upon us, because the Son of God walked those glowing coals in our company. Yes, we can look with resignation upon penury, disease, and even death. For if all comforts be taken from us, we should still be blest so long as we enjoy the presence of the Lord our Savior.

You Need a Personal Experience of God

The infidel says, "There is no God." The atheist would altogether laugh me to scorn. They shall say what they will, but "a bundle of myrrh is my well-beloved *unto me*." Even bishops have been found who will take away a part of his Book, and so rend his garments, and rob him; and there be some who say his religion is out of date, and grace has lost his power; and they go after philosophy and vain conceit, and I know not what, but "a bundle of myrrh is my well-beloved *unto me*." They may have no nostril for him, they may have no desire after him; so let it be, but "a bundle of myrrh is my well-beloved *unto me*." I know there are some who say they have tried him and not found him sweet, and who have turned away from him and gone back to the beggarly elements of the world because they see nothing in Christ that they should desire him; but "a bundle of myrrh is my well-beloved *unto me*."

Christian, this is what you want: a personal experience, a positive experience. You want to know for *yourself*, for there is no religion which is worth a button which is not burnt into you by personal experience; and there is no religion worth a straw which does not spring from your soul, which does lay not hold upon the very vitals of your spirit. Yes, you must say—I hope you can say as you enter into that busy, giddy world—you must say, "Let the whole world go astray, 'a bundle of myrrh is my well-beloved unto *me*.'"

SONG OF SOLOMON 2

SONG OF SOLOMON 2:1–7

1 I am the rose of Sharon,
And the lily of the valleys.
2 As the lily among thorns,
So is my love among the daughters.
3 As the apple tree among the trees of the wood,
So is my beloved among the sons.
I sat down under his shadow with great delight,
And his fruit was sweet to my taste.
4 He brought me to the banqueting house,
And his banner over me was love.
5 Stay me with flagons, comfort me with apples:
For I am sick of love.
6 His left hand is under my head,
And his right hand doth embrace me.
7 I charge you, O ye daughters of Jerusalem,
By the roes, and by the hinds of the field,
That ye stir not up, nor awake my love, till he please.

EXPOSITION

1 **I am the rose of Sharon** It is our Lord who speaks: "I am the rose of Sharon." How is it that he utters his own commendation, for it is an old and true adage that "self praise is no recommendation"? None but vain creatures ever praise themselves, and yet Jesus often praises himself. He says, "I am the good shepherd" (John 10:11, 14); "I am the bread of life" (John 6:35); "I am meek and lowly in heart" (Matt 11:29), and in diverse speeches he is frequently declaring his own excellencies, yet

Jesus is not vain! Scorned be the thought! Yet I said if any *creature* praised itself it must be vain, and that, too, is true.

How then shall we solve the riddle? Is not this the answer that he is no creature at all, and therefore does not come beneath the rule? For the creature to praise itself is vanity, but for the Creator to praise himself, for the Lord God to manifest and show forth his own glory, is becoming and proper. Hear how he extols his own wisdom and power in the end of the book of Job, and see if it is not most seemly, as the Lord himself proclaims it! Is not God constantly ruling both providence and grace for the manifestation of his own glory, and do we not all freely consent that no motive short of this would be worthy of the divine mind? So, then, because Christ talks thus of himself, since no man dare call him vainglorious, I gather an indirect proof of his deity, and bow down before him, and bless him that he gives me this incidental evidence of his being no creature, but the uncreated one himself.

He compares himself here, not as in other places to needful bread and refreshing water, but to lovely flowers, to roses and lilies. What is the use of roses and lilies? I know what the use of corn is. I must eat it; it is necessary to me for food. I know why barley and rye and all sorts of roots and fruits are created; they are the necessary food of man or beast. But what do we want with roses? What do we want with lilies? They are of no use at all except for joy and delight. With their sweet form, their charming color, and their delicious fragrance we are comforted and pleased and delighted; but they are not necessaries of life. A man can live without roses; there are millions of people, I have no doubt, who live without possessing lilies of the valley. There are all too few roses and lilies in this smoky Babylon of ours; but, when we do get them, what are their uses? Why, they are things of beauty, if not "a joy for ever." Jesus is all that and more; he is far more than "a thing of beauty," and to all who trust him he will be "a joy for ever."

ILLUSTRATION

J. M. W. Turner's Eye

Preaching Themes: Beauty, Creation, Holy Spirit, Jesus

Eyes need to be trained to see beauty. No man sees half or a thousandth part of the beauty even of this poor, natural world. But the painter's eye—the eye of Turner, for instance—can see much more than you or I ever saw. "Oh!" said one, when he looked on one of Turner's landscapes, "I have seen that view every day, but I never saw as much as that in it." "No," replied Turner, "don't you wish you could?"

And, when the Spirit of God trains and tutors the eye, it sees in Christ what it never saw before. But, even then, as Turner's eye was not able to see all the mystery of God's beauty in nature, so neither is the most trained and educated Christian able to perceive all the matchless beauty that there is in Christ.

And the lily of the valleys "I am the rose." That is *the emblem of majesty*. The rose is the very queen of flowers; in the judgment of all who know what to admire it is enthroned above all the rest of the beauties of the garden. But the lily—what is that? That is *the emblem of love*. The psalmist hints at this in the title of the forty-fifth psalm: "Upon Shoshannim ... a Song of love." Shoshannim signifies lilies, so the lily-psalm is the love song, for the lilies, with their beauty, their purity, their delicacy, are a very choice emblem of love.

Are you not delighted when you put these two things together, majesty and love? A King upon a throne of love, a Prince whose very eyes beam with love to those who put their trust in him, a real Head united by living bonds of love to all his members—such is our dear Lord and Savior. A rose and yet a lily; I do not know in which of the two I take the greater delight; I prefer to have the two together. When I think that my Savior is King of kings and Lord of lords, I shout, "Hallelujah!" But when I remember that he loved me, and gave himself for me, and that still he loves me, and that he will keep on loving me forever and ever, there is such a charm in this thought that nothing can excel it.

ILLUSTRATION

Hearing the Song of the Nightingale

Preaching Themes: Love of God, Music, Presence of God

Traveling on the Lake Lugano one morning, we heard the swell of the song of the nightingale, and the oars were stilled on the blue lake as we listened to the silver sounds. We could not see a single bird, nor do I know that we wished to see—we were so content with the sweetness of the music.

Even so it is with our Lord; we may enter a house where he is loved, and we may hear nothing concerning Christ, and yet we may perceive clearly enough that he is there, a holy influence streaming through their actions pervades the household; so that if Jesus be unseen, it is clear that he is not unknown. Go anywhere where Jesus is, and though you do not actually hear his name, yet the sweet influence which flows from his love will be plainly enough discernible.

---

2 **As the lily among thorns, so is my love among the daughters** Notice the first verse of the chapter, wherein the bridegroom speaks: "I am the rose of Sharon, and the lily of the valleys." He is the lily, but his beloved is like him; for he applies his own chosen emblem to her: "As the lily among thorns, so is my love among the daughters." Notice that he *is* the lily, she is *as* the lily—that is to say, he has the beauty and *she* reflects

it. She is comely in his comeliness which he puts upon her. If any soul has any such beauty as is described here, Christ has dowered that beloved soul with all its wealth of charms, for in ourselves we are deformed and defiled. What is the confession of this very spouse in the previous chapter? She says, "I am black"—that is the opposite of a lily. If she adds, "but comely," it is because her Lord has made her comely. There is no grace but what grace has given, and if we are graceful it is because Christ has made us full of grace. There is no beauty in any one of us but what our Lord has wrought in us.

It is the nature of love to make the thing beloved like itself. If Christ be a lily, he makes his people lilies too. Certainly, he is the lily of the valley, and before long his church is able to say, "As the lily among the thorns, so am I," while for the present Jesus says it. She is among the thorns, thorns that hurt and vex her. The people of God are still in the tents of Kedar, still among the wicked, having their ears vexed with their filthy conversation. But the lily is all the more beautiful on account of the thorns that make the background, and so your piety may be all the more resplendent because of the evil men among whom you sojourn.

3 **As the apple tree among the trees of the wood, So is my beloved among the sons** By the apple tree would probably be intended by the oriental writer either the citron, or the pomegranate, or the orange. I suppose he did not refer to the apple tree of our gardens, for it would scarcely be known to him. The word would not, however, be properly rendered if we confined it to any of the three fruit trees we have mentioned, or if we excluded our own apple from it, for the term apple comprehends all large round fruit not enclosed in a shell; and so we may, without making any mistake, think of the apple tree of our own English orchards, and yet the metaphor will stand good, except that the shadow of our apple tree at home is hardly so excellent a retreat from the sun as the shadow of the other trees included under the term. Our own apple tree will suffice us, however, and we shall not need to enter into any minute distinctions, or to carry you away to Palestine;

we can sit at home in England, and can say with great propriety, if we love the Lord Jesus Christ, "As the apple tree among the trees of the wood, so is my beloved among the sons." The point of the metaphor is this. There are many trees of the forest, and they all have their uses, but when one is hungry, and faint, and thirsty, the forest trees yield no succor, and we must look elsewhere; they yield shelter, but not refreshing nutriment. If, however, in the midst of the wood one discovers an apple tree, he there finds the refreshment which he needs; his thirst is alleviated, and his hunger removed. Even so the church here means to say that there are many things in the world which yield us a kind of satisfaction—many men, many truths, many institutions, many earthly comforts, but there are none which yield us the full solace which the soul requires; none which can give to the heart the spiritual food for which it hungers; Jesus Christ alone supplies the needs of the sons of men. As the apple tree is the exception to the forest trees in bearing its fruit, as it stands on that account in contrast to the trees of the wood, so does Jesus our Beloved contrast with all others, and transcendently excel them.

ILLUSTRATION

No Help from the Trees

Preaching Themes: Creation, False Teaching

Imagine yourself, upon some sultry day in autumn, as a wanderer in the leafy lanes of a great forest, where the grand cathedral aisles reach before you to lengths immeasurable, or huge domes of foliage rise above you like a second sky. Imagine yourself roaming amidst the ferns and brakes, trampling on the briars and hollies, or sitting down on mossy banks and knolls soft with layers of sere leaves. Suppose also that you are hungry and thirsty, and that no rippling streams offer their cooling floods, while you are so far away from human call that, hungry though you might be even to death, there would be no eye to see you, and consequently no hand outstretched for your help. In such a plight it needs no imagination to conceive you as glancing to the trees, your only companions, and silently appealing to them for aid. Some of them look as if their bowing branches would sympathize if they could, others grotesquely grin at you, and the most of them sternly refuse you succor by their solemn silence. You will ask in vain of oak, or ash, or elm. Suppose you appeal to yonder stately tree which is *the greatest* of them all, the king of the forest, unequaled in greatness or girth; admire its stupendous limbs, its gnarled roots, its bossy bark, the vast area beneath its boughs. You look up at it and think what a puny creature you are, and how brief has been your life compared with its duration. You try to contemplate the storms which have swept over it, and the suns which have shone upon it. Great, however, as it is, it cannot help you: if it were a thousand times higher, and its topmost boughs swept the stars, yet it could minister no aid to you.

This is a fit picture of the attempt to find consolation in systems of religion which are recommended to you because they are greatly followed.

I sat down under his shadow with great delight She who said, "I sat down under his shadow with great delight," was *one who had known before what weary travel meant, and therefore valued rest*. The man who has never labored knows nothing of the sweetness of repose. The loafer who has eaten bread he never earned, from whose brow there never oozed a drop of honest sweat, does not deserve rest, and knows not what it is. It is to the laboring man that rest is sweet; and when at last we come, toilworn with many miles of weary plodding, to a shaded place where we may comfortably "sit down," then are we filled with delight.

The spouse had been seeking her Beloved, and in looking for him she had asked where she was likely to find him. "Tell me," says she, "O thou whom my soul loveth, where thou feedest, where thou makest thy flock to rest at noon." He told her to go and seek him by the footsteps of the flock. She did go her way, but after a while she came to this resolution: "I will *sit down* under his shadow."

She who said, "I sat down under his shadow with great delight," *could appreciate shade, for she had been sunburnt*. This was her exclamation, "Look not upon me, because I am black, because the sun hath looked upon me." She knew what heat meant, what the burning sun meant; and therefore shade was pleasant to her. You know nothing about the deliciousness of shade till you travel in a thoroughly hot country; then you are delighted with it.

Mark well these two things concerning the spouse. She knew what it was to be weary, and she knew what it was to be sunburnt; and just in proportion as you, also, know these two things, your valuation of Christ will rise.

And his fruit was sweet to my taste *She did not feast upon the fruit of the tree till first she was under the shadow of it*. There is no knowing the excellent things of Christ till you trust him. Not a single sweet apple shall fall to the lot of those who are outside the shadow.

Now it would appear, as we read the text, that *she obtained this fruit without effort*. The proverb says, "He who would gain the fruit must climb the tree." But she did not climb, for she says, "I sat down under his shadow." *The spouse rested while feasting;* she sat, and ate.

Further, notice that, *as the spouse fed upon this fruit, she had a relish for it*. It is not every palate that likes every fruit. Never dispute with other people about tastes of any sort, for agreement is not possible. That dainty which to one person is the most delicious is to another nauseous; and if there were a competition as to which fruit is preferable to all the rest, there would probably be almost as many opinions as there are fruits. But blessed is he who has a relish for Christ Jesus!

4 **He brought me to the banqueting house** That, I trust, he will again do, as he has often done before, both while we are hearing his word and when we approach his table.

And his banner over me was love Not the fiery ensign of war, but the peaceful banner of love. You have had enough of the world, beloved, during the past six days; you will again have enough of it in the six days yet to come. But just now, let love's royal banner wave over you, and give up your thoughts entirely to him who has loved you with an everlasting love, and sealed his love to you by the blood that streamed from his pierced heart.

5 **Stay me with flagons, comfort me with apples: For I am sick of love** The soul overjoyed with the divine communications of happiness and bliss which came from Christ, the body scarcely able to bear the excessive delirium of delight which the soul possessed, she was so glad to be in the embraces of her Lord, that she needed to be stayed under her overpowering weight of joy.

The love of Christ shed abroad in our hearts sometimes quite overpowers us. It is very possible to be so delighted, so full of joy with a sense of the love of Jesus, that one feels unable to bear any more of it. Oh, for more of this blessed sickness!

6 **His left hand is under my head, And his right hand doth embrace me** The hand with which he smites his enemies cannot smite me, for it is under my head, my sweet support. And his right hand, the hand with which he blesses, the hand of his power and his glory, embraces each one of his people.

The soul hath come to its resting place in God, and feels itself to be supported by the divine strength. The heart has learned to abide in Christ Jesus to go no more out forever, but to lean on his bosom both day and night. It is somewhat in the condition of Noah's dove which, when weary, was about to drop into the all-destroying waters, but Noah put out his hand and plucked her in unto him into the ark; and when she was all safe, in the hollow of his hands, held by her preserver with a firm but tender grasp, she found in that place a refuge which surrounded her and upheld her from below. The hands covered her on all sides and came beneath her too. Even thus the hand of God sustains all those who dwell in the secret place of the Most High and abide under the shadow of the Almighty.

7 **I charge you, O ye daughters of Jerusalem, By the roes, and by the hinds of the field** The spouse was in the full enjoyment of fellowship with her Beloved. Her joy was so great as almost to overpower her, and yet, so nearly does fear tread upon the heels of joy, she was filled with dread lest her bliss should come to an end. She feared lest others should disturb her Lord, for if he were grieved she would be grieved also, and if he departed the banquet of her delight would be over. She was afraid even of her friends, the daughters of Jerusalem; she knew that the best can interrupt fellowship as well as the worst, and therefore she adjured even Zion's daughters not to sin against Zion's King. Had they aroused her Beloved and broken his sacred peace she would not have found a recompense in their company, but would rather have regarded them with aversion, for having robbed her of her chief delight. The adjuration which she used is a choice specimen of oriental poetry: she charges them, not as we should prosaically do, by everything that is sacred and true, but "by the roes, and by the hinds of the field."

"The roes and the hinds of the field" are creatures of great *beauty*. Who can gaze upon them as they wander among the bracken without an inward admiration? Now, since nothing can be more lovely than communion with Jesus, the spouse exhorts the daughters of Jerusalem by all the loveliest objects in nature to refrain from disturbing it. No one would wish to drive away the gazelle, but would feast his eyes upon it, and yet its graceful elegance can never be compared with that beauty of holiness, that comeliness of grace which are to be seen in fellowship with Jesus. It is beautiful from both sides; it is a lovely display of condescension for our beloved Lord to reveal himself to us, and on the other hand, it is a charming manifestation of every admirable virtue for a believer to enter into fellowship with his Lord. He who would disturb such mutual intercourse must be devoid of spiritual taste, and blind to all which is most worthy of admiration.

As one delights to see the red deer in the open glades of the forest, and counts them the finest ornaments of the scene, so do men whose eyes are opened rejoice in the saints whose high communion with heaven renders them beings of superior mold to common mortals. A soul in converse with its God is the admiration of angels. Was ever a lovelier sight seen than Jesus at the table with the beloved disciple leaning on his bosom? Is not Mary sitting at the Master's feet a picture worthy of the choicest art? Do nothing, then, O you who joy in things of beauty, to mar the fellowship in which the rarest beauty dwells. Neither by worldly care, nor sin, nor trifling make even the slightest stir which might break the Beloved's repose. His restful presence is heaven below, and the best antepast of heaven above; in it we find everything that is pure, and lovely, and of good report. It is good, and only good. Why, then, O daughters of Jerusalem, should ye stir up our Beloved, and cause his adorable excellency to be hidden from us? Rather join with us in preserving a joy so fair, a bliss so comely.

The next thought suggested "by the roes, and by the hinds of the field" is that of *tender innocence*. These gentle creatures are so harmless, so defenseless, so timid, that he must have a soulless soul who would do them harm or cause them fright. By all, then, that is tender the spouse beseeches her friends not to disturb her Beloved. He is so good, so kind, so holy, harmless, and undefiled, that the most indifferent ought to be ashamed to molest his rest. About him there is nothing to provoke offense, and everything to forbid it. He is a man of sorrows and acquainted with grief; he gave his back to the smiters, and his cheeks to them that plucked off the hair, he hid not his face from shame and spitting. Being reviled he reviled not again, but in his death agonies he prayed for his enemies. Who, then, could find cause for offense in him? Do not his wounds ward off the blows which might be challenged had he been of another character? Who will wish to vex the Lamb of God? Go elsewhere, ye hunters! "The hind of the morning" has already sweated great drops of blood falling to the ground. When dogs compassed him and the assembly of the wicked enclosed him he felt the full of grief—will ye afflict him yet again?

A third thought most certainly had a place in the mind of the anxious spouse; she meant to adjure and persuade her friends to silence by everything which sets forth *love*. The lilies and the roes have always been sacred to love. The poet of the Canticles had elsewhere used the symbol of the text to set forth married love. "Let her be as the loving hind and pleasant roe" (Prov 5:19). If ever there was true love in all this selfish world, it is the love of Jesus first, and next the love of his people. As for his love, it passes the love of women, many waters cannot quench it, neither can the floods drown it; and as for the love of the church, he who best knows it says, "How fair is thy love, my sister, my spouse! How much better is thy love than wine! and the smell of thine ointment than all spices!" (Song 4:10). If love, therefore, may plead immunity from war, and ask to have its quietude respected, the spouse used a good argument when she pleaded "by the roes and by the hinds of the field," that her royal Bridegroom's rest of love might not be invaded.

That ye stir not up, nor awake my love, till he please If he be with me, may nothing disturb him—nothing cause him to withdraw himself. Our Lord Jesus is very jealous, and when he manifests himself to his people, a very little thing will drive him away like the hinds and the roes that are very timid, so is communion a very delicate and dainty thing. It is soon broken. Oh! May God grant that nothing may happen to the thoughts of any of you by which your fellowship with Christ should be destroyed.

APPLICATION

Christ Is Accessible and Abundant

I have been talking about my Master, and I want to show you that *he is accessible*. He is meant to be plucked and enjoyed as roses and lilies are. He says in the text, "I am the rose of Sharon." What was

Sharon? It was an open plain where anybody might wander, and where even cattle roamed at their own sweet will. Jesus is not like a rose in Solomon's garden, shut up within high walls, with broken glass all along the top. Oh, no! He says, "I am the rose of Sharon," everybody's rose, the flower for the common people to come and gather. "I am the lily." What lily? The lily of the palace of Shushan, enclosed and guarded from all approach? No, but "I am the lily of the valleys," found in this glen, or the other ravine, growing here, there, and everywhere: "I am the lily of the valleys."

Then *Christ is as abundant as a common flower*. Whatever kind of rose it was, it was a common rose. Whatever kind of lily it was, it was a well-known lily that grew freely in the valleys of that land. Oh, blessed be my Master's name, he has brought us a common salvation, and he is the common people's Christ! Men in general do not love him enough, or else they would have hedged him in with all sorts of restrictions. They would have made a franchise for him, and nobody would have been able to be saved except those who paid I know not how much a year in taxes. But they do not love our Lord enough to shut him in, and I am glad they have never tried to do so. There he stands, at the four-crossroads, so that everybody who comes by and wants him may have him. He is a fountain, bearing this inscription, "Let him that is athirst come. And whosoever will, let him take the water of life freely" (Rev 22:17). "I am the rose of Sharon, and the lily of the valleys."

Why do roses grow in Sharon? Why do lilies grow in the valleys? Why, to be plucked, of course! I like to see the children go down into the meadow when it is decked in grass, and adorned with flowers, gilded with buttercups, or white with the day's-eyes. I love to see the children pluck the flowers, and fill their pinafores with them, or make garlands, and twist them round their necks, or put them on their heads. "O children, children!" somebody might cry, "do not spoil those beautiful flowers, do not go and pick them." Oh, but they may! Nobody says they may not. They may not go into our gardens and steal the geraniums and the fuchsias, but they may get away into the meadows or into the open fields and pluck these common flowers to their heart's content.

And now, poor soul, if you would like an apronful of roses, come and have them. If you would like to carry away a big handful of the lilies of the valleys, come and take them, as many as you will. May the Lord give you the will! That is, after all, what is wanted. If there be that grace-given will, the Rose of Sharon and the Lily of the Valleys will soon be yours. They are common flowers, growing in a common place, and there are plenty of them. Will you not take them?

The Christian as a Lily among Thorns

Many saints reside in families where they will never be appreciated any more than the lily is appreciated by the thorns. This is painful, for the sympathy of our fellows is a great comfort. Lilies of the valley love to grow in clusters, and saints love holy company, and yet in some cases it must not be; they must live alone. Nor need we think that this loneliness is unrelieved, for God goes out of the track of men, and he visits those whom his own servants are passing by. The poet says, "Full many a flower is born to blush unseen, And waste its sweetness on the desert air."[1]

But the poet forgot that God is in the wilderness, and the solitary place, and the sweetness of lonely flowers is his. He who planted the lily among thorns sees its beauty. It is God's flower, and does it waste its sweetness because no human nostril smells at it? It would be blasphemous to count that wasted which is reserved for the great King. The Lord understands the incense of nature better than we do, and as he walks abroad he rejoices in his works. Grace struggling in loneliness is very choice in God's esteem. If man does not see you, O lonely believer, you may nevertheless sing, "You, God, see me." The flower which blooms for God alone has a special honor put upon it, and so has the saint whose quiet life is all for Jesus. If you are unappreciated by those around you, do not therefore be distressed, for you are honorable in the sight of God.

The lily is altogether unassisted too by its surroundings—"the lily among thorns" borrows nothing from the growth which gathers about it. A genuine Christian is quite unhelped by ungodly men; what is worse, he is cumbered by them. Yet through divine grace he

1. A quote from Thomas Gray's "Elegy Written in a Country Churchyard." —ed.

lives and grows. You know how the good seed could not grow because of the thorns which sprang up and choked it, but here is a good seed, a choice bulb, which flourishes where you could not have looked for it to do so. God can make his people live and blossom even among the thorns, where the ungodly by their evil influences would choke and destroy it. Happy it is when the gracious one can overtop the thorn-thicket that would check his growth and make his influence to be known and felt above the grossness of surrounding sin.

We should not do justice to this text if we failed to see in it a reminder of the persecution to which many of the best of God's people are subjected. They live all their lives long like the lily among thorns. Some of you, dear friends, are in this condition. You can hardly speak a word but what it is picked up and made mischief of; you cannot perform an action but what it is twisted, and motives imputed to you that you do not know. Nowadays persecutors cannot drag men to the stake, but the old trial of cruel mockings is still continued; in some cases it rages even more fiercely than ever. God's people have been a persecuted people in all times, and you only fare as they fare. Bear well the burden common to all the chosen! Make no great wonder of it; this bitter trial has happened to many more before, and you may well rejoice that you are now in fellowship with apostles and prophets and honorable men of all ages. The lily among thorns should rejoice that it is a lily and not a thorn, and when it is wounded it should consider it a matter of course, and bloom on.

But why does the Lord put his lilies among thorns? It is because he works transformations, singular transformations, by their means. He can make a lily grow among thorns till the thorns grow into lilies. Remember how it is written, "The wilderness and the solitary place shall be glad for them; and the desert shall rejoice, and blossom as the rose" (Isa 35:1). He can set a Christian in a godless family till first one and then another shall feel the divine power, and shall say, "We will go with you, for we perceive that God is with you." It cannot happen in nature, but it does happen in grace perpetually, that the sweet perfume of the lily believer, shed abroad upon the thorn-brake of the ungodly, turns it into a lily-garden. Such holy work among ungodly people is the truest and best "Flower Mission." They do well who give flowers to cheer the poor in their dreary habitations, but they do better still who are themselves flowers in the places where they live. Be lilies, my dear brothers; preach by your actions, preach by your kindness, and by your love, and I feel quite sure that your influence will be a power for good.

Tell Others about the Apple Tree

I am sure, if there were an apple tree in any forest, and it were once found out, everybody would be taken to see it, it would be such an attraction. There would be many paths to it, and everybody who had been in the forest and seen it would tell his neighbors.

Now, I beseech you who have found the Savior to be telling others what you know about him and try to lead others to look at him. You cannot make them feed upon him, but God can, and if you can lead them to the tree, who knows but God will give them spiritual hunger and will lead them to feed as you have fed. O you silent Christians, you silent Christians, who neither by your tongue, nor your pen, nor by any other way, ever tell about Christ, I do not know what to make of you. I wonder the seats you sit on do not push you off and speak instead of you, and that the stones of the street do not cry out against you as you pass over them. Why, what can you be made of, to be saved from going down to hell, and not want others to be saved too! Shame on you! Shame on me also whenever I am silent about such a blessed salvation, such a divine redemption. I want to set your tongues going about this blessed apple tree among the trees of the wood. There is nothing about which you can speak so freely without fear of exaggeration.

All the world has been talking about the Shah of Persia; I wish they would talk half as much about the Christ of God. All the good you will ever get out of the Shah you may see with your eyes shut, but the benefit that will come from the King of heaven to your own souls, and ten thousands of other souls, is unlimited.

Cry the Savior up, beloved. Set him on a high throne; give him the best of your thoughts, the best of your words, the best of your actions. Give him of your time and your substance. He deserves to have honor above all the sons of men, for he is the best of all. As the apple tree to the hungry man excels all other trees, so does Jesus excel all other loves. Let us give him today our hearts' warmest love, and praise him forever and forever. God grant it, for his name's sake.

SONG OF SOLOMON 2:8–17

8 The voice of my beloved! behold, he cometh
Leaping upon the mountains, skipping upon the hills.
9 My beloved is like a roe or a young hart:
Behold, he standeth behind our wall,
He looketh forth at the windows,
Shewing himself through the lattice.
10 My beloved spake, and said unto me,
Rise up, my love, my fair one, and come away.
11 For, lo, the winter is past,
The rain is over *and* gone;
12 The flowers appear on the earth;
The time of the singing *of birds* is come,
And the voice of the turtle is heard in our land;
13 The fig tree putteth forth her green figs,
And the vines *with* the tender grape give a *good* smell.
Arise, my love, my fair one, and come away.
14 O my dove, *that art* in the clefts of the rock, in the secret *places* of the stairs,
Let me see thy countenance, let me hear thy voice;
For sweet *is* thy voice, and thy countenance *is* comely.
15 Take us the foxes,
The little foxes, that spoil the vines:
For our vines *have* tender grapes.
16 My beloved *is* mine, and I *am* his:
He feedeth among the lilies.
17 Until the day break, and the shadows flee away,
Turn, my beloved,
And be thou like a roe or a young hart
Upon the mountains of Bether.

EXPOSITION

8 **The voice of my beloved!** The spouse knows it at once; her ear is so trained that she recognizes it as soon as she hears it. Jesus said that his sheep follow him, for they know his voice, and he added, "A stranger will they not follow, but will flee from him: for they know not the voice of strangers" (John 10:5).

behold, he cometh "I thought my sins would keep him back, for they seemed like great mountains; how could he come to me? But, 'behold,' he makes nothing of those barriers: 'he cometh leaping upon the mountains, skipping upon the hills.' "

Leaping upon the mountains, skipping upon the hills Jesus can come to us when we cannot go to him. The roe and the young hart, or, as you may read it, the gazelle and the ibex, live among the crags of the mountains, and leap across the abyss with amazing agility. For swiftness and sure-footedness they are unrivaled. The sacred poet said, "He maketh my feet like hinds' feet, and setteth me upon my high places" (Ps 18:33), alluding to the feet of those creatures which are so fitted to stand securely on the mountain's side. Our blessed Lord is called in the title of the twenty-second psalm, "the hind of the morning," and the spouse in this golden Canticle sings, "My Beloved is like a roe or a young hart; behold, he cometh leaping upon the mountains, skipping upon the hills."

9 **My beloved is like a roe or a young hart: Behold, he standeth behind our wall, He looketh forth at the windows, Shewing himself through the lattice** When we observe the ordinances aright, they are like latticed windows. We cannot see our Lord through them as clearly as we would, but still, we do see him, and we are thankful for these windows until we get up yonder, where we shall see him face to face.

10 **My beloved spake, and said unto me, Rise up, my love, my fair one, and come away** To everything there is a time and a purpose, and every season has its special labor. It seems from

the text, that whenever it is springtide in our hearts, then Christ's voice may be heard saying, "Arise, my love, my fair one, and come away." Whenever we have been delivered from a dreary winter of temptation or affliction, or tribulation—whenever the fair spring of hope comes on us, and our joys begin to multiply, then we should hear the Master bidding us seek after something higher and better, and we should go forth in his strength to love him more, and serve him more diligently than before.

11 **For, lo, the winter is past, The rain is over and gone** We do not usually call our friends to look at things which we do not ourselves admire, so here the Bridegroom calls his spouse to share in his joy in these tokens of the heavenly life of the church of God.

12 **The flowers appear on the earth; The time of the singing of birds is come, and the voice of the turtle is heard in our land** The history of Christ's church is a varied year of many seasons. She has had her high and noble processions of victory; she has had her sorrowful congregations of mourners during times of disaster and apparent defeat. Commencing with the life of Christ, what a smiling spring it was for the world when the Holy Spirit was poured out in *Pentecost*. Then might the saints sing with sweet accord—

> The Jewish wintry state is gone,
> The mists are fled, the spring comes on;
> The sacred turtle dove we hear,
> Proclaim the new, the joyful year;
>
> The immortal vine of heavenly root,
> Blossoms and buds and gives her fruit;
> Lo, we are come to taste the wine,
> Our souls rejoice and bless the vine.[1]

1. These lines are quoted from the Isaac Watts hymn "The Voice of My Beloved Sounds." —ed.

The winter was over and past—that long season in which the Jewish state lay dead, when the frosts of Pharisaism had bound up all spiritual life. The rain was over and gone, the black clouds of wrath had emptied themselves upon the Savior's head. Thunder and tempest and storm, all dark and terrible things were gone forever. The flowers appeared on the earth; three thousand in one day blossomed forth, baptized in the name of the Lord Jesus Christ. Fair promises created for beauty and delight sprang up and with their blessed fulfillment clothed the earth in a royal garment of many colors. The time of the singing birds was come, for they praised God day and night, eating their bread with joy and singleness of heart. The voice of the turtle was heard, for the Spirit—that hallowed dove from heaven—descended with tongues of fire upon the apostles, and the gospel was preached in every land. Then had earth one of her joyous Sabbaths; the fig tree put forth her green figs; in every land there were some converts; the dwellers in Mesopotamia, Medes, Parthians, Elamites—some of all—had been converted to God, and the tender grapes of newborn piety and zeal gave forth a sweet smell before God.

13 **The fig tree putteth forth her green figs, and the vines with the tender grape give a good smell** The vine is of all trees the most useless unless it bears fruit. You cannot make hardly anything of it; you would scarcely be able to cut enough wood out of a vine to hang a pot upon; you cannot turn it into furniture, and barely could you use it in the least degree for building purposes. It must either bear fruit, or else it must be consumed in the fire. The branches of the vine that bear no fruit are necessarily cut off, and they are used, as I have seen them used in the South of France many a time, in little twisted bundles for kindling the fire. They burn very rapidly, so there is soon an end of them, and then they are gone.

The vine is constantly used in Scripture as a picture of the nominal church of Christ; so, like the vine, we must either bring forth fruit or we shall be accounted as good for nothing. Christ forms a correct, condescending, wise estimate of these vines with the tender grape. He calls his church to look at them, he calls them tender, he says that they have a sweet smell, and then he shows that he cares very much about them, for he says, "Take us the foxes, the little foxes, that spoil the vines: for our vines have tender grapes." He does not want even the tender grapes to be spoiled.

14 **O my dove, that art in the clefts of the rock, in the secret places of the stairs, let me see thy countenance, let me hear thy voice** Christ calls you out, you hidden ones. You who are half ashamed to be seen, he bids you come to him. Come away from your doubting and your fearing, your halting and your hesitating. It is Jesus who calls you, therefore come to him at once.

For sweet is thy voice, and thy countenance is comely The Lord so loves his people that he is never long away from them. You know that dear relationship into which our Lord has entered with his church; she is his bride, he loves her as he loves his own soul. In some respects, he loves her better than he loves himself, for he gave himself for her; and do you think that he is happy away from his bride, his spouse? It is not so; he saith to her, "Let me see thy countenance, let me hear thy voice; for sweet is thy voice, and thy countenance is comely"; and whenever she calls for him, saying, "Let my beloved come into his garden" (Song 4:16), his quick answer is, "I am come into my garden, my sister, my spouse" (Song 5:1). He so loves us that, when we shut the door against him, he stands and knocks, and cries to us, "Open to me, my sister, my love, my dove, my undefiled; for my head is filled with dew, and my locks with the drops of the night" (Song 5:2). Do not think that he has gone from you when he loves you so as your Father, and as the Husband of your soul. Moreover, he will be with his church in her work, because her work is his work; and wherever there is a heart on the earth, sanctified by the Holy Ghost, in sympathy and harmony with the heart of Christ, depend upon it he is assuredly there, for that sympathy and that harmony are created by his very presence.

15 **Take us the foxes, the little foxes, that spoil the vines** In the spiritual vineyard there are foxes of many kinds. There is, first, *the hard censurer*. He will spoil the vines if he can, and especially the vines that have the tender grapes. He finds fault with everything that he can see in you who are but young believers.

A worse fox even than that one, however, is *the flatterer*. He comes to you smiling and smirking, and he begins to express his approval of your religion, and very likely tells you what a fine fellow you are. Indeed, you are so good that he thinks you are rather too precise, you have gone a little over the line! He believes in religion, he says, fully; though, if you watch his life, you will not think so; but he says that he does not want people to be righteous overmuch; he knows that there is a line to be drawn, and he draws it. I never could see where he drew it; but still he says he does, and he thinks that you draw the line a little too near the cross.

Then there comes another foul fox, *Mr. Worldly-wiseman*. He says, "You are a Christian, but do not be a fool. Carry your religion as far as you can make it pay; but if it comes to losing anything by it, well then, don't you do it. You see, this practice is the custom of the trade; it is not right, I know, but still, other people do it, and you ought to do it. If you do not, you will never get on in business." Mr. Worldly-wiseman further says, "Never mind if you tell a lie or two, make your advertisements say what is not true; everybody else does it as a matter of course, and why should not you? Then try whether you cannot get a slice out of your customer here and a slice there when he does not know it, it is the custom of the trade; it is the way other people do, and, as it is the custom, of course you must do it." To all such talk I reply that there is another custom, a custom that God has, of turning all liars into hell; mind that you do not come under that divine rule and law. There is another custom that God has, namely, that of cutting down as hypocrites those who do not walk honestly and uprightly towards their fellow men.

There is another ugly fox about, and that is, *a doubting fox*. He comes and says, "You seem very happy, and very joyful; but is it true? You appear to have become quite a different person from what you used to be; but is there, after all, such a thing as conversion?" This fox begins nibbling at every doctrine, he even nibbles at your Bible, and tries to steal from you this chapter and that verse. God save you young people from all these foxes!

There are some foxes of *evil doctrine*. They say, "Now, you are a person of considerable breadth of thought, you have an enlarged mind, you are a man of culture; it is a pity that you should cling to those old-fashioned beliefs, which really are not consistent with modern progress"; and the foolish young fellow thinks that he is a wonder, and so is puffed up with conceit. When a man has to talk about his own culture, and to glory in his own advancement, it is time that we suspected the truth about him. When a man can despise others who are doing vastly more good than he ever dreamed of doing, and call such people antiquated and old-fashioned, it is time that he should get rebuked for his impudence, for that is what it really is. Get out of the way of that fox, or else he will do much mischief to the tender grapes.

For our vines have tender grapes We try all we can to stop the gaps in the hedge, that we may keep the foxes out; but they are very crafty, and they manage to get in sometimes. The foxes in the East are much smaller than ours, and they seem to be even more cunning and more ferocious than those we have in this country, and they do much mischief to the vines.

16 **My beloved is mine** The spouse makes this the first of her joy notes, the cornerstone of her peace, the fountain of her bliss, the crown of her glory. Observe here that where such an expression is truthfully used the existence *of the Beloved is matter of fact*. Skepticism and questioning have no place with those who sing in this way. There are dreamers nowadays who cast doubt on everything; taking to themselves the name of philosophers, and professing to know something of science, they make statements worthy only of idiots, and demand for their

self-evidently false assertions the assent of rational men. The word "philosopher" will soon come to mean a lover of ignorance, and the term "a scientific man" will be understood as meaning a fool, who has said in his heart there is no God. Such attacks on the eternal verities of our holy faith can have no effect on hearts enamored of the Son of God, for, dwelling in his immediate presence, they have passed the stage of doubt, left the region of questioning far behind, and in this matter have entered into rest. The power of love has convinced us; to entertain a doubt as to the reality and glory of our Well-beloved would be torment to us, and therefore love has cast it out. We use no perhapses, buts, or ifs concerning our Beloved, but we say positively that he is, and that he is ours. We believe that we have better evidence of his being, power, Godhead, and love to us than can be given for any other fact. So far from being abashed by the cavils of skeptics or quailing beneath the question, "Is there such a Beloved?" we are not careful to answer in this matter, for we know that there is. Our love laughs at the question, and does not condescend to answer it save by bidding those who seriously inquire to "come and see" for themselves.

and I am his Christ is mine, but if I were not his it would be a sorry case, and if I were his and he were not mine it would be a wretched business. These two things are joined together with diamond rivets—"My beloved is mine, and I am his." Put the two together, and you have reached the summit of delight.

That we are his is a fact that may be proven—indeed, it should need no proving, but be manifest to all that "I am *his*." Certainly we are his by creation: he who made us should have us. We are his because his Father gave us to him, and we are his because he chose us. Creation, donation, election are his triple hold upon us. We are his because he bought us with his blood, his because he called us by his grace, his because he is married to us, and we are his spouse. We are his, moreover, to our own consciousness, because we have heartily, from the inmost depths of our being, given ourselves up to him, bound by love to him forever. We feel we must have Christ, and be Christ's, or die—"For me to live is Christ" (Phil 1:21).

ILLUSTRATION

Refusing to Begin at the Beginning

Preaching Themes: Election, Salvation

We have scores of people who will not come to Christ because they cannot understand election. Meet a boy in the street and invite him to go to a two-penny school. "No," says the boy, "I don't feel fit to go to a national school, to learn to read and write, for, to tell you the truth, I don't understand the Hebrew language." You would reply, "But my good lad, you will learn Hebrew afterward, if you can; but that is no reason, at any rate, why you should not learn English first. Come first to the little school; you shall go afterward to the grammar school; if you get on, you shall go to the University, take your BA degree, and perhaps come out as a Master of Arts." But here we have poor souls that want to be MAs before they have gone to the penny school. They want to read the tomes before they will read the hornbook. They are not content to spell A, B, C—"I am a sinner, Christ is a savior"—but they long to turn over the book of decrees and find out the deep things of God. You shall find them out afterward; you shall go step by step, while the master shall say to you, each time, "Friend, come up higher." But if you begin with election, you will have to come down again, for there will be a more honorable man than you who will come in, and you will begin with shame to take the lowest room.

He feedeth among the lilies The spouse in the seventh verse had charged her companions by all things of gentleness, delicacy, and timidity—"by the roes, and by the hinds of the field" (Song 2:7)—to refrain from offending her beloved while he deigned to abide with her; she had also compared him to a roe or a young hart, rather hiding than revealing himself; and here she likens him to the same roe, quietly pasturing in the gardens, so gently moving that he does not break or even bruise a lily, but softly insinuates himself among their delicate beauties, as one of the same dainty mold. This hints in poetic imagery at the solemn and sacred truth that the dearest fellowship with Jesus can never be known by the rough and the coarse, the hard and the restless, but remains the priceless heritage of the lowly and meek; and these can only retain it by a studious care which cherishes love, and guards it from even the least intrusion. A gazelle among the lilies would start at the bark of a fox, and be gone at the voice of a stranger, and therefore soft whispers of inward love must say, "Take us the foxes, the little foxes" (Song 2:15), and nimble hands with noiseless fingers must draw up the lattice that kindly eyes may look forth at the windows, and may be seen of him who delights in love.

What are these lilies? Do not these lilies represent the pure in heart, with whom Jesus dwells? The spouse used the imagery which her Lord had put into her mouth. He said, "As the lily among thorns, so is my love among the daughters" (Song 2:2), and she appropriates the symbol to all the saints. A preacher who is great at spiritualizing has well said on this verse, "The straight stalk, standing up erect from the earth, its flowers as high from the ground as possible, do they not tell us of heavenly-mindedness? Do they not seem to say, 'Set your affection on things above, not on things on the earth'? And if the spotless snow of the leaves teaches us of grace, then the gold of the anthers tells us of that crown which shall be the reward of grace."[2] The violet and the primrose in spring nestle close to the earth, as if in sympathy with her chill condition, but the lily lifts up itself towards heaven in sympathy with the summer's light and splendor. The lily is frail, and such are the saints of God; were not Jesus among them to protect them the wild beast would soon tread them down. Frail as they are, they are surpassingly lovely, and their beauty is not that which is made with hands. It is a beauty put upon them by the Lord,

2. Spurgeon is quoting from John Mason Neale, *Sermons on the Song of Songs.* —ed.

for "they toil not, neither do they spin, and yet ... Solomon in all his glory was not arrayed like one of these" (Matt 6:28–29). The saints work not for life, and spin no righteousness of their own, and yet the royal righteousness which adorns them far surpasses all that wisdom could devise or wealth procure.

Where, then, is my Lord today? He is up and away, among the lilies of Paradise. In imagination I see those stately rows of milk-white lilies growing no longer among thorns: lilies which are never soiled with the dust of earth, which forever glisten with the eternal dews of fellowship, while their roots drink in unfading life from the river of the water of life which waters the garden of the Lord. There is Jesus! Can you see him? He is fairer even than the lilies which bow their heads around him. But he is here too where we are, like lilies which have scarce opened yet, lily buds as yet, but still watered by the same river, and yielding in our measure the same perfume.

But *what is he doing* among the lilies? It is said, "He feedeth among the lilies." He is feeding himself, not *on* the lilies, but *among* them. Our Lord finds solace among his people. His delights are with the sons of men; he joys to see the graces of his people, to receive their love, and to discern his own image in their faces. As he said to the woman of Samaria, "Give me to drink," so does he say to each one of his people, "Give me to drink" (John 4:7), and he is refreshed by their loving fellowship. But the text means that he is feeding his people. He feeds that part of his flock redeemed by blood of which we read that "the Lamb which is in the midst of the throne shall feed them and shall lead them into living fountains of waters" (Rev 7:17). Nor does he forget that part of his flock which is in the low lands of earth, but he gives them also their portion of food.

17 **Until the day break** In a certain sense the Christian is now in the light, for he is a child of light, and he walks in the light, and he may walk in the light as God is in the light, and so have fellowship with the Father, and feel that the blood of Jesus Christ his Son cleanses us from all sin. But Paul, in some passages, calls this present estate darkness. "For," he says, "the night is far spent, the day is at hand" (Rom 13:12), meaning thereby

this present state of life to the believer, which is far spent, and the daylight, the glorious daylight of eternity, is near at hand. "The day break." Why, this represents to the most of us, probably, the moment of death. To as many as shall be alive and remain at the coming of the Lord, it represents the coming of the Lord, and the glory of his people.

"The day break!" *It is the hour of joy*. During the night the earth seems sad; she has covered herself with sackcloth, her eyes are full of the drops of the night. There is silence over the plain; the woods send not forth their grateful music. There is only heard the hooting of the owl, with, perhaps, now and then a stray note from the nightingale as though she remembered the day. Night is the time of the world's gloom, but daybreak is the time of her festival. Then is her splendor abroad. Then

> Morn, her rosy steps in the eastern clime
> Advancing, sowed the earth with orient pearl.[3]

Ten thousand winged songsters of the grove, waking up from their slumber, begin to pour forth incessant streams of music. Every creature, beholding the light of the sun, wakes up itself and is full of joy.

and the shadows flee away The spouse sings, "Until the day break, and the shadows flee away," so that the beloved of the Lord may be in the dark. It may be night with her who has a place in the heart of the Well-beloved. A child of God, who is a child of light, may be for a while in darkness—first, darkness comparatively, as compared with the light he has sometimes enjoyed, for days are not always equally bright. Some days are bright with a clear sunshine, other days may be overcast. So the child of God may one day walk, with full assurance of faith, in close fellowship with the Father and with his Son Jesus Christ, and at another time he may be questioning his interest in the covenant of grace, and may be rather sighing

3. A quotation from John Milton's *Paradise Lost*, book V, lines 1–2. —ed.

than singing, rather mourning than rejoicing. The child of God may be, then, in comparative darkness.

Yes, and he may be in positive darkness. It may be very black with him, and he may be obliged to cry, "I see no signs of returning day." Sometimes, neither sun nor moon appears for a long season to cheer the believer in the dark. This may arise partly through sickness of body. There are sicknesses of the body which in a very peculiar way touch the soul; exquisite pain may yet be attended with great brightness and joy, but there are certain other illnesses which influence us in another way. Terrible depressions come over us; we walk in darkness and see no light. I should not like to guess how heavy a true heart may sometimes become; there is a needs-be that we be in heaviness through manifold trials. There is not only a needs-be for the trials, but also for the heaviness which comes out of them. It is not always that a man can gather himself together, and defy the fierce blasts, and walk through fire and through water with heavenly equanimity. No, "a wounded spirit who can bear?" (Prov 18:14). And that wounded spirit may be the portion of some of the very fairest of the sons of God; indeed, the Lord has some weakly, sickly sons who, nevertheless, are the very pick of his family. It is not always the strong ones by whom he sets the most store, but, sometimes, those that seem to be driven into a corner, whose days are spent in mourning, are among the most precious in his sight. Yes, the darkness of the child of God may be comparative darkness, and it may to a great extent be positive darkness.

But yet it can only be temporary darkness. The same text which suggests night promises dawn: "Until the day break, and the shadows flee away," says the song of the spouse. Perhaps no text is more frequently upon my lips than is this one; I do not think that any passage of Scripture more often recurs to my heart when I am alone, for just now I feel that there is a gathering gloom over the church and over the world. It seems as if night were coming on, and such a night as makes one sigh and cry, "Until the day break, and the shadows flee away."

Turn, my beloved The spouse had lost the company of her Bridegroom: conscious communion with him was gone, though she loved her Lord, and sighed for him. In her loneliness she was sorrowful; but *she had by no means ceased to love him*, for she calls him her Beloved, and speaks as one who felt no doubt upon that point. Love to the Lord Jesus may be quite as true, and perhaps quite as strong, when we sit in darkness as when we walk in the light. Nay, *she had not lost her assurance of his love to her*, and of their mutual interest in one another; for she says, "My beloved is mine, and I am his"; and yet she adds, "Turn, my beloved." The condition of our graces does not always coincide with the state of our joys. We may be rich in faith and love, and yet have so low an esteem of ourselves as to be much depressed. It is plain, from this sacred Canticle, that the spouse may love and be loved, may be confident in her Lord, and be fully assured of her possession of him, and yet there may for the present be mountains between her and him. Yes, we may even be far advanced in the divine life, and yet be exiled for a while from conscious fellowship.

And be thou like a roe or a young hart Upon the mountains of Bether Our text gives us sweet assurance that *our Lord is at home with those difficulties which are quite insurmountable by us*. Just as the roe or the young hart knows the passes of the mountains, and the stepping-places among the rugged rocks, and is void of all fear among the ravines and the precipices, so does our Lord know the heights and depths, the torrents and the caverns of our sin and sorrow. He carried the whole of our transgression, and so became aware of the tremendous load of our guilt. He is quite at home with the infirmities of our nature; he knew temptation in the wilderness, heartbreak in the garden, desertion on the cross. He is quite at home with pain and weakness, for "himself took our infirmities, and bare our sicknesses" (Matt 8:17). He is at home with despondency, for he was "a man of sorrows, and acquainted with grief" (Isa 53:3). He is at home even with death, for he gave up the ghost, and passed through the sepulchre to resurrection.

It is easy, too, for Christ to come over the mountains for our relief. It is easy for the gazelle to cross the mountains, it is made for that end; so is it easy for Jesus, for to this purpose was he ordained from of old that he might come to man in his worst estate, and bring with him the Father's love.

ILLUSTRATION

Struggling to Be Hatched

Preaching Themes: Freedom, Perseverance

This seems to be a world of trying rather than of accomplishing. We are straining to be able to serve God. I feel myself constantly, if I can imagine such an experience, like the chick within the shell—chipping it, wanting to get out of it, doing all it can. No, not do all it can—but doing somewhat, and desiring to do more, feeling its circle to be circumscribed, and itself to be cribbed, cabined, and confined. But what a glorious thing it will be when the young eaglets hatch themselves, and leave the nest, and try their wings!

Such is the happiness we are looking forward to—the daybreak; that we shall serve God day and night in his temple without any weariness, that we shall serve him without any sin, that we shall adore him without any wandering thoughts, that we shall be dedicated to him without anything that can stir the jealousy of his holy mind.

APPLICATION

The Least Sin Will Grieve the Holy Spirit

The Lord our God is a jealous God, and that jealousy is most seen where most his love is displayed. The least sin, willfully indulged in, will grieve the Holy Spirit; slights, forgetfulnesses, and neglects will cause him to turn away. If we would remain positively and joyously assured that the Beloved is ours and that we are his, we must use the utmost circumspection and holy vigilance. No man gains full assurance by accident or retains it by chance. As the gentle hind wanders in lovely spots where grow the pure white lilies, and as he shuns the places profaned by strife, and foul with rank weeds and nettles, so does the Lord Jesus come to holy minds perfumed with devotion and consecrated to the Lord, and there in sacred quiet he finds solace and abides with his saints.

May the Lord preserve us from pride, from self-seeking, from carnality, and wrath, for these things will chase away our delights even as dogs drive off the hind of the morning. Both our inward and outward walk must be eagerly watched, lest anything should vex the Bridegroom. A word, a glance, a thought may break the spell, and end the happy rest of the heart, and long may it be ere the blessing be regained. We have some of us learned by bitter experience that it is hard to establish a settled peace, and easy enough to destroy it. The costly vase, the product of a thousand laborious processes, may be broken in a moment; and so the supreme delight of communion with the Lord Jesus, the flower of ten thousand eminent delights, may be shattered by a few moments' negligence.

The Shadows Shall All Flee Away

This is the valley of shadows. Surely every man walks in a vain show, and disquiets himself in vain. Some shadows we have are precious. There are the shadows of the ordinances—baptism and the Lord's Supper. I speak of them with the highest reverence; yet they are but shadows in themselves, and we need them because we are in the shadowland. He that is immersed in water is not, therefore, buried with Christ. The burial with Christ is the reality; the burial in water is but the shadow. He that eats and drinks at the table of the Master does not, therefore, eat his flesh and drink his blood. The bread and the wine, though they look substantial, are but the shadows. The real flesh and blood of Jesus—these are the inner substance, and only to faith is it given to feed upon these celestial viands. These things are only intended to last until the daybreak, for note, "As often as ye eat this bread and drink this cup, ye do show forth the Lord's death until he come" (1 Cor 11:26). Then when he comes the day breaks, and the shadow even that blessed shadow, must flee away.

Other shadows we have that we shall be more glad to lose—shadows of frightful things which haunt especially the timid, nervous, and faint-hearted people of God. Some of the Lord's people spend their lives in fighting shadows. They make troubles. They sit down and imagine disasters which cannot occur. They bind heavy burdens and put them upon their own shoulders—burdens which God never intended them to bear, and burdens which, in fact, do not exist. Some of them even create actual trouble by foolish anxiety to escape from an imaginary trouble. Well, poor trembler, poor Mr. Fearing, and you, Miss Much-afraid, and Miss Despondency, the shadows will flee away soon. Though you generally go halting to heaven, with weak hands and feeble knees, and as many sighs as breaths, and as many tears as minutes, there is an end coming to all these, and you shall be as merry as any of them by and by. You shall be as near the eternal throne as the apostles themselves and have as much of the divine love and enjoyment as the strongest believers in Christ ever had. Be of good courage. Strive against those fears now. They weaken you; they dishonor your Master. Repent of ever having indulged them, for they are wicked. Still, let this encourage you, they shall all flee away at the daybreak. Do not, therefore, dread dying when with that comes the daybreak. Expect it, even long for it, since then the shadows which oppress you from morn till night shall flee away.

So, too, those doubts and fears which are made of sterner stuff, those deeper shadows and heavier glooms, shall all flee away. There may be some who never have a doubt about their acceptance in Christ, but I am afraid I cannot count myself as one of them. For the most part I know whom I have believed, and I am persuaded that he is able to keep that which I have committed to him until that day; but when it comes to close heart work sometimes, and self-examination, I cannot give up Cowper's hymn:

> 'Tis a point I long to know,
> Oft it causes anxious thought;
> Do I love the Lord or no?
> Am I his, or am I not?

If I love, why am I thus?
  Why this cold and lifeless frame?
Hardly, sure, could they be worse
  Who have never known his name.[4]

Not that it is of any use having such a hymn as that in the hymn-book, for you never ought to sing it. It is not a thing to sing but to groan out all alone before our God. I think most of us are compelled to do that sometimes. Well, blessed be God, at the daybreak all these fears will be gone. We shall never be able then to doubt our interest in Christ, because we shall be with him where he is, and shall behold his glory. We shall never then have any fear lest after having preached to others we ourselves should be cast away. We shall not be afraid lest we should be shipwrecked, for though it may be but on boards and broken pieces, yet we shall then have come safe to land. All these fears will have vanished forever.

Is He Your Beloved?

If this were the day of judgment—if tonight you stood, fresh risen from your graves—if now you heard the trumpet sound—if now you saw the King in his beauty sitting upon the great white throne, I know that many of you would say, "My beloved is mine, and I am his." If this day the millennial reign of Christ had begun—if the vials had been opened, the plagues poured out, and if now Christ were come, that the wicked might be driven out and that his saints might reign, I am sure there are many of you who would say, "Welcome, welcome, Son of God; my Beloved is mine, and I am his." And there are many of you, too, who if the angel of death should pass the pew, and flap his black wing into you face, and the cold air of death should smite you, would say, "It is well, for my Beloved is mine, and I am his." You could shut your eyes and your ears to the joys and to the music of earth, and you could open them to the splendors and melodies of heaven. To be fearless of death should always be the mark of the Christian. Sometimes a sudden alarm may rob us of our presence of mind; but no believer is in a healthy state, if he be not

4. These lines appear in *Olney Hymns*, written by William Cowper and John Newton. —ed.

ready to meet death at any hour and at any moment. To walk bravely into the jaws of the dragon—to go through the iron gates, and to feel no terror—to be ready to shake hand with the skeleton king, to look on him as a friend, and no more a foe—this should be the habitual spirit and the constant practice of the heir of heaven. Oh! if this be written on my soul, "My Beloved is mine, and I am his," come, welcome death!

> Come, death, and some celestial band,
> I'll gladly go with you.[5]

But—and a solemn "but"—pass the question around these galleries, and in this area, and how many among you must say, "I never thought of that. I never thought whether I was Christ's, or Christ mine." I will not rebuke you tonight. I will not thunder at you. God's grace to me forbids that *this* should be a day of thunder. Let it be a day of feasting to everyone, and of sorrow to none. What shall I say to you, then, but this? O that Christ *may* be yours. When he was here on earth he chose to go among sinners—sinners of the blackest hue; and now he is in heaven, up yonder he loves sinners as much as ever he did. He is as willing to receive you tonight as to receive the thief. It will give as much joy to his heart to hear your cry tonight, as when he thanked God that these things were revealed unto babes. It is to his honor that you should be his; it is to his joy that he should be yours. Sinner! If you will have Christ—if now the Spirit of God makes you willing—there is no bar on God's part, when the bar is taken away on yours. If you are willing, he is more willing than you are. If the gate of your heart is on the latch, the gate of heaven is wide open. If your soul only yearns after Christ, his bowels have long yearned after you. If you have but a spark of love to Christ, he has a furnace of love to you. And if you have none at all—no love, no faith—oh! may you have it now! "Believe in the Lord Jesus Christ, and you shall be saved" (Acts 16:31). *You*; yes, *you!*

---

5. These are the final lines in the Isaac Watts hymn "Death Dreadful or Delightful." —ed.

SONG OF SOLOMON 3

SONG OF SOLOMON 3:1–5

1 By night on my bed I sought him whom my soul loveth:
I sought him, but I found him not.
2 I will rise now, and go about the city
In the streets, and in the broad ways
I will seek him whom my soul loveth:
I sought him, but I found him not.
3 The watchmen that go about the city found me:
To whom I said, Saw ye him whom my soul loveth?
4 It was but a little that I passed from them,
But I found him whom my soul loveth:
I held him, and would not let him go,
Until I had brought him into my mother's house,
And into the chamber of her that conceived me.
5 I charge you, O ye daughters of Jerusalem,
By the roes, and by the hinds of the field,
That ye stir not up, nor awake my love, till he please.

EXPOSITION

1 **By night on my bed I sought him** As it were on her bed of sloth and idleness, she *dreamed of a happiness she was far from enjoying*. But we shall never get the privilege of close communion with Christ by merely wishing for it. It was not because she sought him by night that she did not find him, for Jesus is often found by his people in the dark. When no rays of light, no gleams of comfort, can steal over our senses, still if we seek Jesus with our whole heart, though to our own apprehension we grope about like blind men, we shall find him, to the joy of our spirits. It was not the night that

prevented her finding him; it was the bed—her supineness, her languor, and her sloth.

whom my soul loveth Four times, I think, does this benighted spouse cry, "Him whom my soul loveth." She cannot see him, but *she cherishes a tender affection for him*. She does not enjoy his presence just now, but her heart cleaves to him and appreciates his excellence. What though she may have been idle and slothful, or though her spirit may be heavy and hazy, one thing she knows, she does love her Lord; about that there can be no mistake. Publicly in the streets, in the hearing of the watchmen, before the ministers and messengers of the gospel, she does not blush to say, "Him whom my soul loveth." So it was with Peter. When he had much to regret, much to reprove himself for, he could say, "Lord, thou knowest all things, thou knowest that I love thee" (John 21:17).

Though the spouse does not just now enjoy communion with Christ, she knows its sweetness, and she *feels uneasy until she partakes of it again*. As the needle cannot stop until it points to the pole, so she trembleth until her soul rests in personal communion with Jesus. Next best to present fellowship is to hunger and thirst after it. And you note, too, in this case, and in the case of every true believer in Jesus, not only is love constant, and desire after Christ earnest, but there remaineth sufficient strength resolutely to seek for him.

I sought him, but I found him not The spouse sings of her Beloved, "I sought him." Then comes in a little minor or mournful music, for the next clause is, "I sought him, *but I found him not*." The spouse is so sad about it that she tells out her woe twice, "I sought him, but I found him not."

Sometimes, the most eager search does not at once obtain its end. For wise reasons, Christ sometimes hides himself from his seeking people.

2 **I will rise now** I may be wrong in my conjecture, but to me the words, "I will rise now," sound a little like dependence upon her own exertions. "I will rise now" has not half so grateful a

ring about it, nor is it half so graceful, as "Draw me, we will run after thee" (Song 1:4). This confiding rather than that confidence seems to be the impression which becomes the saint when cold and crushed he keenly feels how desolate he is.

In the streets, and in the broad ways I will seek him whom my soul loveth: I sought him, but I found him not Once again, *in trusting in the scrupulous using of the means* the bride seems to have thoroughly relied upon attaining her end. Lest I should seem too censorious of her conduct, allow me to say that my criticism of the text is bent on taking and applying the rebukes to ourselves. Do you not notice, however, how sure she seems of finding him if she goes about the city, in the streets and in the broad ways, and if she meets the watchmen and inquires of them? But it does not appear that the fitness of the places to seek, or the persons to inquire of, were of much avail. She went down one street, and another, as we may resort to the street of private prayer, a narrow and little-frequented way, and she said, "I shall find him there." But after she had walked through it she said, "He is not here; my chamber is not a palace as it used to be; no more is it the privy-closet of the King of Kings, the audience-chamber royal." So she saw a wider way, and she said, "I will walk down here," as we may go to the prayer meeting. "What blessed hours I have oft enjoyed there," said she; "I shall find him in that highway I feel sure." But after traversing all its length she said: "I go where others go, but find not Jesus there." Then she says, "I will go into the broad places where the preaching of the gospel is to be heard. I will go with the throng; where God speaks through his servants I will be." But service after service, and sermon after sermon, were like clouds without rain, and wells without water. Others were refreshed, but she, trusting in the means, came away without a blessing.

3 **The watchmen that go about the city found me** We shall now hold her up as an example which you will do well to imitate. With *what constancy* she sought this communion. She

began at dead of night, as indeed it is never too late to seek renewed fellowship. Yet she sought on. The streets were lonely, and it was a strange place for a woman to be at such a strange time, but she was too earnest in seeking to be abashed by such circumstances. The watchmen met her, and they were astonished, as well they might, how she came to be there at that hour. But she sought on; she would never rest until she had found him. Believer, if you would have fellowship with Christ, you must be in continual quest after it. Your soul must get a craving for the one thing, and such a craving as nothing but that one thing can satisfy. I wish my own soul were like Anacreon's harp, only in a better sense. You know he says, though he wished to sing of Cadmus, his harp would sing of love alone. Oh, that we might sing of the love of Jesus and of his love alone, then it would not be long before our fellowship with him would be renewed.

To whom I said, Saw ye him whom my soul loveth? The same question over and over again—only that one thought, "Where is he?" Ministers were nothing, streets of ordinances were nothing. What the soul wanted was to find a personal Christ, and to have personal fellowship with him.

Why did they not answer? Perhaps because they were blind and never did see themselves. Alas! that some watchmen on the walls need to watch for their own souls rather than for the souls of others. *Still, not the best of the watchmen there could console her* with a smile of Jesus's face.

4 **It was but a little that I passed from them, but I found him whom my soul loveth** Notice what the spouse said: "I found *him*." She was not satisfied with finding anything else: "I found him." If she had found her nearest and dearest friend, if the mother of whom she speaks had met her, it would not have sufficed. She had said, "I love him, I sought him," and she must be able to add, "I found him." Nothing but Christ consciously enjoyed can satisfy the craving of a loving heart which once sets out to seek the King in his beauty.

The city watchmen found the spouse, and she spoke to them; she inquired of them, "Saw ye him whom my soul loveth?" She did not sit down and say to any one of them, "O watchman of the night, your company cheers me! The streets are lonely and dangerous; but if you are near, I feel perfectly safe, and I will be content to stay awhile with you." No, she leaves the watchmen, and still goes along the streets until she finds *him* whom her soul loves. I have known some who love the Lord to be very happy while the preacher is proclaiming the truth to them, but they have stopped with the preacher and have gone no further. This will never do, dear friends; do not be content to abide with us, who are only watchmen, but go beyond us, and seek till you find our Master.

I held him, and would not let him go The only way to hold Christ is to hold him by his own power. I smiled to myself as I read my text, and tried to make it all my own: "I held him, and would not let him go." I thought to myself, the spouse said of her Bridegroom that she would not let him go; and shall I ever say to my Lord that I will not let him go? He is the King of kings, the omnipotent Jehovah; can I hold him? He is the mighty God, and yet a poor puny worm like myself says, "I would not let him go." Can it be really so? Well, the Holy Ghost says that it is, for he guided the pen of the writer of this Song when he wrote, "I held him, and would not let him go." Think of poor Jacob, who, when the angel did but touch him, felt his sinews shrink directly, yet he said, "I will not let thee go" (Gen 32:26). And I, a poor trembling creature, may hold the Omnipotent himself, and say to him, "I will not let thee go."

How is that wonder to be accomplished? I will tell you. If Omnipotence helps you to hold Omnipotence, why, then, the deed is done! If Christ, and not you alone, holds Christ, then Christ is held indeed, for shall he vanquish his own self? No, Master, you could slay death, and break the old serpent's head, but you cannot conquer your own self; and if you are in me, I can hold you, for it is not I, but Christ in me, that holds Christ, and will not let him go. This is the power which enables us, with the apostle, to say, "I am persuaded that neither death, nor life, nor angels, nor principalities, nor powers, nor things present, nor things to come, nor height, nor depth, nor any other creature, shall be able to separate us from the love of God, which is in Christ Jesus our Lord" (Rom 8:38–39).

Until I had brought him into my mother's house I do not believe in any reverence for mere material buildings, but I have great reverence for the true church of the Living God. The church is the house of God, and the mother of our souls. It was under the ministry of the word that most of us were born to God; it was in the assembly of the saints that we heard the message which first of all quickened us into newness of life, and we may well be content to call the church of Christ our mother, since our elder Brother—you know his name—when one said to him, "Behold, thy mother and thy brethren stand without, desiring to speak with thee," pointing to his disciples, answered, "Behold, my mother, and my brethren. For whosoever shall do the will of my Father which is in heaven, the same is my brother, and sister, and mother" (Matt 12:47–50). Surely, where Jesus chooses to call the assembly of the faithful by the sacred name of mother, we may rightly do the same.

And into the chamber of her that conceived me Jacob's wrestlings are succeeded by Jacob's vows. Fellowship that is sweet to me must be sweet to others of my brothers; therefore, will I bring him to the church, and tell to all the assembled people how sweet, how delightful he is to my soul.

5 **I charge you, O ye daughters of Jerusalem, by the roes, and by the hinds of the field** "By everything that is timid, and delicate, and pure, and full of love, I charge you, O ye daughters of Jerusalem."

ILLUSTRATION

Jesus Like a Gazelle

Preaching Themes: Repentance, Sin, Purity

In ancient times gazelles were often tamed and were the favorite companions of Eastern ladies. The gazelle might be standing near its mistress, fixing its loving eyes upon her, but if a stranger clapped his hands it would hasten away. The roes and hinds *of the field* are even yet more jealous things. A sound will startle them, even the breath of the hunter tainting the gale puts them to speedy flight.

Even thus is it with Jesus. A little thing, a very little thing, will drive him from us, and it may be many a day before our repentance shall be able to find him again. He has suffered so much from sin that he cannot endure the approach of it. His pure and holy soul abhors the least taint of iniquity.

that ye stir not up, nor awake my love, till he please Observe, then, that *the Lord Jesus in his church is not indifferent to the conduct of his people*. We are not to suppose that because the sin of all God's elect is pardoned, therefore it is of small consequence how they live. By no manner of means. The Master of this great house is not blind nor deaf, neither is he a person who is utterly careless as to how the house is managed; on the contrary, as God is a jealous God, so is Christ a jealous husband to his church. He will not tolerate in her what he would tolerate in the world. She lies near his heart, and she must be chaste to him.

What a solemn work the Lord did in the early church. That story of Ananias and Sapphira—it is often used most properly to illustrate the danger of lying, but that is not the point of the narrative. Ananias and Sapphira were members of the church at Jerusalem, and they did not lie to men, which would have been sin enough, but in lying to the church officers they lied to God, and the result was their sudden death. Now, you are not to suppose that this was a solitary case. Wherever there is a true church of God, the judgments of God are always going on in it.

I speak now not only what I have read but what I have known and seen with my eyes—what I am as sure of as I am sure of any fact in history. The apostle Paul, speaking of the same in his day, said that in a certain church there was so much sin that many were weak and sickly among them, and many slept; that is to say, there was great sickness in the church, and many died. Judgments are begun in the house of God and are always going on there. I have seen men in the church who have walked at a distance from God, who have been visited with severe chastisements; others, who have been of hot and proud spirit, have been terribly humbled; and some who have arrogantly touched God's ark, and the doom of Uzzah has befallen them. I have seen it and do know it. And so it always will be. The Lord Jesus Christ looking around his church, if he sees anything evil in it, will do one of two things: either he will go right away from his church because the evil is tolerated there, and he will leave that church to be like Laodicea, to go on from bad to worse, till it becomes no church at all; or else he will come and he will trim the lamp, or to use the figure of John 15, he will prune the vine branch and with his knife will cut off this member, and the other, and cast them into the fire, while, as for the rest, he will cut them till they bleed again because they are fruit-bearing members, but they have too much wood and he wants them to bring forth more fruit. It is not a trifling matter to be in the church of God. God's fire is in Zion and his furnace in Jerusalem. "His fan is in his hand, and he shall thoroughly purge"—what? The world? Oh no, "his floor," the church (Matt 3:12). And then, again, "He shall sit as a refiner and purifier of silver, and he shall purify"—what? The heathen nations? No, "the sons of Levi"—his own people (Mal 3:3). So Christ is not indifferent to what is going on in the church, and it is needful that when he comes to the church to take his repose, and solace himself there, we should not stir him up nor awake him till he please.

APPLICATION

Diligently Seek Jesus

Ardent lovers of Jesus *must diligently seek him*. The chapter before us says that the spouse sought him, sought him on her bed, sought him in the streets, sought him in the broadways, sought him at last at the lips of the watchmen, sought him everywhere he was likely to be found. We *must* enjoy the perpetual fellowship of Jesus. We who love him in our souls cannot rest until we know that he is with us. I fear that with some of us our sins have grieved him, and he has betaken himself to the far-off "mountain of myrrh and hill of frankincense" (Song 4:6). It may be our lax living, our neglect of prayer, or some other fault has taken from us the light of his countenance. Let us resolve that there shall be no rest to our souls until once again he has returned to us in the fullness of his manifested love, to abide in our hearts. Seek him, brother, seek him, sister. He is not far from any of you, but do seek him with an intense longing for him, for until you do, you are not the man to bring him into the assembly. Labor to bring Jesus into the chambers of the church, but first be sure that you have him yourself, or your zeal will be hypocrisy.

In seeking our Lord, we must *use all ministries*. The spouse inquired of the watchmen. We are not to despise God's servants, for he is usually pleased to bless us through them, and it would be ungrateful both to him and to them to pass them by as useless. But, while we use the ministries, *we must go beyond them*. The spouse did not find her Lord through the watchmen. But she says, "It was but a little that I passed from them, that I found him whom my soul loveth." I charge you, never rest content with listening to me. Do not imagine that hearing the truth preached simply and earnestly will by itself be a blessing to your souls. Far, far beyond the servant, pass to the Master. Let this be the longing of each heart, each Sabbath day, "Lord, give me fellowship with yourself." True, we are led to see Jesus sometimes, and I hope often, through listening to the truth proclaimed, but, O Lord, it is no outer court worship that will satisfy us. We want to come into the holy of holies and stand at the mercy seat itself. It is not seeing you afar off and hearing about you that will content our spirits; we must draw near to you and behold you as the world cannot. Like Simeon, we must take you into our arms or we cannot say that we have seen God's salvation. Like John, we must lean our heads upon your bosom or we cannot rest. Your apostles are well enough, your prophets well enough, your evangelists well enough. But oh, we feel constrained to go beyond them all, for we thirst after fellowship with you, our Savior. Those who feel this way will bless the church, but only such.

Sin Causes Christ to Withdraw

May each one of us be more watchful lest the Bridegroom should withdraw from us. He will go away if we grow proud. If we are boastful, and say, "There is some reason why God should bless us," and should begin to speak hectoringly towards weaker brethren, the Lord will let us know that not unto us, not unto us, but unto his name shall be all the glory (Ps 115:1).

Again, if there is a lack of love among us, the Lord of love will be offended. The holy dove does not love scenes of strife; he frequents the calm still waters of brotherly love. There the Lord commanded the blessing, even life forevermore, where brothers dwelled together in unity. If any of you have half a hard thought toward another, get rid of it; if there are the beginnings of anything like jealousy, quench the sparks. "Leave off contention," says Solomon, "before it be meddled with" (Prov 17:14), as if he said, "End it before you begin it," which, though it seems strangely paradoxical, is most wise advice. "Little children, love one another." "Walk in love, as Christ also hath loved us" (Eph 5:2). May discord be far from us.

Let us gather from the text that there are some things in the true church which give our Lord rest. He is represented here as though he slept in the church, "That ye stir not up nor awake my love till he please." Wherever he sees true repentance, real faith, holy consecration, purity of life, chastity of love, there Christ rests. I believe he finds no sweeter happiness even in heaven than the happiness of accepting his people's prayers and praises. Our love is very sweet to him; our deeds of gratitude are very precious, the broken alabaster boxes of self-sacrifices done for him are very fair in his esteem. He finds no rest in the world—he never did—but he finds sweet rest on the bosoms of his faithful ones. He loves to come into a pure church, and there to say, "I am at home." "I will declare thy name unto my brethren: in the midst of the congregation will I praise thee" (Ps 22:22).

Hold on to Jesus

Jesus will go away if he is not held. "I held him and I would not let him go," as if he would have gone if he had not been firmly retained. When he met with Jacob that night at the Jabbok, he said, "Let me go." He would not go without Jacob's letting him, but he would have gone if Jacob had loosed his hold. The patriarch replied, "I will not let thee go, except thou bless me" (Gen 32:26). This is one of Christ's ways and manners; it is one of the peculiarities of his character. When he walked to Emmaus with the two disciples, "he made as if he would have gone further" (Luke 24:28). They might have known it was none other than the angel of the covenant by that very habit. He would have gone further, but they constrained him, saying, "Abide with us for the day is far spent." If you are willing to lose Christ's company, he is never intrusive. He will go away from you, and leave you till you know his value and begin to pine for him. "I will go," says he, "and return to my place, till they acknowledge their offence, and seek my face: in their affliction they will seek me early" (Hos 5:15). He will go unless you hold him.

But note, next, *he is very willing to be held.* Who could hold him if he were not? He is the omnipotent Savior, and if he willed to withdraw he could do so: let us hold him as we might. But mark his condescension. When his spouse said, "I held him, and I would not let him go," he did not go, he could not go, for his love held him as well as her hands. Christ is willing to be held. He loves that sacred violence which takes him by force, that holy diligence which leaves not a gap open by which he may escape, but shuts every door, bars every bolt, and says, "I have you now and I will take care that if I lose you it shall be through no fault of mine." Jesus is willing enough to be retained by hearts which are full of his love.

And, whenever you have Christ, remember that *you are able to hold him.* She who held him in the Song was no stronger than you are; she was but a feeble woman, poorly fed under the Old Testament dispensation. You have drunk the new wine of the new covenant, and you are stronger than she. You can hold him, and he will not be able to go from you. "How," you say, "shall I be able to hold him?" Oh, have you grasped him? Is he with you? Now, then, hold him fast by your faith; trust him implicitly, rest in him for every day's cares, for every moment's ills. Walk by faith and he will walk with you. Hold him also with the grasp of love. Let your whole heart go out towards him. Embrace him with the arms of mighty affection, enchain him with ardent admiration. Lay hold on him by faith, and clasp him with love. Be also much in prayer. Prayer casts a chain about him. He never leaves the heart that prays. There is a sweet perfume about prayer that always attracts the Lord; wherever he perceives it rising up to heaven, there will he be. Hold him, too, by your obedience to him. Never quarrel with him. Let him have his way. He will stop in any house where he can be master; he will stay nowhere where some other will lords it over his. Watch his words; be careful to obey them all. Be very tender in your conduct, so that nothing grieves him. Show to him that you are ready to suffer for his sake. I believe that where there is a prayerful, careful, holy, loving, believing walk towards Jesus, the fellowship of the saint with his Lord will not be broken, but it may continue for months and years. There is no reason, except in ourselves, why fellowship with Jesus should not continue throughout an entire life; and oh, if it did, it would make earth into heaven, and lift us up to the condition of angels, if not beyond them, and we should be the men who would bring Christ into the church, and through the church into the world. The church would be blessed, and God would be glorified, and souls would be saved, if there were some among us who thus held him, and would not let him go.

SONG OF SOLOMON 3:6–11

6 Who *is* this that cometh out of the wilderness like pillars of smoke,
Perfumed with myrrh and frankincense,
With all powders of the merchant?
7 Behold his bed, which *is* Solomon's;
Threescore valiant men *are* about it,
Of the valiant of Israel.
8 They all hold swords, *being* expert in war:
Every man *hath* his sword upon his thigh because of fear in the night.
9 King Solomon made himself a chariot of the wood of Lebanon.
10 He made the pillars thereof *of* silver,
The bottom thereof *of* gold,
The covering of it *of* purple,
The midst thereof being paved *with* love, for the daughters of Jerusalem.
11 Go forth, O ye daughters of Zion, and behold king Solomon
With the crown wherewith his mother crowned him
In the day of his espousals,
And in the day of the gladness of his heart.

EXPOSITION

6 **Who is this that cometh out of the wilderness** Great princes in the East are in the habit of traveling in splendid palanquins, which are at the same time chariots and beds. The person reclines within, screened by curtains from public view; a bodyguard protects the equipage from robbers, and blazing torches light up the path along which the travelers proceed. King Solomon, in this Song, describes the church of

Christ, and Christ himself, as traveling through the world in such a palanquin.

The equipage excites the attention of the onlooker; his curiosity is raised, and he asks, "*Who is this?*" Now, in the first progress of the Christian church, in her very earliest days, there were persons who marveled greatly; and though they set down the wonders of the day of Pentecost to drunkenness, yet "they were all amazed, and were in doubt, saying one to another, What meaneth this?" (Acts 2:12). In after years, many a heathen philosopher said, "What is this new power which is breaking the idols in pieces, changing old customs, making even thrones unsafe—what is this?" By-and-bye, in the age of the Reformation, there were cowled monks, cardinals in their red hats, and bishops, and princes, and emperors, who all said, "What is this? What strange doctrine has come to light?" In the times of the modern reformation, a century ago, when God was pleased to revive his church through the instrumentality of Whitfield and his brethren, there were many who said, "What is this new enthusiasm, this Methodism? Whence came it, and what power is this which it wields?" And, doubtless, whenever God shall be pleased to bring forth his church in power, and to make her mighty among the sons of men, the ignorance of men will be discovered breaking forth in wonder, for they will say, "Who is this?" Spiritual religion is as much a novelty now as in the day when Grecian sages scoffed at it on Mars Hill. The true church of God is a stranger and pilgrim still; an alien and a foreigner in every land; a speckled bird; a dove in the midst of ravens; a lily among thorns.

like pillars of smoke When great personages traveled in their palanquins, and more especially on marriage processions, they were attended by a number of persons who, at night, carried high up in the air burning cressets which gave forth a blaze of light. Sometimes these lights were simply torches carried in the hands of running footmen; at other times they were a sort of iron basket lifted high into the air, upon poles, from which went up a pillar of smoke and flame. Our text says, "Who is this that cometh out of the wilderness like pillars of smoke?" a beautiful illustration of the fact that wherever Christ and his cause are carried, light is a sure accompaniment. Into whatsoever region the gospel may journey, her every herald is a flash of light, her every minister a flaming fire. God makes his churches the golden candlesticks and says unto his children, "Ye are the lights of the world" (Matt 5:14). As certainly as ever God said "Let there be light," and there was light over the old creation, so does he say, whenever his church advances, "Let there be light," and there is light. Dens of darkness, where the bats of superstition had folded their wings and hung themselves up for perpetual ease, have been disturbed by the glare of these divine flambeaux; the innermost caverns of superstition and sin, once black with a darkness which might be felt, have been visited with a light above the brightness of the sun. "The people which sat in darkness have seen a great light, and to them which sat in the region and shadow of death light has sprung up" (Matt 4:16). Thus saith the Lord unto the nation where his kingdom cometh, "Arise, shine, for thy light is come, and the glory of the Lord hath risen upon thee!" (Isa 60:1).

But you will tell me that our text rather speaks of "*pillars of smoke*" than of sparkling lamps. The smoke is but the effect of the flame, and even the pillar of smoke is luminous. What is the smoke that has attended the church? What but the deaths of her martyrs, the sufferings of her confessors, the patient endurance of her valiant sons? Wherever she goes, the thick smoke of her suffering goes up to heaven. "We ... are alway delivered unto death" (2 Cor 4:11), said the apostle. The cause of truth involves a perpetual sacrifice; her smoke ascends forever. Black smoke I say it is in the eye of man, but unto God it is a sweet-smelling savor. Never did fat of rams, or the fat of kidneys of fed beasts, smell so sweetly before the Most High as the faith, the love, the courage, which has ascended up to heaven from the dauntless heroes of the church in past ages when at the stake they have been faithful even unto death.

Perfumed with myrrh and frankincense, with all powders of the merchant? It often happens that oriental monarchs of immense possessions are not content with burning common coals in these cressets, but frequently consume sandalwood and other woods which give forth a delightful smell; or else, if they use ordinary coals, they sprinkle upon them frankincense and myrrh, so that a delicious perfume is spread on all sides. In the olden times, they also went to great expense in obtaining drugs, which the merchants collected from all parts of the earth, and these were carefully compounded into the renowned *"powders of the merchants,"* which yielded a delicious variety of delicate perfumes, not to be produced by any one aromatic essence. Our inspired poet describes the traveling procession of the royal pair, and fails not to dwell upon the delightful perfume of myrrh and frankincense, with all the powders of the merchant, "which make the wilderness smell as a garden of roses." Wherever the church of Christ proceeds, though her pathway is a desert, though she marches through a howling wilderness, she scatters the richest perfume. The page of history would be only worthy to be blotted in oblivion were it not for the sweet odors which the church has left upon it. Look at all past ages, and the track of the church is still redolent with all the richest fragrance of human virtue and divine grace. Wherever the church advances she makes manifest the savor of the knowledge of Christ in every place! Men believe in Jesus, and unto the Lord faith has all the fragrance of myrrh. They love Jesus; and love in the esteem of heaven is better than frankincense. Loving Christ they endeavor to be like him, till patience, humility, brotherly-kindness, truthfulness, and all things that are honest, lovely, and of good repute, like "powders of the merchant," are spread abroad throughout the whole earth. Tell me where the church is not, and I will tell you where sin reigns; tell me where Christ and his church are carried, and I will tell you where you shall find every virtue that can adorn humanity, and every excellence that can magnify the excellence of the grace of God.

7 **Behold his bed, which is Solomon's** This palanquin or traveling chariot in which the king is carried represents the

covenant of grace, the plan of salvation, and, in fact, the whole system by which the Lord Jesus comes down in mercy among men, and by which he bears his people along with himself through the wilderness of this world, onward to the rest which he has prepared for them. It is, in a word, the mediatorial work of Jesus. The ark was carried through the wilderness preceded by the pillar of cloud and fire, as the symbol of the divine presence in mercy, and here we have a somewhat similar representation of the great King of grace, borne in regal splendor through the world, and bearing his elect spouse with him. May it be ours to be made to ride like Jeshurun, upon the high places of the earth in happy fellowship with him whose goings forth were of old, even from everlasting.

The description advances step by step, each sentence mentioning an additional and far-enhanced preciousness. Thus do those who study the work of salvation prize it more and more. At the first glance the sweet singer who speaks in this song perceived that the chariot was made of cedar, a costly wood; a closer view revealed "the silver pillars, beauteous to behold": further observation showed "the basis all of burnished gold." From cedar to silver, and from silver to gold, we have a clear advance as to precious material. On looking again, the observer remarks "the top of princely purple," which is yet more precious as the type of imperial dignity, and the token of that effectual atonement which was wrought out by the ensanguined stream of Calvary. The blood which dyed that purple canopy is much more precious than gold that perishes, though it be tried with fire. And then, though one would think there could be no advance beyond the precious blood, the song proceeds yet one step further, for we find that "the midst thereof was paved with love, for the daughters of Jerusalem."

Threescore valiant men are about it, of the valiant of Israel Of course when traveling through a wilderness, a royal procession was always in danger of attack. Arabs prowled around; wandering Bedouins were always prepared to fall upon the caravan; and more especially was this the case with a marriage procession, because then the robbers might expect to obtain many jewels, or, if not, a heavy ransom for the redemption of the bride or bridegroom by their friends. What shall I say of the attacks which have been made upon the church of Christ, and upon Christ himself? They have been incessant. When one form of evil has been routed, another has presented itself. Evil teems with children. The frogs and lice of Egypt were not more numerous than the enemies of the Lord's anointed and his bride. Every day produces new battles. These attacks arise from all quarters; sometimes from the world, and sometimes, alas, from even professed members of the church. Adversaries lurk everywhere, and until the church and her Lord shall be revealed in the splendor of the Millennium, having left the wilderness forever, we must expect to find her molested on every side. My dear brethren, we know that Christ's cause in the world is always safe because of divine protection, and because the legions of God's angels keep watch and ward over the saints. But we have something more tangible than this. Our gracious God has been pleased to commit unto *men* the ministry of Christ. "Unto the angels hath he not put in subjection the world to come, whereof we speak" (Heb 2:5). The Lord ordains that chosen men should be the protectors of his church; not that they have any power as of themselves to do anything, but he girds the weak with strength and makes the feeble mighty; so then, men, even the sons of men stand in array around the traveling palanquin of Christ, to guard both the bridegroom and the bride.

Read verses 7 and 8 carefully, and you will notice *that there are enough swordsmen.* "Threescore valiant men are about it." There are always enough men chosen of God to guard the church. Poor Unbelief holds up her hands and cries, "The good men are all dead; Zion is under a cloud; the Lord has taken away the great men; we have no valiant defenders of the faith, none such as this crisis may require!" Unbelief, let the Lord say unto you as he did unto Elias—"Yet have I left me seven thousand in Israel, all the knees which have not bowed unto Baal" (1 Kgs 19:18). There shall be just as many warriors as the crisis shall require. We do not know where the men are to come from, but the Lord will provide. There may be sitting in the Sunday school today a child who shall one day shake this nation from one end to the other; there may be, now unknown, obscure, and unobserved, the man whom God will make strong to rebuke the infamous infidelity of our age. We know not where the anointing rests. We, in our folly, would anoint Eliab or Abinadab, but God has chosen David, the shepherd's boy, and he will bring him forth and teach him how to hurl the stone at Goliath's brow. Do not tremble, neither be afraid; God who makes man and makes man's mouth will find the sixty men when the sixty shall be needed. "The Lord gave the word, great was the company of them that published it" (Ps 68:11). The glory of the Lord shall be revealed, and all flesh shall see it together, for the mouth of the Lord has spoken it.

Observe that these warriors *are men of the right mettle*. "Yes," says poor trembling Little-Faith, "we have hosts of men, but they are not like the great hearts of old; they have not the qualifications which the age requires." But remember, about the bed of Solomon there are "threescore *valiant* men." And glory be unto my Master, while I may not flatter the ministry, I must not dishonor him by believing that he has left his church without *valiant* defenders. There are Luthers still living who bid defiance to all adversaries; men who can say, "We do not count our lives dear unto us that we may finish our course with joy, and fulfill the ministry which the Lord has delivered unto us." Fear not; you may not at present know the valor of the Lord's bodyguard, but when the church's battle grows hotter than just now, suddenly there shall be seen a champion stalking to the front of the battle, and men shall say, "Who is this? How he wields that battle axe! How he splits the armor of his foes! See how he piles them heaps on heaps, and mounts that hill of slaughtered enemies to smite a greater foe! Who is this?" And the answer shall be, "This is a man whom God has found; the world knew not of him, but God has trained him in the camps of Dan, and now the Spirit moves him to smite the Philistines."

I think I hear you say, "But though there may be so many men, and men of the right sort, I am afraid *they are not in the right place*." Look again at the text. It is written, "Threescore valiant men are *about it*"; that is, there are some on that side, and some on this, some before, and some behind; they are all around the traveling chariot of Christ. "I wish there might be one in our parish," says one. Pray for him, and he who has promised to send you all good things may yet send him to you. "Pray ye the Lord of the harvest that he may send forth labourers into his harvest" (Matt 9:38). It is singular how God sometimes raises a mighty man, in this denomination, then in that, and then in the other. Suppose any body of Christians should try to monopolize all the valiant men themselves; why, they could not do it, because every side of the royal bed must be guarded, and in his own place each man is set for the defense of the gospel. The church is compassed about with mighties who are under God to do great exploits. If the Lord guides the flight of sparrows, surely he knows how to dispose his ministers, and let the church be well-content to let them occupy their posts until the wilderness is past and the glory shall be revealed. The church often makes mistakes, and thinks she can make ministers, or at least choose their position. She can do no such thing. God sends the valiant man; all you can do is to recognize his valor and accept him as your champion. Beyond that you cannot go; this is God's work, not man's. A minister made by men, made valiant by human strength, had better betake himself at once ignominiously to his tent, for his disgrace will be certain. God who sends the men knows where to put them, so that they may stand round about the bed and leave no corner unprotected.

8 **They all hold swords, being expert in war** Notice that these men *are all well-armed*. The text says expressly, "They all hold swords." What swords are these? Every valiant man in Christ's Israel holds the sword of the Spirit, which is the Word of God. A man who is a good textuary will usually be a good divine; he who draws from the treasury of the written word will find his spoken word to be fruitful in profit to the people of God. If

we use carnal reason; if we rely upon refinement, argument, eloquence, or any other form of the wisdom of man, we shall soon find our enemies will defeat us. But to ply the Word right and left, to give gospel cuts and strokes such as the devil himself cannot parry, this is to overcome the world through the Word of God. Besides this, and here is an opportunity for you all to carry swords—every valiant man in God's Israel carries the sword of prayer, which is comparable to those huge two-handed swords of the olden time, which the soldier lifted up and brought down with such tremendous force, as to cleave a man in halves: prayer is a weapon which no man can effectually resist.

Further, these men are not only well-armed, *but they are well-trained*. They are all expert in war; men who have endured temptations themselves; men whose souls have been exercised; men who have slain both the lion and the bear and are men of war from their youth. Christian ministers especially should be no novices, but both in the school of temptation and in some school of the prophets, they should be disciplined for fight.

Every man hath his sword upon his thigh Further, these men were not only well-trained, but you will see *that they were always ready*. Each man has his sword upon his thigh, ready to be drawn forth.

because of fear in the night Observe also that these men were *watchful*, for "they had their sword on their thigh because of fear *in the night*." They never sleep, but watch always for the church's interest. Pray that the Lord may raise up many such, who night and day with tears shall watch for the souls of men, and against the enemies of our Israel.

9 **King Solomon made himself a chariot of the wood of Lebanon** It is not difficult to convey to persons the most unacquainted with Eastern manners and customs, an idea of what this palanquin is. It is a sort of large sedan in which one or two persons may recline with ease. Of course, this palanquin

could not be made of gold or silver, because then it would be too heavy for carriage; it must be made of wood; hence King Solomon made a bed, or chariot, or palanquin, of the wood of Lebanon. Then there needs to be four pillars supporting the covering and the curtains; the pillars of it are of silver. The bottom of it should be something massive, in order to sustain the weight of the person; the bottom of it is of gold. The canopy on the top is a covering of purple. Since to lie on gold would be very unpleasant, it is covered with delicate, daintily wrought carpets; and so we have the bottom thereof paved, or rather carpeted with love for the daughters of Jerusalem. Some delicate devices of needlework adorn the bottom of this bed-chariot in which the king and his spouse recline during their journey.

The doctrines of the gospel are comparable, for their antiquity, for their sweet fragrance, for their incorruptibility, to the wood of Lebanon. The gospel of Christ never decays; Jesus Christ the same yesterday, today, and forever. Not one single truth, bears any sign of rot. And to those souls that are enlightened from above, the gospel gives forth a fragrance far richer than the wood of Lebanon.

10 **He made the pillars thereof of silver** As for the silver pillars which bear up the canopy, to what should I liken them but to *the attributes of God* which support and guarantee the efficiency of the great atonement of Christ beneath which we are sheltered. There is the silver pillar of God's *justice*. He cannot, he will not smite the soul that hides beneath the cross of Christ. If Christ hath paid the debt, how is it possible that God should visit again a second time the iniquity of his people, first on their Surety, and then again on themselves? Then stands the next, the solid pillar of his *power*. "They shall never perish, neither shall any man pluck them out of my hand; my Father, which gave them me, is greater than all; and no man is able to pluck them out of my Father's hand" (John 10:28). Then on the other side is the pillar of his *love*, a silver pillar indeed, bright and sparkling to the eye; love unchanging and eternal,

strong as the power and fast as the justice which bear up the canopy on the other side. And here on this side stands *immutability*, another column upon which the atonement rests. If God could change, then might he cast away his blood-bought; but because I am God and change not, therefore ye sons of Jacob rejoice (Mal 3:6).

The bottom thereof of gold As for the *bottom of this palanquin*, which is of gold—may not this represent the eternal purpose and counsel of God, that purpose which he formed in himself "or ever the earth was" (Prov 8:23)? Pure was the decree of God, holy, wise, just, for his own glory, and most true; and as the precious things of the temple were all of gold, well may the basis of eternal love, an immutable and unchangeable decree, be compared to much fine gold.

The covering of it of purple As for the *covering of the chariot*, it is of purple. I need not tell you where it was dyed. No Tyrian hues are mingled here. Look up, Christian, and delight yourself in that bloodred canopy which shelters you from the sun by day and from the moon by night! From hell and heaven, from time and from eternity, are you secured by this covering which is of purple.

The midst thereof being paved with love Metaphor is suddenly dropped in this last item, and the result is a complicated, but very expressive form of speech. Some regard the expression as signifying a pavement of stone, engraved with hieroglyphic emblems of love, which made up the floor of this traveling chariot; but this would surely be very uncomfortable and unusual, and therefore others have explained the passage as referring to choice embroidery, and dainty carpets, woven with cost and care, with which the interior of the traveling chair was lined. Into such embroidery sentences of love-poetry may have been worked. Needlework was probably the material of which it was composed; skillful fingers would therein set forth emblems and symbols of love. As the spouse in the second chapter sings, "His banner over me was love," probably alluding to some love-word upon the banner; so, probably, tokens of love were carved or embroidered, as the case may have been, upon the interior of the chariot, so that "the midst thereof was paved with love, for the daughters of Jerusalem."

ILLUSTRATION

Seeing but Not Tasting

Preaching Themes: Foolishness

A man may pass the door of the London Tavern or the Mansion House for years, and yet have no notion of the banquets within, for these are indoors, and you must enter to partake of them. Savory vapors floating from the festive board may awaken a transient imagination, but no more.

The cock on the dunghill turned over the diamond, and, according to the fable, remarked that he cared very little for it. He would sooner have found a grain of barley. So, many hear of the sweetness of true religion, but they have not the taste or the ability to perceive its sweetness.

---

for the daughters of Jerusalem Our Lord finds rest in the love of his people. "Here will I dwell for ever." They do, as it were, make these carpets of needlework in their love and affection for him, and in their trust and confidence in him; and here he rests. On the other hand, our Beloved spent his life to work for us our bed of rest, so that we must translate it "love *of*," as well as "love *for* the daughters of Jerusalem." We rest in Christ's love; *he* rests in our love.

11 **Go forth, O ye daughters of Zion, and behold king Solomon** It is not King David; King David is the type of Christ up to the time of his crucifixion: "despised and rejected of men, a man of sorrows and acquainted with grief" (Isa 53:3), and yet king of the Jews. King Solomon is the type of Christ ever since the day when

> They brought his chariot from above,
> To bear him to his throne,[1]

and, with sound of trumpet, conducted him to his Father's presence-chamber above. Now it is King Solomon—King Solomon for wealth, for wisdom, for dignity, for honor, for peace. He is the Wonderful Counselor, the Mighty God, the Everlasting Father, the Prince of Peace, and therefore is he King Solomon going forth.

With the crown wherewith his mother crowned him in the day of his espousals and in the day of the gladness of his heart Let your eye rest upon him. Let your eye behold the head that today is crowned with glory, wearing many crowns. Behold, too, his hands which once were pierced, but are now grasping the scepter. Look to his girdle where swing the keys of heaven, and death, and hell. Look to his feet, once pierced with iron, but now set upon the dragon's head. Behold his legs, like fine brass, as if they glowed in a furnace. Look at his heart, that bosom which heaves with love to you, and when you have surveyed him from head to foot exclaim, "Yea, he is the chief among ten thousand, and altogether lovely." Does sin prevail? Behold King Solomon. Have doubts and fears arisen? Behold King Jesus. Are you troubled, and does your enemy annoy you? Look up to him; behold King Solomon. I pray you remember the light in which you are to behold him. Do not think that Christ has lost his former power. Behold him as he was at Pentecost, *with the crown wherewith his mother crowned him in the day of his espousals*.

APPLICATION

Look into the Heart of God

When the Christian stands apart from his Lord, and judges by outward appearances, he cannot perceive, as once he did, the

1. These lines are from the hymn "Beyond the Glittering Starry Sky" by James Fanch and Daniel Turner. —ed.

loving-kindness of the Lord. Providence grows dark as a winter's day. The tried believer cries, "My wife has been taken from me; my property is melting away, my business fades; I am sick in body and weary in soul; I cannot see a trace of the love of God to me in all this." Brother, the description in the Song does not say that the chariot is plated with love on the outside, but it is paved with love *within*, "in the midst of it." Oh that you had faith to believe that the heart and real core of every providence is love. The exterior of it may be as a thorn hedge, but sweet fruit ripens within. "Oh," you say, "but I have looked at the Bible lately, and as I have glanced over its once-cheering promises they appear to smile at me no more. Some of the words grate very harshly on my ear, and almost condemn me." I do not wonder, for although I can at this moment see love in the very outside of Scripture, yet there are times when I cannot, when I can only feel as if every text thundered at me, and out of God's own mouth came heavy sentences against me. Beloved, it does not say, I repeat it, that the exterior part of this palanquin was adorned with self-apparent love, but that love was in the midst. If you stand examining the exterior of providence, and the mere letter of the word, and begin to judge and try your God, I should not wonder if little enough of love should be conspicuous to you. Look into the heart of God and read what he has written there. When faith takes a step upward, and mounts to the inside of the chariot of grace, she finds that it is paved with love for the daughters of Jerusalem.

Come and sit side by side with Jesus in his chariot of grace, his bed of rest. Come and recline with him in hallowed fellowship. There is room enough for you, and strength enough to bear your weight. Come now and be carried with him who carried all your cross. Sit down with him who on his hands, and on his side, bears the memorials of his dying love to you. What company you have, and what royal accommodation is provided for you!

Jesus Reigns in Love

The chariot was a royal one, and as the king rode along he was reigning, but he was reigning in love, and it is so with Jesus. All things are in his hands, and he governs all things in love to his people. Heavenly principalities serve him, and angels are his willing messengers. But there is no power Jesus has which he does not wield in love to us. Has his power seemed sometimes to be exercised harshly? It is not so; it cannot be so. He reigns in love. Our Joseph is lord over all Egypt, and since Joseph loves his brothers, the good of all the land of Egypt is theirs. Jesus rules all the world for his people's benefit; all things are theirs, whether things present or things to come, all are theirs. Jesus reigns in love.

And Jesus rests in love. This chariot was a place for the traveler to rest in; he reclined as he was carried along. Nothing gives Jesus such rest as his love for his people. It is his solace and his joy. It is almost inconceivable by us that Jesus should derive joy from the fact that he loves us, but so it is. That text in Zephaniah comes again to our recollection—"He will rest in his love, he will joy over thee with singing" (Zeph 3:17). It is a joy to Christ to love his people. His own heart finds a joy in their joy, a heaven in their heaven. To see them saved is bliss to him. Oh, how glad we ought to be of this. Jesus rests in love.

But as the traveler rested he also proceeded on his way; the bearers carried the palanquin from place to place, and the traveler made progress, but always with the same surroundings within his curtained bed. So Jesus in all his glorious marching, in everything he does or is to do, still marches on in love. Read the book of Revelation, and think of the trumpets, and the falling stars, and the opened vials full of judgments, and you may well tremble. But then fall back upon the doctrine of the Scriptures, and say, "These are the goings forth of my Lord the King, but he always rides in a chariot which is paved with love for the daughters of Jerusalem. So let him come: with earthquake and with flame, if so he chooses, let him come; let him even loose destroying angels to smite the earth; and let the whole world before his coming rock and reel, and all men's hopes depart like visions of the night. I will not fear, for sure am I that he cannot come except in love to me. No judgment can bear wrath to his people, no overturning can overturn their hopes, no rod of iron can shatter their bliss." This is surely a thought which should make your spirit glad.

Now notice that as Jesus rides in this chariot, so do you, O believer, and at this moment your standing is upon love. You stand up in this palanquin upon love. You are accepted in the Beloved: you are not judged according to the law, but you are judged according to grace: you are not estimated at the judgment seat by what you have done, but according to his abounding mercy. Recline this morning in the love of God. Ah, take your rest in it. As the rich man tries to find solace in his riches, and the strong man in his strength, and the great man in his fame, so stretch yourselves and lie at ease upon this glorious bed of almighty love.

And, beloved, take care that when you labor to make progress, you still make it in the power and energy of his love. Do not strive after virtue and grace by the law, for you will never get them. The chariot in which you rest is also the chariot in which you are to be carried forward towards perfection. Grow in grace, but keep to the cross. Cling still to the love of God in Christ Jesus, for that keeps you always safe. You sleep in it; you wake in it; you eat and you drink in it. Wherever you are, love surrounds you. It is in the atmosphere you breathe; it is to be found in every place, wherever you roam. You are never out of the love which is in the midst of the chariot.

Attacks on the Bible

Some of you may at times be alarmed when you hear of attacks made upon the Bible. At one time it was thought that ethnology would prove that the human race could not be one; and Moses was terribly abused by some who said it was not possible that all of us could have come of one pair. That battle was fought, and you hear nothing of it now; it is over; learning and argument in the hand of God has routed those antagonists. Then they pelted us with shells, and bones of lizards. Geology threatened to dig our graves. But we have lived all through that struggle, and we have found geology to be a great blessing, for it has shed a new light on the first chapter of Genesis and made us understand a great deal better what it meant. Another Amalekite advances to combat; this time it is with figures and numbers. We are to be speared with arithmetic, and slain with algebra! And what will be the result of it? Why, it will do the Bible a world of good, for we shall understand it better. I thank God whenever the Bible is attacked. For all those who know the times and seasons, begin to study just that part of Scripture more carefully, and then we get a clearer light shed upon it, and we find ourselves more confirmed than ever that this is the very truth, and that God has revealed it to us. "Well, but who will take this matter up?" I do not know, and I do not particularly care, but I know my Master has his threescore valiant men round about his bed, and that each man has his sword upon his thigh because of fear in the night, and never mind what the battle may be, the end of it will be for God's glory, and there shall be progress with the chariot of Christ through that which seemed as if it must overthrow it. Cast aside your fears; rejoice, and be glad, O daughter of Zion! Your Lord is with you in the traveling chariot, and the threescore valiant men are watching against thy foes.

SONG OF SOLOMON 4

SONG OF SOLOMON 4:1–16

1 Behold, thou *art* fair, my love; behold, thou *art* fair;
Thou *hast* doves' eyes within thy locks:
Thy hair *is* as a flock of goats, that appear from mount Gilead.
2 Thy teeth *are* like a flock *of sheep that are even* shorn, which
came up from the washing;
Whereof every one bear twins, and none *is* barren among them.
3 Thy lips *are* like a thread of scarlet, and thy speech *is* comely:
Thy temples *are* like a piece of a pomegranate within thy locks.
4 Thy neck *is* like the tower of David
Builded for an armoury,
Whereon there hang a thousand bucklers, all shields of mighty men.
5 Thy two breasts *are* like two young roes that are twins,
Which feed among the lilies.
6 Until the day break, and the shadows flee away,
I will get me to the mountain of myrrh, and to the hill of frankincense.
7 Thou *art* all fair, my love; *there is* no spot in thee.
8 Come with me from Lebanon, *my* spouse, with me from Lebanon:
Look from the top of Amana, from the top of Shenir and Hermon,
From the lions' dens, from the mountains of the leopards.
9 Thou hast ravished my heart, my sister, *my* spouse;
Thou hast ravished my heart with one of thine eyes,
With one chain of thy neck.
10 How fair is thy love, my sister, *my* spouse!
How much better is thy love than wine!
And the smell of thine ointments than all spices!
11 Thy lips, O *my* spouse, drop *as* the honeycomb:
Honey and milk *are* under thy tongue;
And the smell of thy garments *is* like the smell of Lebanon.

12 A garden inclosed *is* my sister, *my* spouse;
A spring shut up, a fountain sealed.
13 Thy plants *are* an orchard of pomegranates, with pleasant fruits;
Camphire, with spikenard,
14 Spikenard and saffron;
Calamus and cinnamon, with all trees of frankincense;
Myrrh and aloes, with all the chief spices:
15 A fountain of gardens, a well of living waters,
And streams from Lebanon.
16 Awake, O north wind; and come, thou south;
Blow upon my garden, *that* the spices thereof may flow out.
Let my beloved come into his garden,
And eat his pleasant fruits.

EXPOSITION

1 **Behold, thou art fair, my love; behold, thou art fair** "Twice fair; first, through being washed in my blood, and next, through being sanctified by my Spirit!"

This is a chapter which is, perhaps, more adapted for private meditation than for reading in public. It is a love song, the song of the loves of Jesus. As he sets forth the beauties and charms of his church, may the like beauties and charms be found in every one of us through the grace which he imparts to us by his Spirit! May we, as parts of his mystical body, be fair and lovely in his esteem because he has bestowed upon us so much of his own loveliness! Let us walk so carefully with God that there may be nothing to put even a spot upon our garments, or to defile our grace-given comeliness.

Thou hast doves' eyes within thy locks Jesus prizes the love of his people which flashes forth from their eyes as they look upon him. The good works of his people, like the locks of hair which are the beauty and glory of the female form, are the beauty of the church, and of every individual believer. It is a beautiful thing to have the eyes of faith glistening between the locks of our good works to the praise and glory of God.

Thy hair is as a flock of goats, that appear from mount Gilead O my soul, see that you have many such acceptable works of faith and labors of love!

2 **Thy teeth** Those parts of our spiritual being with which we feed upon Christ, and masticate and assimilate the Word.

are like a flock of sheep that are even shorn, which came up from the washing; Whereof every one bear twins, and none is barren among them We should seek so to feed upon the Word as to become fruitful by it. If we spiritually feed upon the flesh of Christ, we shall afterward be the means of bringing forth an abundant harvest of holiness to his praise and honor.

3 **Thy lips are like a thread of scarlet** And well they may be, for what is there for the believer to talk about but the scarlet of the Savior's blood, that matchless bath in which we are washed whiter than snow? My mouth, be filled with the praises of the Lord, that my lips may be like a thread of scarlet!

and thy speech is comely There is always a comeliness in that conversation which is full of Christ. So, beloved, let your conversation ever be such as becometh the gospel of Christ; but that cannot be the case unless there is much of Christ in it.

Thy temples are like a piece of a pomegranate within thy locks Those parts of us with which we think upon God's Word should ever be surrounded by good works. Doctrines in the head, without holiness in the life, are of no service. But when the temples are covered with the locks of righteousness, then are they like a piece of a pomegranate, acceptable both to God and men.

4 **Thy neck is like the tower of David Builded for an armoury** And what is this but our faith? Does not the neck join the body to the head, and is not faith that connecting link by which we are united to Christ? Oh, for that faith which is like the tower of David built for an armory! It is sure to be assaulted; let it, therefore, be firmly founded, and fully armed.

Whereon there hang a thousand bucklers, all shields of mighty men They hung up their bucklers in memory of their triumphs. Read the eleventh chapter of the Epistle to the Hebrews, which is a record of the victories of faith. The promises of God are also like these bucklers which are hung up in the armory. Let us be so familiar with them that we shall have them ready for use in every emergency.

5 **Thy two breasts are like two young roes that are twins, which feed among the lilies** The ordinances of God's house are very delightful to Christ, and to his people too. Consequently, that part of our spiritual being which seeks to feed others, and specially to nourish the young believer, is very precious in Christ's esteem.

6 **Until the day break, and the shadows flee away, I will get me to the mountain of myrrh, and to the hill of frankincense** Our Beloved has gone away from us until the day of his reappearing—until the night of his church's anxiety is over, and the Sun of righteousness shall arise with healing in his wings. Jesus has gone from earth, but where is he? He has gone to intercede for us before the throne of his Father above. He has gone to where there are mountains of myrrh. Think, beloved, of the sweet perfume that ever arises from his one great sacrifice for sins; well may he compare it to a mountain of myrrh and to a hill of frankincense.

7 **Thou art all fair, my love** *Christ has a high esteem for his church.* He does not blindly admire her faults, or even conceal them from himself. He is acquainted with her sin, in all its heinousness of guilt, and desert of punishment. That sin he does not shun to reprove. His own words are, "As many as I love, I rebuke and chasten" (Rev 3:19). He abhors sin in her as much as in the ungodly world, nay even more, for he sees in her an evil which is not to be found in the transgressions of others—sin against love and grace. She is black in her own sight, how much more so in the eyes of her omniscient Lord. Yet there it stands, written by the inspiration of the Holy

Spirit, and flowing from the lips of the bridegroom, "Thou art all fair, my love; there is no spot in thee." How then is this? Is it a mere exaggeration of love, an enthusiastic canticle which the sober hand of truth must strip of its glowing fables. Oh, no. The king is full of love, but he is not so overcome with it as to forget his reason. The words are true, and he means us to understand them as the honest expression of his unbiased judgment, after having patiently examined her in every part. He would not have us diminish anything, but estimate the gold of his opinions by the bright glittering of his expressions; and therefore in order that there may be no mistake, he states it positively, "Thou art all fair, my love," and confirms it by a negative, "there is no spot in thee."

When he speaks positively, how complete is his admiration! She is "fair," but that is not a full description; he styles her "all fair." He views her in himself, washed in his sin-atoning blood and clothed in his meritorious righteousness, and he considers her to be full of comeliness and beauty. No wonder that such is the case, since it is but his own perfect excellencies that he admires, seeing that the holiness, glory, and perfection of his church are his own garments on the back of his own well-beloved spouse, and she is "bone of [his] bone and flesh of [his] flesh" (Gen 2:23). She is not simply pure, or well-proportioned; she is positively lovely and fair! She has actual merit! Her deformities of sin are removed; but more, she has through her Lord obtained a meritorious righteousness by which an actual beauty is conferred upon her.

there is no spot in thee When the bride extols her Lord there is no wonder, for he deserves it well, and in him there is room for praise without possibility of flattery. But does he who is wiser than Solomon condescend to praise this sunburnt Shulamite? It is even so, for these are his own words, and were uttered by his own sweet lips. No, do not doubt, for we have more wonders to reveal. There are greater depths in heavenly things than you have at present dared to hope. The church not only *is* all fair in the eyes of her beloved, but in one sense she always was so. He delighted in her before she had either a natural or a spiritual being, and from the beginning could he say, "My delights were with the sons of men" (Prov 8:31). Having covenanted to be the surety of the elect, and having determined to fulfill every stipulation of that covenant, he from all eternity delighted to survey the purchase of his blood, and rejoiced to view his church in the purpose and decree, as already by him delivered from sin and exalted to glory and happiness.

8 **Come with me from Lebanon, my spouse, with me from Lebanon: look from the top of Amana, from the top of Shenir and Hermon** My heart, leave the world; leave its sweet places; though Lebanon be full of fragrance, leave it. Leave the world's high places; though the top of Amana may seem to reach to heaven, leave even that to have communion with your Lord. "Come out from among them, and be ye separate, saith the Lord, and touch not the unclean thing" (2 Cor 6:17). The best spots in the world are to you, O Spouse of Christ, but lions' dens and mountains of leopards. You are always in danger while you consort with worldlings, you are ever in peril while you are entangled with the world. So come away from Lebanon, from Amana, from Shenir and Hermon; leave everything for your Lord.

From the lions' dens, from the mountains of the leopards When Christ came the first time, he met with fierce opposition, from sin, and death, and hell. These were the lions; these were the leopards; and our great Champion had to go hunting them, and they hunted him. You know how these grim lions met him, and how they tore him; they rent his hands, and his feet, and his side. Do you not remember how that great lion of the pit came leaping upon him, how he received him upon his breast, like a greater Samson, and though he fell in the death-struggle, he tore that lion asunder, as though he had been a kid, and cast him down? As for his other enemies, he could truly say, "O death, where is thy sting? O grave, where is thy victory?" (1 Cor 15:55).

9 **Thou hast ravished my heart** I think the Septuagint reads it, "Thou hast unhearted me," as if Christ's people had taken away his heart, so that it was all theirs, and not his any longer.

Thou hast ravished my heart with one of thine eyes, With one chain of thy neck The eye of love, and the neck of faith with its chain, hold captive the heart of Christ.

> So dear, so very dear to Christ,
> Dearer I cannot be;
> The love wherewith God loves his sons,
> Such is Christ's love to me.[1]

Oh, what a miracle of mercy it is that Christ himself should be unhearted by such foul and loathsome creatures as we were. Yet he loved us so that he would have us. Having determined to do so, he put a beauty upon us that is really now worthy of his love. I speak advisedly, for the righteousness of Christ and the sanctification of the Spirit have in them something really so fair that Christ does not now love that which is unworthy of his love. That righteousness which he has himself wrought in us now rightly claims his affection.

10 **How fair is thy love, my sister, my spouse!** I have said that this is Jesus speaking to his church. Now when the church praises Jesus, you do not wonder, for he deserves all she can say of him, and ten thousand times more. When she uses such large expressions concerning his loveliness, you feel that she falls far short of her mighty theme—that she does but demean him by her comparisons. For she can but compare the greater with the less, and the beautiful and the eternal, with that which is mutable and transient. But hear Christ turn around upon his church, and seem to say to her: "You have praised me; I will praise you. You think much of me; I think quite as much of you. You use great expressions to me; I will use just the same to you. You say my love is better than wine; so is

1. These lines are from the Catesby Paget hymn "A Mind at Perfect Peace with God." —ed.

yours to me. You tell me all my garments smell of myrrh; so do yours. You say my word is sweeter than honey to your lips; so are yours to mine. All that you can say of me, I say it back to you; I see myself in your eyes; I can see my own beauty in you; and whatever belongs to me belongs to you. Therefore, O my love, I will sing back the song: you have sung it to your beloved, and I will sing it to my beloved. You have sung it to your Ishi; I will sing it to my Hephzibah. You have sung it to your husband; I will sing it to my sister, my spouse."

Your love, poor, feeble, and cold though it be, is very precious unto the Lord Jesus; in fact it is so precious that he himself cannot tell how precious it is. He does not say how precious, but he says, "how fair." This is an expression that men use when they do not know how to describe anything. They lift up their hands, they put in a note of exclamation, and they say, "How fair! How precious! How much better is thy love than wine!" The fact is that Jesus values our love at such a price that the Holy Spirit, when he dictated this Song of Solomon, could not see any word in all human language that was large enough to set forth Christ's estimation of our love.

How much better is thy love than wine! Jesus Christ is delighted with the thought that his people love him, this cheers and gladdens him. Just as the thought of his love gladdens us, so the thought of our love gladdens him. Notice how he puts it, he says, "How much better is thy love than wine!" Now wine when used in Scripture, frequently signifies two things, a great luxury, and a great refreshment. Wine is a luxury, especially it is so in this country, and even in the East, where there was more of it, good wine was still a dainty thing. Now Jesus Christ looks upon his people's love as being a luxury to him; and I will show you that he does. When he sat at the feast of Simon the Pharisee, I have no doubt there were sparkling wine cups on the table, and many rich dainties were there. But Jesus Christ did not care for the wine, nor for the banquet. What did he care for them? That poor woman's love was much better to him than wine. He could say to Simon the Pharisee, if he had chosen, "Simon, put away thy wine cups, take away thy dainties; this is my feast, the feast of my people's love." I told you also that wine was used as an emblem of refreshment. Now, our Savior has often been refreshed by his people's love. "No," says one, "that cannot be." Yes! You remember once he was weary and thirsty, and sat upon the well of Samaria. He needed wine then indeed to refresh him, but he could not get so much as a drop of water. He spoke to a woman whom he had loved from before all worlds, he put new life into her, and she at once desired to give him drink; but she ran away first to tell to the Samaritans what she had heard. Now the Savior was so delighted at her wishing to do good that when his disciples came, they expected to find him fainting, for he had walked many a weary mile that day, so they said, "Whence hath he meat?" and he said, "I have meat to eat that ye know not of" (John 4:32). It was that woman's love that had fed him. He had broken her heart, he had won her to himself, and when he saw the tear roll from her eye and knew that her heart was set upon him, his spirits all revived, and his poor flagging strength grew strong. It was this encouraged him.

No, I will go further. When Christ went to his cross there was one thing that cheered him even in the agonies of death; it was the thought of his people's love. Are we not told in Hebrews that our blessed and divine husband, the Lord Jesus, "for the joy that was set before him endured the cross, despising the shame" (Heb 12:2)? What was that joy? Why, the joy that he should see his seed, and that seed should love him, and that he should have his love written in their hearts, in remembrance of his dying pains and agonies. Jesus was cheered, even in his death agonies, by the thought of the love of his people, when the bulls of Bashan roared upon him, and the dogs bayed him, when the sun was put out in darkness, when his Father's hand was heavy upon him, when the legions of hell compassed him, when the pangs of body and the tortures of spirit all beset him. It was this that cheered him: "My people they are dear to me; for them I stretch these bleeding hands; for them shall this heart be pierced, and oh, how they will love me, how they will love me on earth! How they will love me spiritually in

Paradise!" This was the wine the Savior had to drink; this was the cup of his delightful joy that made him bear all these pains without a murmuring, and this was the meaning of these words of Jesus: "How much better is thy love than wine!"

ILLUSTRATION

A Child with a Flower

Preaching Themes: Grace, Giving, Love

Have you never known a little child when he feels love in his heart go into the garden or the field and bring you a little flower? It may be but a little buttercup or a daisy, a great thing to him, perhaps, but a trifle to you—worthless, in fact. You have taken it, and you have smiled and have felt happy because it was a token of your child's love.

So, Jesus esteems your graces; they are his gift to you. Mark, first of all, they are very poor things in themselves. Still he esteems them as tokens of your love, and he rejoices in them, and declares they are as sweet to him as all the spices of Araby, and all the rich odors of the merchant.

And the smell of thine ointments than all spices! You know that he has the smell of myrrh, and aloes, and cassia upon his garments when he comes out of the ivory palaces, yet he considers that his people's graces are sweeter than all the spices that ever grew.

11 **Thy lips, O my spouse, drop *as* the honeycomb:** Christ's people are not a dumb people; they were once but they *talk* now. I do not believe a Christian can keep the secret that God gives him if he were to try; it would burst his lips open to get out. When God puts grace into your heart, you may try to hide it, but hide it you cannot. It will be like fire in the bones and will be sure to find its way out. Now the church is a talking

church, a preaching church, and a praising church; she has got lips, and every believer will find he must use his lips in the service of Christ.

Jesus Christ does not find any fault in what the church speaks. He says, "No, 'Thy lips, O my spouse, drop as the honeycomb.' " You know the honey that drops out of the honeycomb is the best—it is called the life-honey. So the words that drop from the Christian's lips are the very words of his life, his life-honey, and they ought to be sweet to everyone. They are as sweet to the taste of the Lord Jesus as the drops of the honeycomb.

ILLUSTRATION

Speaking Only to Plato

Preaching Themes: Prayer, Presence of God, Speech

Plato, we are told, was once listening to an orator, and when all the people had gone away but Plato, the orator went on with all his might. Being asked why he proceeded, he replied that Plato was sufficient audience for any man.

And surely if in preaching, or in praying, all the world should find fault, and all the world should run from it, Jesus is enough to be the hearer for any man. And if he is satisfied, if he says our words are sweeter than the honeycomb, we will not stop; all the devils in hell shall not stop us. We could continue to preach, and praise, and pray, while immortality endures.

Honey and milk are under thy tongue We speak about solemn sounds upon a thoughtless tongue; but the Christian has his words first under the tongue. There they lie. They come from his heart; they do not come from the top of his tongue—they are not superficial service work, but they come from under the tongue—down deep—things that he feels and matters that he knows. Nor is this the only meaning. The things that are under the tongue are thoughts that have never yet been expressed; they do not get to the top of the tongue but lie there half formed and are ready to come out. But either because they cannot come out, or we have not time to let them out, there they remain, and never come into actual words. Now Jesus Christ thinks very much even of these; he says, "Honey and milk are under thy tongue," and Christian meditation and Christian contemplation are to Christ like honey for sweetness and like milk for nourishment. Honey and milk are two things with which the land of Canaan was said to flow; and so the heart of a Christian flows with milk and honey, like the land which God gave to his ancient people.

And the smell of thy garments is like the smell of Lebanon The odoriferous herbs that grew on the side of Lebanon delighted the traveler, and perhaps here is an allusion to the peculiarly sweet smell of the cedarwood. Now, the garments of a Christian are twofold—the garment of imputed righteousness, and the garment of inwrought sanctification. I think the allusion here is to the second. The garments of a Christian are his *everyday actions*—the things that he wears upon him wherever he goes. Now these smell very sweet to the Lord Jesus.

12 **A garden inclosed** We are not only like a garden, but a garden *enclosed*. If the garden were not enclosed, the wild boar out of the wood would bark the vines and uproot the flowers; but infinite mercy has made the church of God an enclosure into which no invader may dare to come. "For I, saith the LORD, will be unto her a wall of fire round about, and will be the glory in the midst of her" (Zech 2:5).

A garden is a place where trees have been planted by a skillful hand; where they are nurtured and tended with care, and where fruit is expected by its owner. Such is the church; such is each renewed soul. But it is a garden enclosed, and so enclosed that one cannot see over its walls—so shut out from the world's wilderness, that the passerby must not enter it—so protected from all intrusion that it is a guarded Paradise—as secret as was that inner place, the holy of holies, within the tabernacle of old.

is my sister, my spouse As if he could not express his near and dear relationship to her by any one term, he employs the two. "My sister"—that is, one by birth, partaker of the same nature. "My spouse"—that is, one in love, joined by sacred ties of affection that never can be snapped. "My sister" by birth, "my spouse" by choice. "My sister" in communion, "my spouse" in absolute union with myself.

The first term, "sister," implies kinship of nature; but *the second term, "my spouse," indicates another kinship, dearer, and, in some respects, nearer:* a kinship undertaken of choice, but, once undertaken, irrevocable and everlasting. This kinship amounts to unity, insomuch that the spouse loses her name, loses her identity, and, to a high degree, is merged in the greater personality to which she is united. Such is our union to Christ, if indeed we be his, that nothing can so well set it forth as marriage union. He loves us so much that he has taken us up into himself by the absorption of love. We may henceforth forgo our name, for "this is the name wherewith *she* shall be called, The Lord our righteousness" (Jer 33:16). Wonderful that the very name which belongs to our Lord Jesus, and one of the most majestic of his names, should yet be used as the name of his church. The Lord Jesus Christ's name is now named upon her, and she is permitted to make use of his name whenever she draws near to the throne of the heavenly grace in prayer. "In his name"—this is to be her great plea whenever she intercedes with heaven. She speaks in the name which is above every name, the name at which angels bow.

ILLUSTRATION

The Church Like a Garden

Preaching Themes: Nature of the Church

A garden in the East is a very needy place. One day's burning sun might suffice to wither all its verdure; but then the Lord has declared of his church, "The sun shall not smite thee by day, nor the moon by night" (Ps 121:6). "I the Lord do keep it; I will water it every moment; lest any hurt it, I will keep it night and day" (Isa 27:3). A garden is a dependent thing, requiring perpetual care from the husbandman; and that care the church of God shall have, for it is written, "He careth for you" (1 Pet 5:7). Jesus says, "My Father is the husbandman" (John 15:1); and surely that is enough.

In a garden weeds spring up; and in the church, and in our hearts, the weeds of sin are plentiful; but there is One who will take care to pluck up evil growths, and cut away all rank shoots, that none of the precious plants may be choked or overgrown. In all ways every single plant, however feeble, shall be tended with all-sufficient skill.

A spring shut up, a fountain sealed Then the Bridegroom calls her "a spring shut up." Otherwise, every beast that passed by might foul her waters, and every stranger might quaff her streams. She is a spring shut up, a fountain sealed, like some choice cool spring in Solomon's private garden around the house of the forest of Lebanon—a fountain which he reserved for his own drinking, by placing the royal seal upon it, and locking it up by secret means, known only to himself. The legend hath it that there were fountains which none knew of but Solomon, and he had so shut them up that, with his ring he touched a secret spring, a door opened, and living waters leaped out to fill his jeweled cup. No one knew but Solomon the secret charm by which he set flowing the pent-up stream, of which no lip drank but his own. Now, God's people are as much shut up, and preserved, and kept from danger by the care of Christ, as the springs in Solomon's garden were reserved expressly for himself.

13 **Thy plants are an orchard of pomegranates, with pleasant fruits; camphire, with spikenard** The Lord has been pleased to separate many of us to himself and bring us into his visible church, so that we dwell within that "garden walled around, chosen and made peculiar ground."[2] Herein is no small deed of love. Aliens are made fellow citizens with the saints and of the household of God. Yet, much more than this has been done for true believers in the blood of Jesus. Not the name only, but the very essence and soul of true piety is ours, so that once again we walk with God; and in communion with the saints and with their Lord, we find a new garden of delight, whose plants are an orchard of pomegranates with pleasant fruits, camphire with spikenard. "Thy plants are an orchard of pomegranates, with pleasant fruits; camphire, with spikenard, spikenard and saffron; calamus and cinnamon, with all trees of frankincense; myrrh and aloes, with all the chief spices: a fountain of gardens, a well of living waters, and streams from Lebanon." We might date our letters from Elysium, for "we which have believed do enter into rest" (Heb 4:3). Yes, we are restored by grace to the King's garden, we have found glory begun below—

> Celestial fruits on earthly ground,
> From faith and hope do grow.[3]

14 **Spikenard and saffron; calamus and cinnamon, with all trees of frankincense; myrrh and aloes, with all the chief spices** Oh, that this were fully true of us—that all our thoughts, and words, and actions, which are like the fruits of the garden, were as full of spices of heavenly fragrance as

2. A quotation from the Isaac Watts hymn "We Are a Garden Walled Around." —ed.
3. A quotation from the Isaac Watts hymn "Come, We That Love the Lord (We're Marching to Zion)." —ed.

Jesus here declares that he thinks them to be! Yet how little we do for him, though he sets such store by our little that he regards it as much.

15 **A fountain of gardens, a well of living waters, and streams from Lebanon** The garden was enclosed before; now it is "a fountain of gardens." The well was shut up, now it is a well of living waters; before we had the fountain sealed, now we have streams dashing adown the sides of Lebanon. So a Christian is to be separate in his inner life; but in the outer manifestations of that inner life, he is to mingle for good among his fellow men.

The garden was shut up—that was to keep it. There are no walls here, so that all may come to it. The streams were shut up before; here it is an open well. The fountain was sealed in the first verse; here it is a flowing stream, which is to teach us this—that the way God keeps his people in security is not by shutting out their enemies from attacking them, but while laying them open to temptation and attack, he yet sustains them. It is not much to preserve oneself behind a wall which cannot be scaled, but to stand where arrows are flying thick as hail, where lances are being pushed with fury, where the sword cuts are falling on every part, to stand, I say, invulnerable, invincible, immortal; this is to wear a divine life which cannot be conquered by human power. Such is the Christian.

16 **Awake, O north wind; and come, thou south; blow upon my garden, that the spices thereof may flow out** The loved one in the text desired the company of her Lord, and felt that an inactive condition was not altogether suitable for his coming. Her prayer is first about her garden, that it may be made ready for her Beloved; and then to the Bridegroom himself, that he would come into his garden, and eat its pleasant fruits. She pleads for *the breath of heaven*, and for *the Lord of heaven*.

First, she cries for the breath of heaven to break the dead calm which broods over her heart. She cannot unlock the caskets of spice, nor cause the sweet odors to flow forth; her own breath would not avail for such an end. She looks away from herself to an unseen and mysterious power. She breathes this earnest prayer: "Awake, O north wind; and come, thou south; blow upon my garden!"

In this prayer there is an evident sense of *inward sleep*. She does not mean that the north wind is asleep; it is her poetical way of confessing that she herself needs to be awakened. She has a sense of *absentmindedness*, too, for she cries, "Come, thou south." If the south wind would come, the forgetful perfumes would come to themselves, and sweeten all the air. The fault, whatever it is, cannot lie in the winds; it lies in ourselves.

Her appeal, as we have already said, is to that great Spirit who operates according to his own will, even as "the wind bloweth where it listeth" (John 3:8). She does not try to "raise the wind"—that is an earthly expression relating to worldly matters; but, alas, it might fitly be applied to many imitations of spirituality! Have we not heard of "getting up revivals"? Indeed, we can no more command the Holy Spirit than we can compel the wind to blow east or west. Our strength lies in prayer. The spouse prays, "Awake, O north wind; and come, thou south!" She thus owns her entire dependence upon the free Spirit. Although she veiled her faith in a divine Worker under the imagery of her song, yet she spoke as to a person. We believe in the personality of the Holy Ghost, so that we ask *him* to "awake" and "come." We believe that we may pray to him, and we are impelled to do so.

Notice that the spouse does not mind what form the divine visitation takes so long as she feels its power. "Awake, O north wind"; though the blast be cold and cutting, it may be that it will effectually fetch forth the perfume of the soul in the form of repentance and self-humiliation. Some precious graces, like rare spices, naturally flow forth in the form of tears, and others are only seen in hours of sorrow, like gums which exude from wounded trees. The rough north wind has done much for some of us in the way of arousing our best graces. Yet it may be that the Lord will send something more tender and cheering; and if so, we would cry, "Come, thou south." Divine love warming the heart has a wonderful power to develop the best part of a man's nature. Many of our precious things are brought forth by the sun of holy joy.

Either movement of the Spirit will sufficiently bestir our inner life, but the spouse desires both. Although in nature you cannot have the north wind and the south blowing at the same time, yet in grace you can. The Holy Ghost may be at one and the same time working grief and gladness, causing humiliation and delight. I have often been conscious of the two winds blowing at once; so that, while I have been ready to die to self, I have been made to live unto God. "Awake, O north wind; and come, thou south!" When all the forms of spiritual energy are felt, no grace will be dormant. No flower can keep asleep when both rough and gentle winds arouse it.

Let my beloved come into his garden and eat his pleasant fruits While the spouse was, as it were, shut up and frozen, and the spices of the Lord's garden were not flowing out, she cried to the winds, "Blow upon *my* garden." She hardly dared to call it her Lord's garden. But now, notice the alteration in the phraseology: "Let my Beloved come into his garden, and eat his pleasant fruits." The wind has blown through the garden and made the sweet odors to flow forth; now it is no longer "my garden" but "his garden." It is wonderful how an increase of grace transfers our properties; while we have but little grace, we cry, "*my*," but when we get great grace, we cry "*his*." Wherein you are sinful and infirm, that is yours, you rightly call it "*my*," but when you become strong, and joyous, and full of faith, that is not yours, and you rightly call it "*his*." Let him have all the glory of the change while you take all the shame and confusion of face to yourself that ever you should have been so destitute of grace. So the spouse says, "Let my Beloved come into his garden. Here are all the sweet perfumes flowing out; he will enjoy them, let him come and feel himself at home amongst them. He planted every flower, and gave to each its fragrance; let him come into his garden, and see what wonders his grace has wrought."

APPLICATION

Talking Too Much?

A little caution to some of you that talk too much. Some of you do not let your words drop as the honeycomb; they gush out as a great stream that sweeps everything before it, so that others could not thrust in a word edgeways. No, not if it were squeezed together and sharpened at one end could it be got in. You must talk; your tongue seems set on a hinge, like a pendulum, forever going on: swing! swing! swing! Now, Christ does not admire that. He says of his church in his commendation, her lips "drop as the honeycomb." Now a honeycomb, when it drops, does not drop so much even as the drops that fall from the eaves of houses, for the honey is thick, and rich, and therefore it takes some time. One drop hangs for a time; then comes another, and then another, and does not all come in quick succession. Now when people are often talking a great deal, it is poor and thin, and good for nothing. But when they have something good to say, it drops by slow degrees like the honey from the honeycomb. Mark, I do not want you to say one good word less. They are those other words, those awkward ones. Oh, that we could leave them out! I am as guilty of this myself, I fear, as many others. If we could talk half as much, it would be, perhaps, twice as good. And if we were to say only a tenth of what we do, perhaps we should be ten times better. For he is a wise man that knows how to speak well, but he is a great deal wiser man that knows how to hold his tongue. The lips of the true church, the lips of the true believer drop like the honeycomb, with rich words, rich thoughts, rich prayers, rich praises.

The Separation of the Church from the World

A garden is a plot of ground separated from the common waste for a special purpose; such is the church. The church is a separate and distinct thing from the world. I suppose there is such a thing as "the Christian world," but I do not know what it is or where it can be found. It must be a singular mixture. I know what is meant by a worldly Christian, and I suppose the Christian world must be an aggregate of worldly Christians. But the church of Christ is not of the world. "They are not of the world," says Christ, "even as I am not of the world" (John 17:16). Great attempts have been made of late to make the church receive the world, and wherever it has succeeded it has come to this result: the world has swallowed up the church. It must be so. The greater is sure to swamp the less. They say, "Do not let us draw any hard and fast lines. A great many good people attend our services who may not be quite decided, but still their opinion should be consulted, and their vote should be taken upon the choice of a minister, and there should be entertainments and amusements in which they can assist." The theory seems to be that it is well to have a broad gangway from the church to the world. If this is carried out, the result will be that the nominal church will use that gangway to go over to the world, but it will not be used in the other direction.

It is thought by some that it would perhaps be better to have no distinct church at all. If the world will not come up to the church, let the church go down to the world; that seems to be the theory. Let the Israelites dwell with the Canaanites and become one happy family. Such a blending does not appear to have been anticipated by our Lord in John 15. Read verses 18 and 19: "If the world hate you, ye know that it hated me before it hated you. If ye were of the world, the world would love his own: but because ye are not of the world, but I have chosen you out of the world, therefore the world hateth you." Did he ever say, "Try to make an alliance with the world, and in all things be conformed to its ways"? Nothing could have been further from our Lord's mind. Oh, that we could see more of holy separation, more dissent from ungodliness, more nonconformity to the world! This is "the dissidence of dissent" that I care for, far more than I do for party names and the political strife which is engendered by them.

Let us, however, take heed that our separateness from the world is of the same kind as our Lord's. We are not to adopt a peculiar dress, or a singular mode of speech, or shut ourselves out from society. He did not do this but was a man of the people, mixing with them for their good. He was seen at a wedding feast, aiding the festivities; he even ate bread in a Pharisee's house, among captious enemies. He neither wore phylacteries nor enlarged the borders of his garments nor sought a secluded cell nor exhibited any eccentricity of manner. He was separate from sinners only because he was holy and harmless, and they were not. He dwelt among us, for he was of us. No man was more a man than he; and yet he was not of the world, neither could you count him among them. He was neither Pharisee, nor Sadducee, nor Scribe; and at the same time, none could justly confound him with publicans and sinners. Those who reviled him for consorting with these last did, by that very reviling, admit that he was a very different person from those with whom he went.

We want all members of the church of Christ to be, manifestly and obviously, distinct persons, as much as if they were of a separate race, even when they are seen mingling with the people around them. We are not to cut ourselves off from our neighbors by affectation and contempt. God forbid. Our very avoiding of affectation, our naturalness, simplicity, sincerity, and amiability of character, should constitute a distinction. Through Christians being what they seem to be, they should become remarkable in an age of pretenders. Their care for the welfare of others, their anxiety to do good, their forgiveness of injuries, their gentleness of manner—all these should distinguish them far more than they could be distinguished by a livery, or by any outward signs. I long to see Christian people become more distinct from the world than ever, because I am persuaded that, until they are so, the church will never become such a power for blessing men as her Lord intended her to be. It is for the world's good that there should be no alliance between the church and the world by way of compromise, even to a shade.

You Cannot Attempt Too Much for Christ

A man may attempt too much, they say—but not for Christ. If you should attempt great things, and have great faith, you shall succeed in all that you attempt. There seems to be a fear among some Christian men either of doing too much themselves, or else of letting other people do too much, and I know some to whom that text might *almost* be applied, "They have the key of the kingdom of heaven, but they neither enter themselves, and they that would they hinder" (Luke 11:52). Not content to refuse the burden for themselves, they will not even touch it with one of their little fingers, but they are afraid that others shall carry the burden either. Well, we are not afraid as these are. Blessed be God, if there is a trench to be filled up, let us struggle which shall lead the way. If there is a rampart to be climbed, if there is no other man to throw the irons over with the scaling-ladder, let your minister attempt the deed, and lead the van, for he is well-assured that there are many here who would jostle with him, and say, "Let me come first; let me serve my Master; let me live or let me die, if I may but glorify him." What, bring forth for Christ a little shriveled cluster upon the topmost bough—a cluster which the very birds of heaven will not deign to touch, because it is too little even for their appetites? No, rather let us have every bough weighed down with clusters, like those of Eshcol, which will take two ordinary men to carry, but which we can bear in rich profusion, because the life of the Spirit of God is in us. We are a race of little doers, of little givers, of little thinkers, of little believers. O God, raise us up again giants in these days; give us again the consecrated men who shall stand upon the sword like the old Roman, and say, "For God I devote myself; to Christ I give body, soul, and spirit, and if I be offered up upon the sacrifice of your faith, I joy and rejoice with you all." If the fountain, the secret fountain, were better seen to, I think there would be more of these outward streams; and if the sealed well were better guarded, we should see more of these rapid streams from Lebanon which would make glad the people of God, and the world at large.

And now, how many of you have the secret spring within you? If your soul is not renewed by grace, you cannot do good. "Except a man be born again, he cannot *see* the kingdom of God" (John 3:3). No man enters fully into discipleship with Christ until the water as well as the Spirit has been reverently received: "Except a man be born of water and of the Spirit, he cannot *enter* the kingdom of heaven" (John 3:5). But these two things being done, being born of water and of the Spirit, go forth to show to others the mystery, the *fellowship* of the mystery—to make all men know that God has appeared unto us in Christ Jesus, reconciling the world unto himself, not imputing their iniquities. Preach of Christ when you know Christ, but not until then. Let the streams flow out when you have the inner fountain, but not until then.

SONG OF SOLOMON 5

SONG OF SOLOMON 5:1–8

1 I am come into my garden, my sister, *my* spouse:
I have gathered my myrrh with my spice;
I have eaten my honeycomb with my honey;
I have drunk my wine with my milk:
Eat, O friends; drink, yea, drink abundantly, O beloved.
2 I sleep, but my heart waketh:
It is the voice of my beloved that knocketh, *saying*,
Open to me, my sister, my love, my dove, my undefiled:
For my head is filled with dew,
And my locks with the drops of the night.
3 I have put off my coat; how shall I put it on?
I have washed my feet; how shall I defile them?
4 My beloved put in his hand by the hole *of the door*,
And my bowels were moved for him.
5 I rose up to open to my beloved;
And my hands dropped *with* myrrh,
And my fingers *with* sweet smelling myrrh,
Upon the handles of the lock.
6 I opened to my beloved;
But my beloved had withdrawn himself, *and* was gone:
My soul failed when he spake:
I sought him, but I could not find him;
I called him, but he gave me no answer.
7 The watchmen that went about the city found me,
They smote me, they wounded me;
The keepers of the walls took away my veil from me.
8 I charge you, O daughters of Jerusalem,
If ye find my beloved, that ye tell him,
That I *am* sick of love.

EXPOSITION

1 **I am come into my garden, my sister, my spouse** Our translators, in dividing the Bible into chapters, seem to have been utterly regardless of the connection or the sense, so that they brought down their guillotine between two verses which must not be divided. The church had said, "Awake, O north wind; and come, thou south; blow upon my garden." She had also said, "Let my beloved come into his garden, and eat his pleasant fruits." In answer to that prayer the Beloved replies, "I am come into my garden." Prayer is always heard, and the prayer of faithful souls finds an echo in Jesus's heart. How quickly the spouse was heard! Scarce had the words died away, "Let my Beloved come," before she heard him say, "I am come!" "Before they call, I will answer; and while they are yet speaking, I will hear" (Isa 65:24). He is very near unto his people, and hence he very speedily answers their request. And how fully does he answer it too! You will perhaps say, "But she had asked for the Holy Spirit; she had said, 'Awake, O north wind; and come, thou south,' and yet there is no mention of the heavenly wind as blowing through the garden." The answer is that the Beloved's coming means all that. His visit brings both north and south wind; all benign influences are sure to follow where *he* leads the way; spices always flow out from the heart when Christ's sweet love flows in, and where he is, Christians have all things in him.

If you take each word of this remarkable sentence, you will find a meaning. "*I* am come." There is the *personal* presence of Christ. "I *am come*." There is the *certainty* that it is so. It is no delusion, no dream, no supposition. "I *am* truly come." Note the next word: "I am come *into* my garden." How near is the approach of Christ to his church! He comes not to the garden door, nor to look over the wall, nor in at the gate and out again, but *into* his garden. Down every walk, amidst the green alleys, among the beds of spices he walks, watching each flower, pruning the superfluous foliage of every fruit-bearing plant, and plucking up by the roots such as his heavenly Father has not planted. His delights are with the sons of men.

His intercourse with his chosen is most familiar, so that the spouse may sing, "My beloved is gone down into his garden, to the beds of spices, to feed in the gardens, and to gather lilies" (Song 6:2). Jesus Christ the Lord forgets not his church but fulfills the promise: "I the Lord do keep it, I will water it every moment; lest any hurt it, I will keep it night and day" (Isa 27:3).

"I am come into *my* garden," says he. Note here the *possession which Christ claims in the church*. If it were not *his* garden, he would not come into it. A church that is not Christ's church shall have none of his presence, and a soul that is not Christ's has no fellowship with him. If he reveal himself at all, it is unto his own people, his blood-bought people, the people that are his by purchase and by power, and by the surrender of themselves to him.

The next word denotes *cultivation*. "I am come into my *garden*." The church is a cultivated spot; it did not spring up by chance, it was arranged by himself, it has been tended by himself, and the fruits belong to himself. Christ, the Great Cultivator, exercises care and skill in training his people, and he delights to see his own handiwork in them.

And then there are the two choice words at the close, by which he speaks of his church herself rather than of her work. As if he would draw the attention of his people to themselves and to himself, rather than to their work; he says, "*My sister, my spouse*." There is one name for the garden, but there are two names for herself. The work is his work, the garden is his garden, but see, he wants communion not so much with the work as with the worker, he speaks to the church herself. He calls her, "My sister, my spouse." "Spouse" has something in it of dearness that is not in the first word, for what can be dearer to the husband than the bride? But then there was a time when the spouse was not dear to the bridegroom, there was a period perhaps when he did not know her, when there was no relationship between them twain; though they are made of one flesh by marriage, yet they were of different families; and for this cause he adds the dear name of "sister," to show an ancient relationship to her, a closeness and a nearness by blood, by birth, as well as by betrothal and wedlock. The two words put together make up a confection of such inexpressible sweetness, that instead of seeking to expound them to you, I will leave them to your meditations, and may he who calls the church "Sister" and "Spouse" open up their richness to your souls.

I have gathered my myrrh with my spice Christ is delighted with *the offerings* of his people. He says, "I have gathered my myrrh with my spice." We may consider myrrh and spice—sweet perfumes—offered by way of incense to God as being indicative of the offerings which his people bring to him. What if I say that prayer is like sweet-smelling myrrh, and that the Beloved has been gathering the myrrh of holy prayer, the bitter myrrh of repenting sighs and cries, in the midst of this church, lo, these many months!

And then, may not spice represent our praises? For these, as well as prayer, come up as incense before his throne.

I have eaten my honeycomb with my honey The Savior's satisfaction is found in his people's *love*—"I have eaten my honeycomb with my honey." Shall I be wrong if I believe that this sweetness refers to Christian love, for this is the richest of all the graces, and sweetens all the rest? Jesus Christ finds delightful solace in his people's love, both in the inward love, which is like the honey, and in the outward manifestation of it, which is like the honeycomb. He rejoices in the love that drips in all its preciousness from the heart, and in the honeycomb of organization, in which it is for order's sake stored up and put into his hand. Or, what if it should mean that Christ overlooks the imperfections of his people? The honeycomb is not good eating, but he takes that as well as the honey! "I have eaten my honeycomb with my honey." As he looks upon his people, and sees what he has done for them, his loving heart rejoices in what his grace has accomplished. As a benevolent man who should have taken a child from the street and educated it, would be pleased see it growing up, prospering, happy, well-informed, talented, so when Jesus Christ, remembering what his people were, sees in them displays of grace, desires after holiness, self-denials, communion with God, and the like, this is to him like honey. He takes an intense satisfaction in the sweet fruits which he himself has caused us to produce; notwithstanding every imperfection, he accepts our love, and says, "I have eaten my honeycomb with my honey."

I have drunk my wine with my milk Our Lord's satisfaction is compared to drinking as well as eating, and that drinking is of a twofold character. "I have drunk my wine." Does he intend by this his *joy* which is fulfilled in us when our joy is full? Does he mean that, as men go to feasts to make glad their hearts with wine, so he comes to his people to see their joy, and is filled with exultation? Does he not mean so? Surely he does. And the milk, may not that mean the Christian's common, ordinary *life*? As milk contains all the constituents of nourishment, may he not mean by this the general life of the Christian? Our Lord takes delight in the graces of our lives. One has said that wine may represent those actions resulting from well-considered dedication and deep spiritual thought; for wine must be expressed from the grape with labor and preserved with care, there must be skill, and work, and forethought spent upon it; but milk is a natural production, it flows freely, plentifully, spontaneously; it is a more common and ordinary, yet precious thing. So the Lord delights that his people should give to him these elaborate works which they have to tend with long care and watch over with much anxiety before they are produced. These are the wine; but he would have them give him the simple outgushing of their souls, the ejaculations which flow forth without labor, the little deeds of love which need no forethought, the everyday outgoings of their inner life—these are milk, and are equally acceptable to him. Well, if it be so, it is certain that Christ finds great pleasure in his people, and in their various forms of piety he drinks his wine with his milk.

Eat, O friends; drink, yea, drink abundantly, O beloved In the invitation we see the character of the invited guests; they are spoken of as *friends*. We were once aliens, we are now brought nigh; we were once enemies, we are made servants, but we have advanced from the grade of service (though servants still) into that of friends, henceforth he calls us not servants, but friends, for the servant does not know what his Lord does, but all things that he has seen of his Father he has made known unto us. The friendship between Christ and his people is not in name only, but in deed and in truth. Having laid down his life for his friends, having brought them to know his friendship in times of trial and of difficulty, he at all times proves his friendship by telling his secrets to them, and exhibiting an intense sympathy with them in all their secret bitternesses. David and Jonathan were not more closely friends than Christ and the believer, when the believer lives near to his Lord. Never seek the friendship of the world, nor allow your love to the creature to overshadow your friendship with Christ.

He next calls his people *beloved* as well as friends. He multiplies titles, but all his words do not express the full love of his heart. "Beloved." Oh, to have this word addressed to us by Christ! It is music! There is no music in the rarest sounds compared with these three syllables, which drop from the Redeemer's lips like sweet-smelling myrrh. "Beloved!" If he had addressed but that one word to any one of us, it might create a heaven within our soul, which neither sickness nor death could mar.

2 **I sleep, but my heart waketh** The spouse laments her state, and sighs out, "I sleep." It strikes us at once that her sleep is a *state recognized*. We are astonished that she should say, "I sleep," and we conclude that it is not so profound a sleep as it might be; for when a man can say, "I sleep," he is not altogether steeped in slumber. When children of God perceive their own imperfections and mourn over them, there is evidently a root of virtue in them; when they perceive the decay of their

grace there is some grace left undecayed with which they are bemoaning their decline.

Further, as this sleep is a matter recognized, so is it *a matter complained of*. The spouse is not pleased to sleep; she says, "I sleep," but she does not mention it as a matter for congratulation. She is not pleased with her condition.

We reach the point of the paradox; here is watchfulness claimed by one who confessed to sleep. "My heart waketh," says the Bride. "I sleep, but my heart waketh." It may seem an odd thing to sleep and yet to be awake, but I commenced by saying that the Christian is a great puzzle. There is an inner life within every Christian which can never die, and there is about him an inward death which can never rise to life. Jesus said, "The water that I shall give him shall be in him a well of water springing up into everlasting life" (John 4:14). Hence this divine life, though it may grow weak and feeble and slumbering, yet never passes into the condition of absolute death, or even of complete insensibility. Somewhat of heaven is about the man of God when the earth encompasses him most. "Sin shall not have dominion over you" (Rom 6:14). God has the throne still, even when Satan rages most.

ILLUSTRATION

The Lion of Slumber

Preaching Themes: Good Works, Laziness and Apathy

"The slothful man saith, There is a lion in the way; a lion is in the streets" (Prov 26:13). This was his argument for keeping in the chimney corner. In truth, the lion is about as real as the monster which has been described of late as prowling over this county of Surrey and devouring women and children all the way from Banstead Downs to Clapham Common. Solomon seems to have been very familiar with this fable of the sluggard's lion, for in another proverb he makes the idler cry, "There is a lion without. I shall be slain in the streets" (Prov 22:13). These poor creatures are so dreamy in spirit that they see a lion everywhere, threatening them if they try to do good in any form; they must needs sit quiet and still, and try to enjoy themselves as best their sleep will allow them to do, for they cannot venture out to work because of the lion. They cannot teach a little Sunday school class, for there is a lion there! Nor go out to speak to a dozen people in a village: a furious lion is roaring there! In fact, they will be devoured if they leave their easy retirement and put their heads out of doors. God help us to escape this lazy condition.

It is the voice of my beloved that knocketh Even when half asleep she knew her Lord's voice. You may catch a true believer at his worst, but he still knows the gospel from anything else, and can detect another gospel in a moment. You shall come forth with all your eloquence, your poetry and sweet concocted phrases, with a something that is not the gospel of the blessed God, and you shall for a moment please the ear of the Christian because of the literary excellence of your address, but he soon detects you. It is true of all Christ's sheep, "A stranger will they not follow … for they know not the voice of strangers" (John 10:5). The awakening believer soon perceives that the most musical voice of a stranger has not the charm in it which is found in the voice of his Lord. He soon closes his ear to it in disgust and in holy trembling lest he should be deceived. His resolve is, "I will hear what God the Lord will speak." He determines to be deaf to other voices, but to his Redeemer he says, "Speak, Lord; for thy servant heareth" (1 Sam 3:9). Blessed is he who in his dullest state can still discern and discriminate and cry, "It is the voice of my beloved."

Open to me, my sister, my love, my dove, my undefiled Observe the appeals which the Beloved here makes. He says, "Open to me," and his plea is the love the spouse has to him, or professes to have, the love he has to her, and the relationship which exists between them.

"Open to me, my *sister*." Next akin to me, bone of my bone, flesh of my flesh, born of the same mother; for Jesus is "the seed of the woman," even as we are. One with us in our humanity, he takes each human heart that believes to be his mother, and sister, and brother.

"My dove," my gentle one, my favorite, my innocent. If you are indeed his dove, how can you rest away from the dovecote? How can you be satisfied without your mate? One turtle pines without the other; how is it you do not pine to have fellowship with the dear Husband of your soul?

"My love," Jesus calls us what we profess to be. We say we love him; yes, and unless we have been dreadfully deceived, we do love him. It brings the water into my eyes to think that I should so often be indifferent to him, and yet I can say it as before him, "Thou knowest all things; thou knowest that I love thee" (John 21:17).

The Bridegroom adds another title, *"my undefiled."* There is a spiritual chastity which every believer must maintain; our heart belongs to no one but to Christ. All other lovers must be gone; he fills the throne. He has bought us; no other paid a part of the price; he shall have us altogether. He has taken us into personal union with himself; of his mystical body we make up a part; we ought, therefore, to hold ourselves as chaste virgins unto Christ, undefiled with the pollutions of the flesh and the rivalries of earthly loves. To the undefiled Jesus says, "Open to me."

ILLUSTRATION

Pigeons Know Their Way Home

Preaching Themes: Devil, Spiritual Warfare

When we were ravens we could rest on our own wings, or on the carrion of this world, but now that we have been made doves we must seek our Noah and his ark. A friend at the back of this Tabernacle furnished me with some pigeons but a little while ago. They were taken home to Norwood, and shut up for a few days, and well-fed, in the hope that they would stay with us. But no sooner were they set at liberty than they soared aloft, made three circles in the sky, and then flew direct for this spot. How I wished on my sick bed that I had their wings and could hasten here too.

It is so with believers. The devil may put us in captivity and shut us up a while, but give us the opportunity and our heart knows the way back to Jesus. The spouse has dove's eyes, and she sees from afar. She makes short work of it and is back again with all the speed of the chariots of Ammi-nadib.

For my head is filled with dew, and my locks with the drops of the night She had no right to be asleep, for her Beloved knew no rest. He was standing outside in the cold street, with his head wet with dew, and his locks with the drops of the night, why should she be at ease? He was anxiously seeking her, how was it that she could be so cruel as to yield to slumber!

Those drops were not the ordinary dew that fall upon the houseless traveler's unprotected head. His head was wet with scarlet dew, and his locks with crimson drops of a tenfold night of God's desertion, when he "sweat as it were great drops of blood falling down to the ground" (Luke 22:44). My heart, how vile you are, for you shut out the Crucified. Behold the Man, thorn-crowned and scourged, with traces of the spittle of the soldiery. Can you close the door on him? Will you despise the "despised and rejected of men" (Isa 53:3)? Will you grieve the "Man of sorrows, and acquainted with grief" (Isa 53:3)? Do you forget that he suffered all this for you, for you, when you deserve nothing at his hands? After all this, will you give him no recompense, not even the poor return of admission to your loving communings?

3 **I have put off my coat; how shall I put it on? I have washed my feet; how shall I defile them?** After the knocking and the pleading, the spouse made a most ungenerous excuse. She sat

like a queen and knew no sorrow. She had put off her garments and washed her feet as travelers do in the East before they go to rest. She was taking her ease in full security, and therefore she said to her Beloved, "I have put off my tunic, I cannot robe myself again. As for my feet, I have washed them, and to tread the floor to open the door would defile them; therefore, I pray, have me excused."

A bad excuse was in this case far worse than none, because it was making one sin an apology for another. Why did she put off her coat? The bridegroom had not come; she should have stood with her loins girt about and her lamp trimmed. Why had she washed her feet? It was right to do so if the emblem had indicated purity, but it indicated carnal ease. She had left holy labor for carnal rest. Why did she do this? She thus makes her wicked slumber and inaction to be an excuse for barring out her Husband.

4 **My beloved put in his hand by the hole of the door, And my bowels were moved for him** In the Eastern door there is generally a place near the lock into which a man may put his hand, and there is a pin inside which, if removed, unfastens the door. Each one of these locks is different from another, so that no one usually understands how to open the door except the master. So, the Master in this case did not actually open the door—you notice the spouse did that, but he pulled out the pin so that she could see his hand. She could see that the door was not fast closed now he had removed the bar. "My Beloved put in his hand by the hole of the door."

Does not this picture the work of effectual grace, when the truth does not appeal to the ear alone, but comes to the heart, when it is no longer a thing thought on, and discussed and forgotten, but an arrow which has penetrated into the reins, and sticks fast in the loins to our wounding, and ultimately to our spiritual healing? No hand is like Christ's hand. When he puts his hand to the work, it is well-done. He "put *in* his hand," not his hand on me to smite me, but his hand in me to comfort me, to sanctify me. He put in his hand, and straightway his beloved began to pity him, and to lament her unkindness.

5 **I rose up to open to my beloved; and my hands dropped with myrrh, and my fingers with sweet smelling myrrh, upon the handles of the lock** As she arose, she first buckled on her garments, and then she searched for the alabaster box of precious ointment, that she might anoint his weary feet and dewy locks. No sooner did she reach the door than see the love of God to her! Her "hands dropped with myrrh, and her fingers with sweet smelling myrrh." Here is the Holy Spirit come to help our infirmities. She begins to pray, and the Holy Ghost helps her. She begins already to enjoy the sweetness, not of communion, but of the very desire after communion. For when our tears begin to flow because we are far from Christ, those holy drops have myrrh in them.

6 **I opened to my beloved; but my beloved had withdrawn himself, and was gone: my soul failed when he spake** She was not perfect even in the exhibition of her love to him who had chosen her, for she has to acknowledge, as upon the occasion before us, that she treated him in an unworthy manner. She kept him waiting at her door in the chilly night and grieved him so that he withdrew.

I sought him, but I could not find him; I called him, but he gave me no answer The newly awakened one went to the door, and opened it to her Beloved, for though he was gone, she did not doubt of her love, nor of his love to her. "I opened to my Beloved, but," says the Hebrew, "he had gone, he had gone." The voice of lamentation, the reduplicated cry of one that is in bitter distress. There must have been a sad relief about it to her sinful heart, for she must have felt afraid to look her dear one in the face after such heartless conduct. But sad as it would have been to face him, it was infinitely sadder to say, "He is gone, he is gone." Now she begins to use the means of grace in order to find him. "I sought him," said she, "and I found him not. I went up to the house of God. The sermon was sweet, but it was not sweet to me, for *he* was not there. I went to the communion table, and the ordinance was a feast of fat things to others, but not to me, for *he* was not there. I sought him, but I could not find him." Then she betook herself to prayer. She had neglected that before, but now she supplicated in real earnest, "I called him. I said to him, Come, my Beloved, my heart wakes for you. Jesus, reveal yourself to me as you do not to the world."

7 **The watchmen that went about the city found me, They smote me, they wounded me** He was gone, and all her calling could not bring him back. What did she do then? Why, she went to his ministers, she went to those who were the watchmen of the night, and what did they say to her? Did they cheer her? Perhaps they had never passed through her experience; perhaps they were mere hirelings. However it might be, they smote her. Sometimes the truthful preaching of the gospel will smite a child of God when he gets out of his walk with God, and it is right it should be so. But they did more than smite; they "wounded" her until she began to bleed from the wounds given by the very men whom she hoped would have comforted her. "Surely," she might have said, "you know where the city's king is, for you are the city's guards!" But she received no comfort.

The keepers of the walls took away my veil from me No woman went into the streets of Jerusalem without her veil, except she was of the baser sort, and the watchmen seemed to say to this woman, "You are of ill name, or you would not be here at this time of night crying out for one you have lost." Oh, cruel work to pull off her veil and expose her, when she was already wretched enough!

8 **I charge you, O daughters of Jerusalem** She knew that there were some who had daily fellowship with the King, daughters of Jerusalem who often saw him, and therefore she sent a message by them, "If ye see my Beloved, tell him that I am sick of love." Enlist your brother saints to pray for you. Go with them to their gatherings for prayer.

If ye find my beloved, that ye tell him, that I am sick of love To gather up the causes of this love-sickness in a few words, does not the whole matter spring from *relationship?* She is his spouse; can the spouse be happy without her beloved lord? It springs from union; she is part of himself. Can the hand be happy and healthy if the life-floods stream not from the heart and from the head. Fondly realizing her *dependence*, she feels that she owes all to him, and gets her all from him. If then the fountain be cut off, if the streams be dried, if the great source of all be taken from her, how can she but be sick? And there is besides this, *a life and a nature* in her which makes her sick. There is a life like the life of Christ, nay, her life is in Christ, it is hid with Christ in God; her nature is a part of the divine nature; she is a partaker of the divine nature. Moreover she is in *union* with Jesus, and this piece divided, as it were, from the body, wriggles, like a worm cut asunder, and pants to get back to where it came from. These are the causes of it. You will not understand my sermon this morning, but think me raving, unless you are spiritual men. "But the spiritual judgeth all things, yet he himself is judged of no man" (1 Cor 2:15).

ILLUSTRATION

Your Longings Will Be Satisfied

Preaching Themes: Faithfulness of God, Hope

It is impossible for Christ to set you longing after him without intending to give himself to you. It is as when a great man makes a feast. He first puts plates upon the table, and then afterward there comes the meat. Your longings and desirings are the empty plates to hold the meat. Is it likely that he means to mock you? Would he have put the dishes there if he did not intend to fill them with his oxen and with his fatlings? He makes you long; he will certainly satisfy your longings.

APPLICATION

Be Careful in Imitating the Saints

We must take care that we do not wrongly use the memoirs of saints as recorded in Scripture. They are not all for our imitation, but many of them for our warning. You may not do all that a good man has done. If you were to copy certain of the actions of the most gracious men you would soon find yourself more faulty than they. For you would be sure to throw the emphasis upon their errors, but their graces you would probably miss. You would copy their faults and aggravate them. Follow no man where he does not follow Christ.

Above all, the lives of the saints may never be used as an excuse for our faults. We shall not be justified in following afar off because Peter did so, nor in calling fire from heaven upon our enemies because James and John wished to do so, nor in quarreling because Paul and Barnabas fell into sore contention. We may wisely quote David as an encouragement to a penitent that God will forgive his sin, but not as an apology for ourselves should we be tempted to commit the sin. We must often use even the saints of God rather as beacons than as harbor lights, as lighthouses set upon rocky coasts to advise us of the dangers into which they fell.

Take care that Holy Scripture be used for holy ends, and that holy men are viewed as helps to holiness, and not as excuses for imperfection. Let us learn from their virtues imitation, from their faults warning, and from both instruction. Judgment is profitable to direct. Follow the Lamb wherever he goes, but there is not a sheep of his flock to whom you may do the same. Do whatever Jesus does. Copy the example of Christ in all its touches, so far as it is imitable, but do not the same even towards the beloved John, though his head be fresh from his Master's bosom. No, nor towards Paul, though he be not a whit behind the very chief of the apostles.

Nearness to Christ

"I charge you, O daughters of Jerusalem, if ye find my beloved, that ye tell him, that I am sick of love" (Song 5:8). Such is the language of the believer panting after present fellowship with Jesus: He is sick for his Lord. Gracious souls are never perfectly at ease except they are in a state of nearness to Christ. For when they are away from him, they lose their peace. The nearer to him, the nearer to the perfect calm of heaven. The nearer to him, the fuller the heart is, not only of peace, but of life, and vigor, and joy, for these all depend on constant intercourse with Jesus. What the sun is to the day, what the moon is to the night, what the dew is to the flower, such is Jesus Christ to us. What bread is to the hungry, clothing to the naked, the shadow of a great rock to the traveler in a weary land, such is Jesus Christ to us.

Therefore, if we are not consciously one with him, little marvel if our spirit cries in the words of the Song, "I charge you, O ye daughters of Jerusalem, if ye find my beloved, tell him that I am sick of love." This earnest longing after Jesus has a blessing attending it: "Blessed are they which do hunger and thirst after righteousness" (Matt 5:6); and therefore, supremely blessed are they who thirst after the Righteous One. Blessed is that hunger, since it comes from God. If I may not have the full-blown blessedness of being filled, I would seek the same blessedness in its sweet bud-pining in emptiness and eagerness till I am filled with Christ. If I may not feed on Jesus, it shall be next door to heaven to hunger and thirst after him. There is a hallowedness about that hunger, since it sparkles among the beatitudes of our Lord. But the blessing involves a promise. Such hungry ones "shall be filled" with what they are desiring. If Christ thus causes us to long after himself, he will certainly satisfy those longings; and when he does come to us, as come he will, oh, how sweet it will be!

Trust Jesus and Follow Him

Be very careful when you possess great joys, for in this instance the spouse had been with the Beloved in choice fellowship, and yet was soon drowsy. He had given her to drink abundantly, and he had feasted with her, but no sooner had the sun set than she said, "I sleep." We are singular creatures. Our very perfect brothers, although they do not see it, generally exhibit some glaring imperfection if you let them talk for five minutes. If you knock at the door to see if Mr. Pride is at home, you need not praise them long before he will show his full-length portrait. We are thankful for these brothers so far as they are saints, for good people are scarce. But I wish they would not tell us so much about their saintliness, for I have noticed that great cry often goes with little wool, and the noisiest thing that goes down the street is the dust-cart. He who makes most noise about his own perfection has the least of it. Let us be careful whenever we rise to the summit of the hill; careful to keep up, careful that we so act when we are up that we do not come down with a run. Whenever the Lord visits you entertain him right heartily. Be careful that nothing grieves him, lest he depart. High joys may produce slumber; the chosen three upon the mount Tabor were soon overcome with heaviness. At the too-transporting sight of the transfigured Savior, darkness covered them. Mind what you do when on the mount; be careful to carry a full cup with a steady hand.

Next, *when you are blaming yourselves for your own work, do not forget the work of the Spirit in you*. "I sleep": smite your heart for that, but do not forget to add if it be true, "My heart waketh." Bless God for any grace you have, even if it be but little. What if I am not sanctified as I wish to be and shall be, yet I am perfectly justified! What if I do not exhibit my Father's likeness so completely as I hope to do, yet I am his child! What if as yet I do not produce all the fruits of the Spirit, yet I have the germs of them, the buds and blossoms, and soon I shall have the ripe fruit. In Aaron's rod we see that the same power that could put the buds and blossoms on a dry stick could put the almonds there too.

Lastly, *make sure above all things that you have that true faith which knows the voice of Jesus*. The spouse had not awaked if it had not been for the charm of Jesus's voice which affected even her drowsy faculties. Some persons can be more easily awakened by the voices of those they love than by any other means. The charm of memory, the charm of intimate affection, the charm of delight, gives music to some tongues: let your ear find all its music in the voice of Jesus. Know his voice. He saith, "Incline your ear, and come unto me: hear, and your soul shall live" (Isa 55:3). "My sheep hear my voice, and I know them, and they follow me, and I give unto them eternal life" (John 10:27–28). God bless you, dear friends, with a faith that trusts Jesus, knows his voice, and follows him, and may we be aroused out of all our sleepiness, if we are at all drowsy, into a holy wakefulness, so as to serve the Lord our God with all our heart and soul and strength while we live. Come, Holy Spirit, and give us this privilege, for Jesus's sake. Amen.

Be Satisfied in Christ

Let me say to my brothers, and especially to my fellow workers in the kingdom of Christ, it is for us just now while our Lord is walking in his garden, while he is finding satisfaction in his work and in his people, to beware of taking any satisfaction in the work ourselves, and equally to beware that we do not neglect the appropriate duty of the occasion, namely, that of feasting our souls with our Lord's gracious provisions. You are caring for others, it is well; you are rejoicing over others, it is well; still watch well yourselves, and rejoice in the Lord in your own hearts. What did he say to the Twelve when they came back glorying that even the devils were subject unto them? Did he not reply, "Notwithstanding in this rejoice not … but rather rejoice, because your names are written in heaven" (Luke 10:20)? It is your personal interest in Christ, you being yourself saved, Christ being present with you, that is your main joy. Enjoy the feast for yourselves, or you will not be strong to hand out the living bread to others. See that you are first partakers of the fruit, or you will not labor aright as God's husbandmen. The more personal enjoyment you allow yourself in connection with your Lord, the more strong will you be for his service, and the more out of an experimental sense of his preciousness will you be able to say with true eloquence, "O taste and see that the Lord is good" (Ps 34:8). You will tell others what you have tasted and handled; you will say, "This poor man cried, and the Lord heard him, and delivered him from all his fears" (Ps 34:6). I put this before you with much earnestness, and I pray that none of you may think it safe so to work as to forget to commune, or wise to seek the good of others so as to miss personal fellowship with the Redeemer.

SONG OF SOLOMON 5:9–16

9 What *is* thy beloved more than *another* beloved, O thou fairest among women?
What *is* thy beloved more than *another* beloved, that thou dost so charge us?
10 My beloved *is* white and ruddy,
The chiefest among ten thousand.
11 His head *is as* the most fine gold,
His locks *are* bushy, *and* black as a raven.
12 His eyes *are* as *the eyes* of doves by the rivers of waters,
Washed with milk, *and* fitly set.
13 His cheeks *are* as a bed of spices, *as* sweet flowers:
His lips *like* lilies, dropping sweet smelling myrrh.
14 His hands *are as* gold rings set with the beryl:
His belly *is as* bright ivory overlaid *with* sapphires.
15 His legs *are as* pillars of marble, set upon sockets of fine gold:
His countenance *is* as Lebanon, excellent as the cedars.
16 His mouth *is* most sweet: yea, he *is* altogether lovely.
This *is* my beloved, and this *is* my friend, O daughters of Jerusalem.

EXPOSITION

9 **What is thy beloved more than another beloved, O thou fairest among women? What is thy beloved more than another beloved, that thou dost so charge us?** The daughters of Jerusalem recognized in the spouse an exceeding beauty, which dazzled and charmed them, so that they could not help calling her the "fairest among women." This was not her estimate of herself; for she had said, "I am black, but comely." Nor was it the estimate of her enemies; for they had

smitten her and wounded her. But it was the estimate of fair, candid, and impartial onlookers.

You will observe that it was in consequence of thinking her the "fairest among women" that they asked the spouse, "What is thy beloved more than another beloved?" They thought that one so fair might well have her choice of a Bridegroom, that one so lovely herself would be likely to have an eye to loveliness in her Husband, and consequently they considered her judgment to be worth some attention, and they put to her the question why her Beloved was more than another beloved. Take it for granted, dear friends, as a truth which your own observation and experience will make every day more and more clear, that your power to spread religion in the world must mainly depend upon your own personal character, of course, in absolute reliance upon the Holy Spirit.

ILLUSTRATION

Seeing the Effects of Medicine

Preaching Themes: Conversion, Gospel, Evangelism

A person talks to me about a certain medicine, how it is compounded, what it looks like, how many drops must be taken at a dose, and so on. Well, I do not care to hear all that, and I soon forget it. But he tells me that for many months he was bedridden, he was in sore distress and in great pain, and like to die; and, looking at him as he stands before me in perfect health, I am delighted with the change, and he says that it was that medicine which restored him. If I am a sick man in the same state as he was, I say to him, "Give me the name and address, for I must try that medicine for myself."

I believe that the simple witness of converted boys and girls, converted lads and lasses, especially the witness of converted fathers and mothers and friends beloved, the witness that comes of the gray head that is backed up by years of godly living, has a wonderful power for the spread of the gospel, and we cannot expect that God will give us any very large blessing until the whole of us shall be at work for our Lord.

---

10 **My beloved is white and ruddy** The spouse intends by these words to call attention to two chief characteristics of her Lord's most blessed person. Had not Solomon often seen the snow-white lambs—the emblems of purity—brought up to the temple to be offered in sacrifice? "So," said he, "my Beloved is white." Had he not also seen the uplifted knife in the priest's hand, and then seen the ruby stream as it flowed down at the foot of the altar till the white lamb was stained crimson in its own blood? So he puts the two together, the white, the immaculate purity, the red, the sacrificial blood-shedding; and these two things, whether they are meant in the text or not, are certainly the two essentials of the Christian faith concerning the person of Christ; and he is no Christian, and, indeed, cannot be a Christian, who hath not well-learned and joyously received the two truths which the white and the red here set forth.

The chiefest among ten thousand Is it not incorrect to say "the chiefest"? I do not care if it is, and I would not like to see the word altered into "chief." Human words at best are such poor things that they stagger under the mighty burden of the perfections of Christ. We seem to need some of those huge pillars and pedestals that we sometimes see outside massive piles of architecture that we may bear up the ponderous truth of our text; we must have such words as "chiefest," for common language does not suffice in such a case as this.

If there are ten thousand bishops, he is *the* Bishop of souls. If there are ten thousand fathers, he is "the Everlasting Father." If there are ten thousand teachers, yet they shall not be called Rabbis, for One is our Teacher and Rabbi, even Christ, and at his feet the reverent church adoringly bows, hailing him, and him alone, as Head and Master, "the chiefest among ten thousand."

According to the Septuagint, the text has another meaning. Our Lord in Scripture is called the chosen One, the elect of God. As the psalmist puts it, speaking by prophecy, "I have exalted one chosen out of the people" (Ps 89:19). Christ is chosen out of ten thousand, as the Mediator to stand between God and men. Whoever else might have been employed by God for this service—and we are not able to think of any other—yet first of all was Christ chosen of God; and today we may call him the chosen One because he is the chosen of his church.

11 **His head is as the most fine gold, his locks *are* bushy, *and* black as a raven** By *the head* of Jesus we may understand his deity, "for the head of Christ is God" and then the ingot of purest gold is the best conceivable metaphor, but all too poor to describe one so precious, so pure, so dear, so glorious. Jesus is not a grain of gold, but a vast globe of it, a priceless mass of treasure such as earth and heaven cannot excel. *The bushy locks* depict his manly vigor. There is nothing effeminate in our Beloved. He is the manliest of men. Bold as a lion, laborious as an ox, swift as an eagle. Every conceivable and inconceivable beauty is to be found in him, though once he was despised and rejected of men. The glory of his head is not shorn away, he is eternally crowned with peerless majesty. *The black hair* indicates youthful freshness, for Jesus has the dew of his youth upon him. Others grow languid with age, but he is forever a priest as was Melchizedek; others come and go, but he abides as God upon his throne, world without end.

12 **His eyes are as the eyes of doves by the rivers of waters, washed with milk, and fitly set** That is, eyes of purity, bright sparkling eyes that care not to look upon that which is unclean. The dove is no carrion-loving bird, and you will recollect that it was the only bird that was offered to God in sacrifice under the old dispensation.

13 **His cheeks are as a bed of spices, *as* sweet flowers** The spouse had already spoken upon her Beloved's head, and locks, and eyes, and now she mentions his cheeks. Any sight of

Christ is delightful; a single passing glimpse of him is a foretaste of heaven, the beginning of paradise. The cheek is the place of fellowship where we exchange tokens of love. What a blessing it is that Christ should have had a cheek for the lips of love to approach, and to kiss. Notice, in the metaphors used by the spouse, that there is *a blending of sweetness and beauty:* "as a bed of spices"—there is sweetness, and then, "as sweet flowers"—there is beauty. There is sweetness to the nostrils and beauty to the eye, spice for its fragrance and flowers for their loveliness. In Christ, there is something for every spiritual sense, and for every spiritual sense there is a complete satisfaction and delight in him.

His lips like lilies, dropping sweet smelling myrrh Notice the comparison in the text—lilies; not white lilies, of course, but red lilies, crimson lilies, lilies of such a color as are frequently to be seen, which would be a suitable emblem of the Beloved's lips. Christ's lips are peculiarly delightful to us, for *it is with them that he speaks to us and intercedes with the Father for us*. When he pleads as the Intercessor on behalf of a poor soul like me, his lips are indeed in God's sight like lovely lilies.

But the spouse's comparison fails, for she said, "His lips like lilies, dropping sweet smelling myrrh." This lilies do not do, but Christ does. He is more than a lily, or he is a lily of such a sort as never bloomed on earth except once. He was the only lily that ever dropped sweet smelling myrrh. The spouse says that his lips do that; what does this mean? Does it not mean that his Word is often full of a very sweet, mysterious, blessed influence? For we need this myrrh for the healing of the wounds that sin has made; we need this myrrh in our spiritual worship that we may offer it up unto God; we need this myrrh to perfume us, and make our lives fragrant in the midst of our daily cares; we need this myrrh to kill the contagion that abounds in this wicked world, and we shall get it through the Word, when it comes fresh from the lips of Christ.

14–15 His hands are as gold rings set with the beryl: his belly is as bright ivory overlaid with sapphires His legs are as pillars of marble, set upon sockets of fine gold: his countenance is as Lebanon, excellent as the cedars Surely we can even now conclude the description from our own experience of him; and while we endorse every word which went before, we can end the description by saying, "His mouth is most sweet, yea he is altogether lovely. His matchless beauty is unimpaired; he is still 'the chief among ten thousand,' 'fairest of the sons of men.' " Did the divine John talk of him when he said, "His head and his hairs were white like wool, as white as snow; and his eyes were as a flame of fire; and his feet like unto fine brass, as if they burned in a furnace; and his voice as the sound of many waters. And he had in his right hand seven stars; and out of his mouth went a sharp twoedged sword; and his countenance was as the sun shineth in his strength" (Rev 1:14–16). He is the same; upon his brow there is never a furrow; his locks are gray with reverence, but not with age; his feet stand as firm as when they trod the everlasting mountains in the years before the world was made—his eyes as piercing as when, for the first time, he looked upon a new-born world. Christ's person never changes.

ILLUSTRATION

William Huntington's Farmer

Preaching Themes: Grace, Love

Some of you may remember William Huntington's story that I have sometimes quoted to you about an old farmer, who, when one of his daughters was married, gave her a thousand pounds as a wedding present.[1] There was another daughter, and her father did not give her a thousand pounds when she was married. But he gave her something as a wedding present, and then he kept on pretty nearly every day in the week sending her what he

1. An English preacher and self-described "coalheaver" (1745–1813). —ed.

called "the hand-basket portion, with father's love," and so in the long run she received a great deal more than her sister did. It was not given all of a lump, and then done with. It kept on coming, now a sack of flour, and then this, and that, and the other, always "with father's love," so she had far more than the thousand pounds, and she also had far more of his love.

I do like, when I get a mercy, to have it come to me with my Heavenly Father's love, just my daily portion as I need it; not given all in a lump, so that I might go away with it into a far country, as we are sure to do if we have all our mercy at once. But given day by day, as the manna fell, with our Heavenly Father's love every time, a fresh token of infinite grace and infinite love.

---

16 **His mouth is most sweet: yea, he is altogether lovely This is my beloved, and this is my friend, O daughters of Jerusalem** Of no other being could it be said, "He is altogether lovely." It means, first, that *all that is in him is lovely, perfectly lovely*. There is no point in our Lord Jesus that you could improve. To paint the rose were to spoil its ruddy hue. To tint the lily, for he is lily as well as rose, were to mar its whiteness. Each virtue in our Lord is there in a state of absolute perfection: it could not be more fully developed. If you were able to conceive of each virtue at its ripest stage it would be found in him.

And he is all that is lovely. In each one of his people you will find something that is lovely—in one there is faith, in another abounding love; in one tenderness, in another courage, but you do not find all good things in any one saint—at least not all of them in full perfection; but you find all virtues in Jesus, and each one of them at its best.

APPLICATION

The Need for Consistency in Evangelism

I suppose it is the earnest wish of every Christian to win for Christ some new converts, to bring some fresh province under the dominion of the King of kings. I will tell you how this may be accomplished.

Your power to achieve this noble purpose must largely depend upon your own personal *consistency*. It little avails what I say if I do the reverse. The world will not care about my testimony with the lip, unless there be also a testimony in my daily life for God, for truth, for holiness, for everything that is honest, lovely, pure, and of good report. There is that in a Christian's character which the world, though it may persecute the man himself, learns to value. It is called consistency—that is, the making of the life stand together, not being one thing in one place and another thing in another, or one thing at one time and quite different on another occasion. It is not consistency to be devout on Sunday and to be dishonest on Monday. It is not consistency to sing the songs of Zion today and to shout the songs of lustful mirth tomorrow. It is not consistency occasionally to wear the yoke of Christ and yet frequently to make yourself the serf of Satan. But to make your life all of one piece is to make it powerful, and when God the Holy Ghost enables you to do this, then your testimony will tell upon those amongst whom you live. It would be ludicrous, if it were not so sorrowful a thing, to be spoken of even with weeping, that there should be professed Christians who are through inconsistency among the worst enemies of the cross of Christ.

I heard the other day a story which made me laugh. A poor creature, in a lunatic asylum, had got it into his head that he was some great one, and he addressed a person who was visiting the asylum in the following words: "I am Sir William Wallace.[2] Give me some tobacco!" What a ridiculous contrast between his proud assertion and his poor request! Who but a lunatic would have said such a thing? Yet, alas, we know people who say, by their actions, if not in words, "I am a Christian, but I will take advantage of you when I can. I am one of the blood-royal of heaven, my life is hid with Christ in God, and my conversation is in heaven, but—but—I like worldliness, and sensual

2. A Scottish knight (c. 1270–1305). —ed.

pleasure, and carnal mirth quite as well as other men!" I say again that this kind of thing would be superlatively ludicrous if it were not ineffably sorrowful, and it is, anyhow, utterly contemptible.

If your life is not all of one piece, the world will soon learn how to estimate your testimony and will count you to be either a fool or a knave, and perhaps both.

Sounding the Gun of Revival

Oh, that the Lord would send us times of true revival once again! Run your finger down the page of history till you come to the Reformation; what was there in Luther, in Calvin, in Zwingli, that they should have been able to shake the world any more than there is in men who are living nowadays? Nothing but this, that they believed what they did believe, and they spoke with an awful earnestness, like men who meant what they said, and straightway there arose a noble race of men, men who felt the power of faith, and lived it out, and the world was made to feel that "there were giants in those days." Then, again, in later times, when the church had fallen into a fatal slumber, there came the age of Whitefield and Wesley. What was the power of the early Methodists? Why, simply the power of true sincerity combined with holiness! What if I say that it was the power of intruding religion upon men, of forcing men to hear God's voice, of compelling a sleeping world to wake out of its slumbers?

As I sat, last week, in the hall of the Free Church Assembly in Edinburgh, just beneath the Castle, I started in my seat, I thought the whole hall was going to fall, for at one o'clock the gun on the Castle was fired from Greenwich by electricity. It startled every one of us, and I noticed that nearly everybody took out his watch to see whether it was right by the gun. I thought to myself, "That is just what the Christian church ought to do. It ought, at the proper time, to give a loud, clear, thundering testimony for God and for truth, so that every man might examine his own conscience, and get himself put right where he is wrong." Our testimony for Christ ought not to be like the ticking of an ordinary clock, or as sounding brass, or a tinkling cymbal, but a mighty booming noise that commands and that demands a hearing. Let our soul be but linked with heaven, let the Spirit of the

Lord flash the message along the wires, and our life may be just as accurate and just as startling as that time-gun at Edinburgh.

So, when men ask us, "What is thy Beloved more than another beloved, that thou dost so charge us?" we shall have an answer ready for them, which may God bless to them, for Christ's sake!

Weary of God's People

Oh, that we did but think more highly of Christ! Perhaps it may help us to do so if we consider how worthy he is of that love, and how wondrously his thoughts of us exceed our thoughts of him. I sometimes feel very sad when I think about some who profess to be the Lord's people. There are many who, I hope, may prove to be his people, but they do not reflect much credit on him. Some of God's children are a very queer lot; if we had such sons and daughters as God has, some of us would never be able to bear with them at all. We would be impatient with them, and turn them out of doors, to get on as best they could by themselves.

When you get sick, and sad, and weary of God's people, turn your thoughts to God himself; and if ever you see any spots in the church, Christ's bride, look at her glorious Husband, and you will only love him more as you think of his wondrous condescension in having loved such a poor thing as his church is even at her best. Think how bright he is, how glorious, how surpassing are his charms that they can be seen even through the defects and imperfections of his redeemed ones. We may well marvel that ever such love as his could have been lavished upon such unworthy beings as his people are. Do not get depressed and distressed, dear friends, because of your own imperfections, or the imperfections of others; or if you do, quickly rise again to fight against sin under the blessed conviction that there are no imperfections in him, that he is altogether lovely, altogether sweet, and that the day must come when we, who are one with him even now, shall be like him, for we shall see him as he is. Complete sanctification will be the lot of every redeemed soul. If we have known the Lord, and have already had something of his likeness, we shall go on to know him till we are perfect in that likeness. Let that blessed consummation be the subject of our constant prayer and our confident expectation.

SONG OF SOLOMON 6

SONG OF SOLOMON 6:1–13

1 Whither is thy beloved gone, O thou fairest among women?
Whither is thy beloved turned aside? that we may seek him with thee.
2 My beloved is gone down into his garden, to the beds of spices,
To feed in the gardens, and to gather lilies.
3 I *am* my beloved's, and my beloved *is* mine:
He feedeth among the lilies.
4 Thou *art* beautiful, O my love, as Tirzah,
Comely as Jerusalem,
Terrible as *an army* with banners.
5 Turn away thine eyes from me, for they have overcome me:
Thy hair *is* as a flock of goats that appear from Gilead.
6 Thy teeth *are* as a flock of sheep which go up from the washing,
Whereof every one beareth twins, and *there is* not one barren among them.
7 As a piece of a pomegranate *are* thy temples within thy locks.
8 There are threescore queens, and fourscore concubines,
And virgins without number.
9 My dove, my undefiled is *but* one;
She *is* the *only* one of her mother,
She *is* the choice *one* of her that bare her.
The daughters saw her, and blessed her;
Yea, the queens and the concubines, and they praised her.
10 Who *is* she *that* looketh forth as the morning,
Fair as the moon, clear as the sun,
And terrible as *an army* with banners?
11 I went down into the garden of nuts to see the fruits of the valley,
And to see whether the vine flourished, *and* the pomegranates budded.

12 Or ever I was aware,
My soul made me *like* the chariots of Ammi-nadib.
13 Return, return, O Shulamite;
Return, return, that we may look upon thee.
What will ye see in the Shulamite?
As it were the company of two armies.

EXPOSITION

1 **Whither is thy beloved gone, O thou fairest among women? Whither is thy beloved turned aside? that we may seek him with thee** Be satisfied to go to Christ yourself. If your brothers will go, well and good, but I think their proper answer to your question would be in the language of the women: "Whither is thy beloved gone, O thou fairest among women? Whither is thy beloved turned aside? that we may seek him with thee." They will not seek him *for* us they say, but they can seek him *with* us. Sometimes when there are six pairs of eyes, they will see better than one; and so, if five or six Christians seek the Lord in company, in the prayer meeting, or at his table, they are more likely to find him. "We will seek him with thee."

2 **My beloved is gone down into his garden, to the beds of spices, to feed in the gardens, and to gather lilies** You know the story well. After Jesus had come over the mountains of our sins, after he had killed the lions and the leopards that stood in our way, he gave up his soul into his Father's hands, and loving friends took his body, and wrapped it in white linen, and Joseph of Arimathea and Nicodemus brought myrrh and aloes to preserve his blessed body, that matchless casket of a perfect soul; and, having wrapped him up, they laid him in a new tomb, which thus became the garden or mountain of myrrh.

3 **I am my beloved's, and my beloved is mine: he feedeth among the lilies** The spouse says, "My beloved is mine, and I am his" (Song 2:16). She weaves the two into one. The cause of the church is the cause of Christ; the work of God will never

be accomplished by the church apart from Christ, her power lies in his being in her midst. He "feedeth among the lilies," and therefore those lilies shall never be destroyed, but their sweetness shall make fragrant all the earth. The church of Christ, working with her Lord, must conquer, but never if she tries to stand alone or to compass any end apart from him.

4 **Thou art beautiful, O my love, as Tirzah, Comely as Jerusalem** What is usually the most correct character which is obtainable of a woman? Shall we be guided by the praises of those neighbors who are on good terms with her, or by the scandal of those who make her the subject of ill-natured gossip? No; the most accurate judgment we are likely to get is that of her husband. Solomon says in the Proverbs concerning the virtuous woman, "Her husband also [riseth up], and he praiseth her" (Prov 31:28). Of that fairest among women, the church of Christ, the same observation may be made. It is to her of small consequence to be judged by man's judgment, but it is her honor and joy to stand well in the love and esteem of her royal spouse, the Prince Emmanuel.

Though the words before us are allegorical, and the whole song is crowded with metaphor and parable, yet the teaching is plain enough in this instance. It is evident that the Divine Bridegroom gives his bride a high place in his heart, and to him, whatever she may be to others, she is fair, lovely, comely, beautiful, and in the eyes of his love without a spot. Moreover, even to him there is not only a beauty of a soft and gentle kind in her, but a majesty, a dignity in her holiness, in her earnestness, in her consecration, which makes even him say of her that she is "terrible as an army with banners," "awful as a bannered army." She is every inch a queen. Her aspect in the sight of her beloved is majestic. Take, then, the words of our text as an encomium upon Christ's church, pronounced by him who knows her best, and is best able to judge concerning her, and you learn that to his discerning eye she is not weak, dishonorable, and despicable, but bears herself as one of highest rank, consciously, joyously strong in her Lord's strength.

Terrible as an army with banners Let us note, first of all, why it is that the church of God is said to be an army with banners. That she is *an army* is true enough, for the church is one, but many; and consists of men who march in order under a common leader, with one design in view, and that design a conflict and a victory. She is the church militant here below, and both in suffering and in service she is made to prove that she is in an enemy's country. She is contending for the truth against error, for the light against darkness: till the day break and the shadows flee away, she must maintain her sentinels and kindle her watch flies; for all around her there is cause to guard against the enemy, and to defend the royal treasure of gospel truth against its deadly foes. But why an army *with banners?* Is not this, first of all, for *distinction?* How shall we know to which king an army belongs unless we can see the royal standard?

ILLUSTRATION

You Know an Army by Its Banners

Preaching Themes: Nature of the Church, Spiritual Warfare, War

In times of war the nationality of troops is often declared by their distinguishing regimentals. The gray coats of the Russians were well-known in the Crimea; the white livery of the Austrians was a constant eyesore in bygone days to the natives of Lombardy. No one mistook the Black Brunswickers [Germans] for French Guards, or our own Hussars for Garibaldians [Italians]. Quite as effectively armies have been distinguished by the banners which they carried. As the old knights of old were recognized by their plume and helmet, and escutcheon [shield or emblem with the coat of arms], so an army is known by its standard and the national colors. The tricolor of the French readily marked their troops as they fled before the terrible black and white of the German army.

The church of Christ displays its banners for distinction's sake. It desires not to be associated with other armies, or to be mistaken for them, for it is not of this world, and its weapons and its warfare are far other than those of the nations.

Banners were carried, not merely for distinctiveness, but also to serve the purposes of *discipline*. Hence an army with banners had one banner as a central standard, and then each regiment or battalion displayed its own particular flag. The hosts of God, which so gloriously marched through the wilderness, had their central standard. I suppose it was the very pole upon which Moses lifted up the brazen serpent (at any rate, our brazen serpent is the central ensign of the church); and then, besides that, each tribe of the twelve had its own particular banneret, and with these uplifted in the front, the tribes marched in order, so that there was no confusion on the march, and in time of battle there was no difficulty in marshaling the armed men. It was believed by the later Jews that "the standard of the camp of Judah represented a lion; that of Reuben, a man; that of Joseph, an ox; and that of Dan, an eagle. The Targumists, however, believe that the banners were distinguished by their colors, the color for each tribe being analogous to that of the precious stone for that tribe, in the breastplate of the high priest; and that the great standard of each of the four camps combined the three colors of the tribes which composed it." So, brethren, in the church of God there must be discipline—the discipline not only of admission and of dismission in receiving the converts and rejecting the hypocrites, but the discipline of marshaling the troops to the service of Christ in the holy war in which we are engaged.

An army with banners may be also taken to represent *activity*. When an army folds up its colors the fight is over. Little is being done in military circles when the banners are put away; the troops are on furlough, or are resting in barracks. An army with banners is exercising, or marching, or fighting; probably it is in the middle of a campaign, it is marshaled for offense and defense, and there will be rough work before long. It is to be feared that some churches have hung up their flags to rot in state, or have encased them in dull propriety. They do not look to do great things, or to see great things. They do not expect many conversions; if many did happen, they would be alarmed and suspicious. They do not expect their pastor's ministry to be with power: and if it were attended with manifest effect they would be greatly disturbed, and perhaps would complain that he created too much excitement.

5 **Turn away thine eyes from me, for they have overcome me** Looking on his church has already overcome the heart of our Heavenly Bridegroom. It was so *in the far-distant past,* not when she looked at him, but when he looked at her, that she overcame him. Ages upon ages ago, or ever the earth was, Christ had conceived in his heart the purpose to redeem from among men a people that should be precious in his sight forever and ever. Through the glass of divine foreknowledge, he looked at his people, he recognized the person of every one of them, he saw them all ruined in the Fall, all stained with sin, all contaminated in nature by our first parents' disobedience and rebellion. As he looked at them, with a steady resolve that he would rescue them, and perfect them, and lift them up to a level with himself, and make them into a race that should praise God forever in heaven with hallelujahs and hosannas beyond all the harmonies of angels, his heart so moved towards them that he longed for the time when he should enter upon the great work of their redemption.

You know, too, *when he lived down here among men,* how often his inmost heart was stirred as he looked upon the people whom he loved. And especially do you recollect the scene on that last night when their redemption-price was about to be paid. He took the cup that he was to drink, and sipped at it; but his holy soul revolted from it, and with the bloody sweat upon his face he cried, "O my Father, if it be possible, let this cup pass from me" (Matt 26:39). Then he went back, and looked upon his people. Truly, there was not much to see in them; he had taken three especially privileged apostles to be the representatives of all his chosen, and those three were asleep when he was in his terrible agony; yet, somehow, the sight of them seemed to strengthen him for the awful ordeal that he was enduring. Backward and forward thrice he ran to gaze upon them, and they so overcame him that he turned back, and said to his Father, "Nevertheless not as I will, but as thou wilt" (Matt 26:39); and he went through with that tremendous work of laying down his life for his people, and drinking the cup of wrath that was their due. They had overcome him as he had looked at them.

And, beloved, now that *our Lord is risen from the dead*, he still feels the power of the sight of his redeemed. The great joy of Christ at this moment is found in gazing at his redeemed ones. Look at him as man, if you will; and what a wondrous Man he is! But remember also that God hath highly exalted him, and given him a name which is above every name; and what does the glorified and exalted Christ think as he looks on the myriads in heaven, all of whom would have been in hell but for him? Then he looks down to the saints on earth, and sees the myriads who are all trusting in him, all conquering sin by his might, and all spared from going down to the pit by the merit of his precious blood; and he seems again to say, "Turn away thine eyes from me, for they have overcome me"; as if Christ felt that a glance at his people brought almost too much joy for him.

ILLUSTRATION

Stories of Experiencing the Love of Christ

Preaching Themes: Assurance, Love of God

You may perhaps have read, in the life of holy Mr. Flavell, the extraordinary instance he records of the love of Christ being poured into his soul. He says that he was riding on a horse, going to some engagement, and he had such a sense of the love of Christ that he completely lost himself for several hours; and when he came to himself again, he found his horse standing quite still, and discovered that he had been sitting on horseback all those hours, utterly lost to everything but a special revelation of the wonderful love of Jesus.

You may also have heard of Mr. Tennant, the mighty American preacher and friend of George Whitefield, who was found, lost and absorbed, in a wood, to which he had retired, and his friends had to call him back, as it were, from the sweet fellowship he had been enjoying with Christ.

You may remember, too, John Welsh, the famous Scotch preacher, who had to cry out, "Hold, Lord, hold! I am but an earthen vessel, and if I feel more of thy glorious love, I must e'en die; so stay thy hand a while."

There are such experiences as these; I will not inquire whether you have ever known them. But if you have, I will tell you one thing. All the infidels in the world, and all the devils in hell, will never make you doubt the truth of the Scriptures if you have once been face to face with Christ, and have spoken with your Master as a man speaks with his friend.

6–7 **Thy teeth are as a flock of sheep which go up from the washing, whereof every one beareth twins, and there is not one barren among them As a piece of a pomegranate are thy temples within thy locks** After having surveyed her whole person with rapturous delight, he cannot be satisfied until he takes a second gaze and afresh recounts her beauties. Making but little difference between his first description and the last, he adds extraordinary expressions of love to manifest his increased delight.

The beauty which he admires is universal, he is as much enchanted with her temples as with her breasts. All her offices, all her pure devotions, all her earnest labors, all her constant sufferings are precious to his heart. She is "all fair."

8–10 **There are threescore queens, and fourscore concubines, and virgins without number My dove, my undefiled is but one;**

she is the only one of her mother, she is the choice one of her that bare her The daughters saw her, and blessed her; yea, the queens and the concubines, and they praised her Who is she that looketh forth as the morning, fair as the moon, clear as the sun When God is our health, our whole countenance becomes bright, according to the words of the Song, "Who is she that looketh forth as the morning, fair as the moon, clear as the sun, and terrible as an army with banners." The believer's countenance becomes bright with clearness, as far as he himself is concerned, he is saved and he knows it. It becomes fair as far as others are concerned, for they see the excellence of his character and wonder at it. Then it becomes dazzling to his adversaries, as the sun vanquishes rash gazers by its effulgence. Holiness is to opposers "terrible as an army with banners."

and terrible as an army with banners? Why is the church of Christ terrible as an army with banners? Why is it terrible because of its banners? The whole passage seems to say that the church is terrible as an army, but that to the fullest degree she owes her terribleness to her banners. "Terrible as an army with banners." I believe the great banner of the Christian church to be the uplifted Savior. "I, if I be lifted up from the earth, will draw all men unto me" (John 12:32). Around him then we gather. "Unto him shall the gathering of the people be" (Gen 49:10). As the brazen serpent in the midst of the camp in the wilderness, so is the Savior lifted high, our banner. The atoning sacrifice of Christ is the great central standard of all really regenerate men, and this is the main source of dismay to Israel's foes.

But we shall take the thoughts in order. The church herself is terrible, and then terrible because of her banners. The army itself is terrible. Why? First, because it consists of elect people. Remember how Haman's wife inquired concerning Mordecai whether he belonged to the seed of the Jews; for if he did, then she foretold that her husband's scheme would prove a failure. "If Mordecai be of the seed of the Jews, before whom thou hast begun to fall, thou shalt not prevail against him, but shalt surely fall before him" (Esth 6:13). Now, the church of God as made up of men and women is nothing more than any other organization. Look at its exterior, and you see in it few persons of great education and a great many of no education; here and there a wealthy and powerful person, but hundreds who are poor and despised. It does not possess in itself, naturally, the elements of strength, according to ordinary reckoning. Indeed, its own confession is that in itself it is perfect weakness, a flock of sheep among wolves; but here lies its strength, that each of the true members of the church are of the seed royal; they are God's chosen ones, the seed of the woman ordained of old to break the head of Satan and all his serpent seed. They are the weakness of God, but they are stronger than men; he has determined with the things that are not to bring to naught the things that are.

The church, again, consists of *a praying people*. Now prayer is that which links weakness with infinite strength. A people who can pray can never be overcome, because their reserve forces can never be exhausted. If ten thousand saints were burned tomorrow, their dying prayers would make the church rise like a phoenix from her ashes. Who, therefore, can stand against a people whose prayers enlist God in their quarrel? "The Lord of hosts is with us; the God of Jacob is our refuge" (Ps 46:7).

ILLUSTRATION

A Sword in the Way

Preaching Themes: Mission, War

There is a story of an officer who was rather awkward in his manners, and, upon some great occasion, almost fell over his sword in his haste. His majesty remarked, "Your sword seems to be very much in the way." "So your majesty's enemies have very often felt," was the reply.

So, when the enemies of the truth are finding fault with our procedure, we accept their verdict when we have turned it the other way upwards. If they do not admire our mode of warfare, we think it is in all probability about the best method we could adopt. We would still, God granting us help, continue preaching the "foolishness" of the gospel, and deliver again and again the old truth, that God was in Christ reconciling the world unto himself, not imputing their trespasses unto them.

We are now to observe that the chief glory and majesty of the church lies mainly in the banner which she carries. What cause for terror is there in the banner? We reply, the enemies of Christ dread the cross, because they know what the cross has done. Wherever the crucified Jesus has been preached, false systems have tottered to their fall. Dagon has always fallen before the ark of the Lord. Rage the most violent is excited by the doctrine of the atonement, a rage in which the first cause for wrath is fear.

The terribleness of the church lies in her banners, because those banners put strength into her. Drawing near to the standard of the cross the weakest soldier becomes strong: he who might have played the coward becomes a hero when the precious blood of Jesus is felt with power in his soul. Martyrs are born and nurtured at the cross. It is the blood of Jesus which is the life-blood of self-denial; we can die because our Savior died. The presence of Alexander made the Greeks more than giants: the presence of our Redeemer makes believers swifter than eagles, and stronger than lions.

Moreover, the powers of evil tremble at the old standard, because they have a presentiment of its future complete triumph. It is decreed of God, and fixed by his predestinating purpose, that all flesh shall see the salvation of God. Jesus must reign; the crucified One must conquer.

11 **I went down into the garden of nuts to see the fruits of the valley, and to see whether the vine flourished, and the pomegranates budded** It appears to me that without in the slightest degree wresting the passage, or deviating from an honest interpretation, we may understand that this is the

language of the church concerning Christ. If so, Christ's words conclude at the end of the tenth verse, and it is the church that speaks at the eleventh. There is not an instance in the whole Song, so far as I can remember, of the Prince himself speaking in the first-person singular; either, therefore, this would be a solitary exception, or else, following the current plan, where the same pronoun is used, the church is speaking to Christ, and telling him of herself.

12 **Or ever I was aware, My soul made me** What is most wanted in all religious exercises is the motion, the exercise of the soul. "Or ever I was aware, *my soul* made me"—or *my soul* became—"like the chariots of Ammi-nadib." Soul-worship is the soul of worship, and if you take away the soul from the worship, you have killed the worship; it becomes dead and barren henceforth.

like the chariots of Ammi-nadib We cannot be quite sure at this date what these chariots of Ammi-nadib were to which the inspired poet here refers. Some suppose that he may have alluded to a person of that name, who was renowned, like Jehu of old, for his furious driving. Hence it might have been familiar at the time, and afterward have become proverbial to speak in metaphor of the chariots of Ammi-nadib. The conjecture seems harmless; still, it is only a conjecture and cannot be verified.

It is quite possible, however, that our translators may have retained as a proper name a conjunction of two words, which, taken separately, are capable of being interpreted. You remember the word "Ammi" as it occurs in the prophet Hosea. "Say ye unto your brethren, *Ammi*" (Hos 2:1), which signifies "you are my people," even as before he had said, "Call his name *lo-Ammi*: for ye are not my people" (Hos 1:9). The one word, "Ammi," thus stands for "people," and the other word, "Nadib," means "willing," so that the two united may be rendered "willing people"—"like the chariots of a willing people." Or the words may be read, I think, more correctly, "The chariots of the princely people"—the princely chariots, the chariots of the prince. Some have understood them to mean the chariots of God, of the people that surround the Great Prince himself; that is to say, the chariots of the angels, according as we read, "The chariots of God are twenty thousand, even thousands of angels" (Ps 68:17). In this case, the figure would be a very striking one—"Or ever I was aware, my soul made me like the chariots of the attendants upon the Great King. I was like the cherubim themselves, all aglow with consecrated fire."

In whatever way the critical point is deciphered, the practical solution appears to be this. The writer's soul was quickened, because full of life, full of energy, full of might, full of spirit, and full of princely dignity too, and not only stimulated to a high degree, but also elevated, lifted up from dullness, indifference, and apathy.

ILLUSTRATION

Painting and Prayer

Preaching Themes: Humility, Prayer

One person who thinks himself a painter can paint any day you like anything you ask him—a mountain, a river, a horse, an insect, or a flower—it is all the same to him. He takes a brush and soon produces something, which ordinary people might think to be a picture. But send that daub of his to the Royal Academy, and they will tell you that it may do for a tea tray but not for the walls of a gallery.

But the man that *can* paint, how does he mix his colors? The great painter will tell you that he mixes his brains with his colors. When he takes his brush and dips it into the paint, he lays it on with his soul. In a great picture, such as sometimes we have seen by a Titiens,[1] or a Raphael,[2] it is not the color but the man's heart that has got out on to

1. Or Titian, an Italian painter (d. 1576). —ed.
2. Raffaello Sanzio da Urbino (Raphael in English) was an Italian painter (1483–1520). —ed.

the canvas. Somehow, he has managed to drop his brush into his soul. That is real painting.

And so it is with prayer. The humblest man that prays to God with his soul understands the fine art of prayer; but the man who chants a pompous liturgy, or repeats an extemporaneous effusion, has not prayed. He has dashed off what he thinks to be a picture, but it is not a picture, it is not a prayer. Had it been a prayer it would have had a palpable inspiration in its light and shade. A painting may consist of few lines, but you will see the painter's hand in it. A prayer may consist of only half a dozen words, but you can see the hand of God in it.

---

13 **Return, return, O Shulamite** This verse is not addressed to the church in her doubting state, nor while seeking her absent Lord, but it refers to her in her very best condition, when she has lately come from the enjoyment of fellowship with her divine spouse, and when her soul in consequence is like the chariots of Ammi-nadib. Read the context, and you will perceive that believers, who are rejoicing in the Lord, may look upon this text as their own. Observe *the title* of the person addressed—it is a marriage name. She has been espoused to Solomon, and she has taken his name, and become *Solyma*, for such is the best rendering of the word rendered Shulamite. This name is appropriate to souls who are united to Christ, to those whom Christ has betrothed unto himself in righteousness, who live in union with their Lord. You who abide in the Lord Jesus are, by a mysterious bond, made one with Christ; and he has conferred upon you his own name—he is Solomon, and you are Solyma. That is a remarkable expression in the book of Jeremiah—"This is *her* name wherewith *she* shall be called, the Lord our righteousness" (Jer 33:16). One would have thought that such a title was incommunicable; but yet so close is the union between Christ and his people, that the Holy Spirit actually transfers that dignified expression, "Lord our

righteousness," to his Israel—his beloved. The title Solyma also signifies both perfection and peace. There is *perfection* in every child of God, but not a perfection in the flesh. We are perfect in Christ Jesus; complete in him; spotless, by being washed in his blood; glorious, by being robed in his righteousness. Every child of God is right sumptuously arrayed in the wedding dress of the Savior's righteousness. We may truly say that "Solomon in all his glory was not arrayed like one of these" (Matt 6:29). Every believer stands in Christ perfectly accepted. The sweet name Solyma, signifies also *peace*—"Therefore being justified by faith, we have peace with God through Jesus Christ our Lord" (Rom 5:1). The true heir of heaven is not at enmity with God, nor at war with his own conscience. The silver trumpet has proclaimed an everlasting peace; God's sword has been sheathed in the Savior's heart, and divine justice is on the side of the chosen people.

return, return, that we may look upon thee *The request* of the text next demands a moment's consideration. It is repeated four times. "Return, return, O Solyma; return, return, that we may look upon thee." Does not this request proceed from the daughters of Jerusalem who desire to behold her beauty? Souls that are anxious about their own state may well desire to understand the experience of the true child of God. You want to know whether you also are a Christian, therefore would you know how Christians feel, how they think of Christ, how they are moved by his Spirit, what is their appearance when his love is shed abroad in their hearts. You anxiously desire to see the true Christian that you may measure yourselves and see whether there be the life of God in you. These daughters of Jerusalem also desire to look upon her for their own delight; for, as to gaze upon beauty is exceeding pleasant, so is it specially delightful to the pure in heart to have fellowship with the pure in heart—to see the fruits which the Spirit has brought forth—to behold the cleanness of the believer's walk, and to know the savor of the believer's conversation. No beauty equals the beauty of holiness; nothing is so comely as uprightness; and therefore we wonder not that four times the request is made. Perhaps, too, these daughters wanted to look at her as an example to themselves. Saints look upon the beauty of others that they may be enabled to emulate their excellencies. Let us read with affectionate attention the biographies of holy men that they may be a stimulus to ourselves, exciting us to exert ourselves in the Redeemer's cause, and may afford us some hope that the highest Christian attainments are not altogether beyond our reach. I think this is the reason why the daughters of Jerusalem said, "Return, return, O Solyma": they would comfort themselves by seeing whether they are like her; they would delight themselves by beholding her perfections; they would also stir up their own souls by seeing her example.

What will ye see in the Shulamite? As it were the company of two armies Either the spouse asks the question, which is the most probable—she says, "What shall ye see in Solyma?" She thinks that there is no beauty in her, nothing in her that anyone should delight in her, or fix his eyes upon her, or derive any profit from regarding her. "Why," says she, "all that you will see in me is a company of two armies—a conflict between good and evil. If you look upon me you see nothing but good and evil fighting together, darkness and light contending. I am not worth your looking at." And so she would fain veil her face and go away if it were not for the earnest request which seems to hold her fast.

Or, as some think, this question is asked by bystanders, and is answered by the daughters of Jerusalem: "What shall ye see in the Shulamite?" the giddy crowd inquire, and instructed believers cry, "We shall see in her the concurrence of two triumphant armies returning as choristers, with music and with dancing, from the field of battle; we shall see in her the King immortal, invisible, with all his hosts of grace; we shall see in her the purified soul co-working with the glorious Savior; we shall see in the Christian church the activity of sanctified manhood, combined with the majestic power of deity residing within." This is what *she* might not say of herself; but what they would see in her.

Observe, then, the two meanings, and let us dismiss the second. There is in every Christian a sweet composition of Christ's power and of the activity of his own soul; there is the power of God, and there is the creature himself made willing in the day of God's power. There is in the Christian God working in him to will and to do of his own good pleasure, and the man himself working out his own salvation with fear and trembling. In the Christian church there is man working for God and God working in man, and all this in such a joyful manner as to be rather resembling the triumph of returning conquerors than the going forth to fight of those who make war.

What shall we see in Solyma? We shall see the blessed confluence of the two great armies of sanctified humanity and of God made flesh.

ILLUSTRATION

Progress by the Sea

Preaching Themes: Faith, Grace, Prayer

Along the coast of Essex the sea is greatly encroaching upon the land, and every time we go to some of the watering-places, we perceive that the cliff has fallen, hundreds or thousands of tons have been carried away. Yet if you are there at a tide which has gone far out, you will often think, "Why, surely the land is gaining on the sea! I never walked out so far as this before. I never saw these rocks exposed and dry before." Well, it is a strangely low tide, but at the same time, ask the old fisherman who has lived there all his days, and he will tell you that his mother was married out in a church which stood where that ship is floating, far out to sea, and that all the intervening soil has been washed away. He recollects when this place, which is now a footpath on the cliff's brink, was a quarter of a mile inland. Then you understand that, though on any one occasion the land may apparently have gained, yet, on the whole, there has been a progress in the sea.

And so it is with spiritual life. There are times when it seems as if sin had gained upon you, and you were going back in spiritual things; there is cause for alarm, but not despair; cause for watchfulness, but not for terror. Go to the Lord, and pray to him to send a mightier wave of his irresistible grace, that your soul may be filled with all the fullness of God. The day is often gloomy at eleven o'clock, but that is no proof that you are not getting towards noon. Many a cold wind howls over the days of March and April, colder than there might have been at Christmas, but that is no proof that you are not getting on to summer. There may come a frosty night in May, nipping the flowers, but that is no proof that the frost is all coming back again. So, you may feel within yourself such things as cause you to bow your head in sorrow, and to cry out to God in grief, but even these things shall but speed you on your way towards your desired haven.

APPLICATION

Holding Fast to the Ancient Faith

An army with banners may signify the *constancy* and perseverance in holding the truth. We see before us not an army that has lost its banners, that has suffered its colors to be rent away from it, but an army which bears aloft its ancient standard and swears by it still. Let us be very earnest to maintain the faith once delivered to the saints. Let us not give up this doctrine or that, at the dictates of policy or fashion. But whatever Jesus says unto us, let us receive it as the word of life. Great injury may be done to a church before it knows it, if it shall tolerate error here and there. For false doctrine, like the little leaven, soon leavens the whole lump. If the church is taught by the Spirit to know the voice of the Good Shepherd, a stranger it will not follow; for it does not know the voice of strangers. This is part of the education which Christ gives to his people: "All thy children shall be taught of the LORD" (Isa 54:13). They shall know the truth, and the truth shall make them free.

May we, as a church, hold fast the things which we have learned and have been taught by God. May we be preserved from the philosophies and refinings of these last days. If we give up the things which are truly believed among us, we shall lose our power, and the energy alone will be pleased. But if we maintain them, the maintenance of the old faith, by the Spirit of God, shall make us strong in the Lord and in the power of his might. Wrap the colors round you, you standard bearers, in the day of danger, and die sooner than give them up. Life is little compared with God's loving-kindness, and that is the sure heritage of the brave defender of the faith. Thus, resolute for truth, the church becomes an army with banners.

Service Leads to Joy

Not infrequently have I known that the Lord has appeared to his people and warmed their hearts when they have been working for him. Some idle, indolent, sluggish professors who have used the ordinances have not found benefit in the ordinances, because the Lord has intended to rebuke their sloth. But when they have got up and gone forth among the poor, when they have gone forth to visit the sick, the sorrowful, and the dying, they have heard such delightful expressions from the lips of holy, suffering men and women, or felt their hearts so kindled by a sight of divine compassion in the midst of desperate poverty and gracious pardon for grievous sin, that a quickening has come over them. Whereas they did not seem to care before whether souls were lost or saved, they have gone out into the world with zeal to win fresh trophies for the Messiah, their hearts being like the chariots of Ammi-nadib, through the benefits they have received from Christian service. A great many Christian people never will be happy, and never fully alive to the destinies that wait on their Redeemer, till they get something to do to give them an interest in those mighty issues. The rule of the Christian life is, "If any would not work, neither should he eat" (2 Thess 3:10). If you will not serve God as Christians, you shall not feed upon the sweet things of the kingdom to your own soul's comfort. A little more service, and your soul would become like the chariots of Ammi-nadib.

Beloved, there is no need that I should enlarge. I merely say this to bring up your grateful memories that you may thank God for what he has done, for remember, whatever he has done in the past he will do again in the future.

Jesus Calls Us

Notice that in the text that word "return" is put four times over. Is it not because it is of the highest importance that every child of God should keep returning, and coming nearer to the Father's house? Is it not because it is our highest joy, our strongest security, our best enrichment, to be always coming to Christ as unto a living stone, and getting into closer fellowship with him? As he calls four times, is it not a hint that we are slow to come? We ought to come to Jesus not only at his first call, but even at the glances of his eyes, when he looks as though he longed for our love. It ought to be our rapture to think only of him, and live wholly to him; but as we fail to answer to first pleas, he cries four times, "Return, return, O Solyma; return, return. Come to your own Husband, your own loving Lord." He does not cease to entreat until we do return.

Do not the reduplications of this call hint at his strong desire after us, his condescending love for us? It does seem so wonderful to me that Christ should want our fellowship, but he does: he cannot be happy without us. Still he sits down upon the well when he is thirsty, and looking across to Samaria's fallen daughter he says to her, "Give me to drink" (John 4:7). His people are his fullness; he cannot be filled if they are away. I dared not have said this if the Holy Ghost had not declared it, but it is true. Without his people, Jesus would be a Head without a body, and that is a ghastly object; a King without subjects, and that would have been a wretched parody of royalty; a Shepherd without sheep, and that would have been a dolorous office, having many pains but no reward. Jesus must have us, or he is a Bridegroom without a bride, bereaved and barren.

Oh, how he loves us! How he longs for communion with us! Shall he stand and cry, "Return, return," and will we not come to him at once?

SONG OF SOLOMON 7

SONG OF SOLOMON 7:1–13

1 How beautiful are thy feet with shoes, O prince's daughter!
The joints of thy thighs *are* like jewels,
The work of the hands of a cunning workman.
2 Thy navel *is like* a round goblet, *which* wanteth not liquor:
Thy belly *is like* an heap of wheat set about with lilies.
3 Thy two breasts *are* like two young roes *that are* twins.
4 Thy neck *is* as a tower of ivory;
Thine eyes *like* the fishpools in Heshbon, by the gate
of Bath-rabbim:
Thy nose *is* as the tower of Lebanon which looketh toward Damascus.
5 Thine head upon thee *is* like Carmel,
And the hair of thine head like purple;
The king *is* held in the galleries.
6 How fair and how pleasant art thou, O love, for delights!
7 This thy stature is like to a palm tree,
And thy breasts to clusters *of grapes*.
8 I said, I will go up to the palm tree,
I will take hold of the boughs thereof:
Now also thy breasts shall be as clusters of the vine,
And the smell of thy nose like apples;
9 And the roof of thy mouth like the best wine
For my beloved, that goeth *down* sweetly,
Causing the lips of those that are asleep to speak.
10 I *am* my beloved's, and his desire *is* toward me.
11 Come, my beloved, let us go forth into the field;
Let us lodge in the villages.
12 Let us get up early to the vineyards;
Let us see if the vine flourish, *whether* the tender grape appear,
And the pomegranates bud forth:
There will I give thee my loves.

13 The mandrakes give a smell,
And at our gates *are* all manner of pleasant *fruits*,
New and old,
Which I have laid up for thee, O my beloved.

EXPOSITION

1–3 **How beautiful are thy feet with shoes, O prince's daughter!** Surely it is when the heart is completely at one with God that the true beauty of the Christian character is seen. Then it is that the heavenly Bridegroom cries out, "How beautiful are thy feet with shoes, O prince's daughter!" Then, too, the church in her tribulation becomes bright and glorious, like her Lord, of whom we read, "His feet like unto fine brass, as if they burned in a furnace" (Rev 1:15). Shod with perfect delight in the will of the Lord, we are able to surmount all the difficulties and trials of the way, for it becomes sweet to suffer when we see that it is the will of God. Resignation is good, but perfect acquiescence is better, and happy, thrice happy is the man who feels it. No silver sandals were ever so precious, no buskins of golden mail adorned with precious stones were so glorious to look upon as a mind molded to the divine will, perfectly in tune with the mind of the Lord most high.

4–5 **Thine head upon thee *is* like Carmel, and the hair of thine head like purple; the king *is* held in the galleries** What does your Lord say of us? You know what sort of face he has. Just hear him while he describes ours. You would scarce think that he could mean it; but certainly he does, for he has seen us often, and therefore he should know. He says of us, O prince's daughter, "Thine head upon thee is like Carmel, and the hair of thine head like purple; the king is held in the galleries" (Song 7:5). And again he says, "Thou art all fair, my love; there is no spot in *thee*." When I first had that text laid home to my soul, well do I recollect how it ravished my heart; I could not understand that my Lord and Master should actually look me in the face, and say, "Lo, thou art fair; there is no spot in thee." Oh! it is a grand and noble truth. Faith grasps it; love dotes on it; our hearts treasure it. There is no spot left in a believer now.

6 **How fair and how pleasant art thou, O love, for delights!** At all seasons the believer is very near the heart of the Lord Jesus, he is always as the apple of his eye, and the jewel of his crown. Our name is still on the breastplate, and our persons are still in his gracious remembrance. He never thinks lightly of his people; and certainly in all the compass of his Word there is not one syllable which looks like contempt of them. They are the choice treasure and peculiar portion of the Lord of hosts; and what king will undervalue his own inheritance? What loving husband will despise his own wife? Let others call the church what they may, Jesus abides in his love, and does not differ in his judgment of her, for he still exclaims, "How fair and how pleasant art thou, O love, for delights!"

7–8 **I said, I will go up to the palm tree, I will take hold of the boughs thereof:** We were thinking of the way of climbing a palm tree, and noted how easy it would be to step from the notch of one departed frond to another, but we could not see our way clear to read the lesson of the physical fact till, turning to good Moody Stuart's *Song of Songs*, we found him thus sweetly expatiating upon the eighth verse of the seventh chapter: "'I said, I will go up to the palm tree, I will take hold of the boughs thereof.' This is for the purpose of gathering the fruit, or rather it is the grasping of the fruit itself, for the laden boughs of the palm are little else than vast fruit-stalks. No tree presents a more beautiful picture of abundance; the single, branchless, untapered stem, the magnificent crown of branching leaves at the summit of the stem, and beneath the leaves the boughs or fruit-stalks, each of them clustered round with innumerable dates, and sometimes hanging downward not far from the outstretched hand. The fruit of the palm is so abundant that in some of the cases of the great African desert it is said to form the principal food of those sons of Ethiopia, 'who will soon stretch out their hands to God,' and pluck living fruit from a nobler palm."

9 **And the roof of thy mouth like the best wine For my beloved, that goeth down sweetly, Causing the lips of those that are asleep to speak** There is now upon our Master, and there always has been, a thirst after the love of his people. Do you not remember how that thirst of his was strong in the old days of the prophet? Call to mind his complaint in the fifth chapter of Isaiah, "Now will I sing to my wellbeloved a song of my beloved touching his vineyard. My wellbeloved hath a vineyard in a very fruitful hill: and he fenced it, and gathered out the stones thereof, and planted it with the choicest vine, and built a tower in the midst of it, and also made a winepress therein" (Isa 5:1–2). What was he looking for from his vineyard and its winepress? What except the juice of the vine that he might be refreshed? "And he looked that it should bring forth grapes, and it brought forth wild grapes"—vinegar and not wine, sourness and not sweetness. So he was thirsting then.

10 **I am my beloved's, and his desire is toward me** The daughters of Jerusalem had been praising the church as the fairest among women. They spoke of her with admiring appreciation, extolling her from head to foot. She wisely perceived that it was not easy to bear praise, and therefore she turned aside from the virgins to her Lord, making her boast not of her own comeliness but of her being affianced to her beloved: "I am my beloved's, and his desire is toward me." Solomon has said, in his book of Proverbs, "As the fining pot for silver, and the furnace for gold; so is a man to his praise" (Prov 27:21), meaning to teach us that praise is a serious ordeal. Very many men can bear censure and abuse, for their spirit rises so superior to it all that they are even profited by it. But to be flattered, or even duly honored, is not so easy a thing to endure.

11 **Come, my beloved** The spouse seems abruptly to break off from listening to the song of the virgins, and turns to her own husband-Lord, communion with whom is ever blessed and

ever profitable, and she says to him, "Come, my beloved, let us go forth into the field; let us lodge in the villages." Communion with Christ is a certain cure for every ill. Whether it be the bitterness of woe, or the cloying surfeit of earthly delight, close fellowship with the Lord Jesus will take the gall from the one, and the satiety from the other.

The spouse speaks of "my beloved" as of a real personage, whom she sees, upon whom she leans, and with whom she talks. Christ Jesus is to his church no fiction, no myth, no imaginary hero. Throughout the song both the personages are most real to each other, so real that they both enter into graphic descriptions of each other's beauties, and present us with portraits drawn by the pencil of admiring love. Now, a church will always be strong when the Lord Jesus is real to her; by this, indeed, may her power be estimated. Jesus must be to us no historical personage who was once on earth, but is now dead and powerless; he must be an actual person living still in our midst.

let us go forth into the field The spouse, when she said, "Let us go forth into the field" *knew that the proposal would please her Lord*; for the nature of Christ is a large and loving one, and, therefore, he would bless the far off ones. His is no narrow heart; his thoughts of love are far-reaching, and when the church says, "Let *us* go forth into the field," truly her Lord is not backward to accept the invitation. The spouse does not guess at this, nor does she merely infer it from her Bridegroom's nature, but she has it in express command from his own lips, "Go ye into all the world and preach the gospel to every creature" (Mark 16:15). There stand the orders, and when our largest enterprises shall have been fulfilled we shall not have exceeded them. There is no exclusion put upon any tribe or clan, no classes are laid under ban, no individuals are exempted.

Let us lodge in the villages Note that *the spouse is evidently prepared for any discomfort that may come as the result of her labor*. She needs to leave the fair palaces of her royal husband and lodge in rustic cottages. Poor lodgings there for Solomon's fair spouse; but what does she care? Any roof which covers her from the evening dew, and shields her from the drops of the night, shall quite suffice her. Yes, if *he* is there, the tents of Kedar shall be fair as the curtains of Solomon, for his sake.

Observe, too, *the spouse is quite ready to continue in this uncomfortable service*. She says, "I will *lodge* in the villages," there will she abide awhile, not paying a flying visit, but stopping until the good work is done, for which her Lord and she went forth.

12 **Let us get up early to the vineyards** Nearer the palace there were vineyards, and the spouse said, "Let us get up early to the vineyards." Note, then, that the church does her work at home as well as abroad. When she loves her Lord she works with zeal, *she gets up early*. All men in Holy Scripture who loved God much rose early to worship him. We never read of one saint engaged upon sacred service who rose late. Abraham rose early, David rose early, Job rose early, and so did they all. It is put here as the very type and symbol of an earnest, vigorous service of Christ.

ILLUSTRATION

Candles and Self-Examination

Preaching Themes: Character, Discipline, Holiness

If a candle is guarded on all sides, if there is but one place left open, the wind will find it out, and blow out the light. So, in self-examination, if we find ourselves right in many points, it is not enough. We must seek to be right in all points.

Let us see if the vine flourish Notice that God's people, when they are awake, first *look well to the church*. "Let us see if the vine flourish." The church is Christ's vine. Let us take stock of it.

whether the tender grape appear Then the church *looks after the little ones.* "Let us see if the vine flourish, whether the tender grape appear." No earnest church forgets the children of her Sabbath school, and every other agency for the young, will be sure to be well-minded. An active church seeks to bring Jesus among the children, to see if the tender grape appear. She pays her visits and performs her services, but ever in his dear company.

And the pomegranates bud forth Then the church also *takes notice of all inquiries.* "Let us see whether the pomegranates bud forth." If a church be alive, there will be always many to observe where the first tear of repentance is glistening.

There will I give thee my loves Observe that *the love of the spouse lived in fellowship with the Well-beloved.* "Come, my beloved, let *us* go, let *us* lodge, let *us* get up, let *us* see, "There will I give thee my loves." True love to Jesus grows stronger and stronger in proportion as it abides in him. We are cold in our love because we live at a distance from him. The angel who dwells in the sun has never to complain of an ice-bound heart; and he who lives in Christ and abides in him will blaze and glow with a warmth of love comparable to that of Christ himself.

ILLUSTRATION

The Whiteness of Snow Compared to Christ

Preaching Themes: Purity, Sin

What a delightfully white thing this snow is! When it has newly fallen, take the whitest linen you may have ever seen, and put it down, you will find it looks positively yellow by the side of it. Take the fairest sheet of paper that ever came from the mill, and compare it; it does not look white at all. There is no whiteness, that I know of, which can at all emulate the heavenly whiteness of the snow.

So, if I put my character side by side with another man's, I may say of it, "It will bear comparison." But if I put it by the side of Christ's perfections, since his whole life is like the pure and spotless snow, I discover at once my own failures and spots.

---

13 **at our gates are all manner of pleasant fruits, New and old** Observe that word, "at *our* gates are all manner of pleasant fruits." Love to Jesus constrains us to make over all that we hold to him, while faith appropriates all that Jesus has to itself. Love will not stand to have divided properties. Such was the love of Jesus, that he gave all that he had to us. He could not bear to have anything, not even his throne itself, that should be altogether to himself. He stripped himself to his last rag to clothe us, and then gave us his breath to be our life, his blood to be our health.

Which I have laid up for thee, O my beloved All through these verses the spouse acts with reference to her beloved. It is for him that she goes forth into the field, for the sake of his company, and the quiet enjoyment of his love, she would lodge in the villages; and all manner of pleasant fruits, new and old, which are stored within her gates she declares to be laid up for her beloved. Love, then, is the fittest and most powerful motive to holy service. "The love of Christ constraineth us" (2 Cor 5:14).

APPLICATION

Going Afield in Christ's Service

Love leads us to go afield in the service of Jesus. "Come, my beloved, let us go forth into the field." A *loving church spontaneously puts herself upon widened service*. She has a large heart towards her Lord, and longs to see him reign over all mankind. She does not wait to hear again and again the Macedonian's cry, "Come over ... and help us" (Acts 16:9), but she is prompt in mission enterprise. She does not tarry till she is forced by persecution to go abroad everywhere preaching the Word, but she sends forth her champions far and wide. As sure as ever she loves her Lord. She asks herself the question, "What more can I do for him?" When she looks over the plot of ground which she has been tilling, she says, "It is not large enough; the harvest I can get out of this will not suffice me for my dear Lord." And she says to him, "Let me go to the regions beyond, to break up the fallow ground, and cause the wilderness to blossom."

Now, do you not feel some such desire? It is upon my heart that we should be undertaking larger things for Christ. Keep up the old agencies by all manner of means; quicken them, strengthen them. But does not love suggest that as increasing years add increasing indebtedness to Christ, as we are always receiving fresh mercies, so we should make new and larger returns to our best friend? If by us, as a church, nothing new may be ventured, yet cannot each individual have his own plan and branch out afresh? Will not each man say in his heart, "What can I do for Jesus today, over and above what I should have done if things had gone on in the ordinary course?" Inquire of him you love, and if your hearts are with him, it will not be long before you will discover what he would have you do.

The Work of Self-Examination

Self-examination should always be very *earnest* work. The text says, "Let us get up early." It has been well-observed that all men in Scripture who have done earnest work, rose up early to do it. The dew of the morning, before the smoke and dust of the world's business have tainted the atmosphere, is a choice and special season for all holy work. In this passage, getting up early signifies that the church felt she must give her best hour to this necessary work; and as the work might be long, she gets up early that she may have a long day before her; that before the sun goes down, she may have examined every vine, and looked to every pomegranate, and examined all the mandrakes of the garden. So we must set to work earnestly about self-examination. This is no child's play. If thou wouldst find out the trickery of thy deceitful heart, thou must be very careful and watchful. If thou wouldst know on what foundation thy hope is built, it is a laborer's work to dig out the rubbish, and to find out where the foundation is laid. He who has to prove the title deeds of his estate, doth not always find it an easy business: there are many manuscripts through which he must wade, and numerous title deeds to be read, verified, and collated, before the case will be clear. And so it must be with you. The great matter, "Do I believe in Jesus," needs no hours of deliberation, for if I do not, I will now begin again; but to know the growing state of one's graces is not so easy. After all, you may be deceived; therefore come to it with a soul all glowing with zeal, saying, in earnest prayer, "Search me, O God, and know my heart: try me, and know my thoughts: and see if there be any wicked way in me, and lead me in the way everlasting" (Ps 139:23–24). Now, methinks, there is nothing which can make you do this earnest work so well as to say to your Master and your Lord, "Lord, come with me." "While we examine ourselves, abide with us to help us in the work." I cannot be careless when I hear Christ say, "My meat and my drink is to do the will of him that sent me." I cannot be careless in my own Christian career when I see him straining every nerve that he may run the race and win the crown for me. When I see him sitting yonder, above all principalities and powers, pleading for my soul with never-ceasing intercession, I cannot be dull and sluggish. Wake up, ye drowsy powers; be stirred up, ye sleeping passions, to examine yourselves anxiously and carefully, since Christ for Zion's sake does not hold his peace, and for Jerusalem's sake does not rest.

Fruits Must Be for Christ

We have fruits both new and old, but here is the point—they are all to be for Christ.

Do you not, after doing good service, detect yourself whispering, "I have done that well"? You intended that nobody should know it; you tried to do it as a secret act of devotion; you were half inclined to tell somebody when it was done; and though it came out, you say it was by accident; but you had a finger in that accident, and you did not altogether regret that you had some of the honor of it.

Do not you find when you are really serving your Master, that if somebody does not pat you on the back, you grow cold? I know some Sunday school teachers, who, if they are looked after and encouraged, can do well, but who, if they have no encouragement, could not keep on in their work. It is so easy for us to preach when there are many souls being fed under us, and the Master honors us in the eyes of men. Would it be quite as easy to serve him without honor? I have known brothers who have met with a little bad feeling among their people, and perhaps they have not always been able to keep their own temper, and they have run away from their charge, left the sheep in the wilderness, because in their inmost heart they were serving themselves, at least to a degree.

Truly, beloved, those are the best and most acceptable services, in which Christ is the solitary aim of the soul, and his glory without any admixture whatever, the end of all our efforts. Let your many fruits be laid up only for your beloved. Bring them forth when he is with you; bless *his* name for them. Put jewels into his crown, but never say, "Unto me be honor, and unto my name be praise"; but "Sing unto Jesus, and to Jesus only be glory, while heaven endures."

SONG OF SOLOMON 8

SONG OF SOLOMON 8:1–10

1 O that thou *wert* as my brother, that sucked the breasts of my mother!
When I should find thee without, I would kiss thee;
Yea, I should not be despised.
2 I would lead thee, *and* bring thee into my mother's house, *who* would instruct me:
I would cause thee to drink of spiced wine of the juice of my pomegranate.
3 His left hand *should be* under my head,
And his right hand should embrace me.
4 I charge you, O daughters of Jerusalem,
That ye stir not up, nor awake *my* love, until he please.
5 Who *is* this that cometh up from the wilderness,
Leaning upon her beloved?
I raised thee up under the apple tree:
There thy mother brought thee forth:
There she brought thee forth *that* bare thee.
6 Set me as a seal upon thine heart,
As a seal upon thine arm:
For love *is* strong as death;
Jealousy *is* cruel as the grave:
The coals thereof *are* coals of fire,
Which hath a most vehement flame.
7 Many waters cannot quench love,
Neither can the floods drown it:
If a man would give all the substance of his house for love,
It would utterly be contemned.
8 We have a little sister, and she hath no breasts:
What shall we do for our sister in the day when she shall be spoken for?

9 If she *be* a wall, we will build upon her a palace of silver:
And if she *be* a door, we will inclose her with boards of cedar.
10 I *am* a wall, and my breasts like towers:
Then was I in his eyes as one that found favour.

EXPOSITION

1 **O that thou wert as my brother, that sucked the breasts of my mother! When I should find thee without, I would kiss thee; yea, I should not be despised** We are sometimes, we think, in his company, but still we cannot help feeling that there is a great gulf fixed between us, even when we come the nearest to him. We talk, you know, about laying our head upon his bosom, and sitting at his feet; but alas! We find it after all to be very metaphorical, compared with the reality which we shall enjoy above. We have seen his face, we trust we have sometimes looked into his heart, and tasted that he is gracious, but still long nights of darkness lay between us. We have cried again and again with the bride, "Oh, that thou wert as my brother, that sucked the breasts of my mother! When I should find thee without, I would kiss thee; yea, I should not be despised. I would lead thee, and bring thee into my mother's house, who would instruct me: I would cause thee to drink of spiced wine of the juice of my pomegranate."

2 **I would lead thee, and bring thee into my mother's house, who would instruct me: I would cause thee to drink of spiced wine of the juice of my pomegranate** According to the sacred canticle of love, in the fifth chapter of the Song of Songs, we learn that when he drank in those olden times it was in the garden of his church that he was refreshed. What does he say? "I am come into my garden, my sister, my spouse: I have gathered my myrrh with my spice; I have eaten my honeycomb with my honey; I have drunk my wine with my milk; eat, O friends; drink, yea, drink abundantly, O beloved" (Song 5:1). In the same song he speaks of his church, and says, "The roof of thy mouth is as the best wine for my beloved, that goeth down sweetly, causing the lips of those that are asleep

to speak" (Song 7:9). And yet again in the eighth chapter the bride says, "I would cause thee to drink of spiced wine of the juice of my pomegranate" (Song 8:2).

Yes, he loves to be with his people; they are the garden where he walks for refreshment, and their love, their graces, are the milk and wine of which he delights to drink. Christ was always thirsty to save men and to be loved by men, and we see a type of his lifelong desire when, being weary, he sat thus on the well and said to the woman of Samaria, "Give me to drink" (John 4:7). There was a deeper meaning in his words than she dreamed of, as a verse further down fully proves, when he said to his disciples, "I have meat to eat that ye know not of" (John 4:32). He derived spiritual refreshment from the winning of that woman's heart to himself.

3 **His left hand should be under my head, and his right hand should embrace me** He has kissed us with the kisses of his love, and killed our doubts by the closeness of his embrace. His love has been sweeter than wine to our souls. We felt that we could sing, "His left hand is under my head, and his right hand doth embrace me." Then all earthly troubles were light as the chaff of the threshing floor, and the pleasures of the world as tasteless as the white of an egg.

4 **I charge you, O daughters of Jerusalem, that ye stir not up, nor awake *my* love, until he please** The spouse is particularly anxious that her communion with her Lord might not be disturbed. Her language is intensely earnest, "I charge you, O daughters of Jerusalem, that ye stir not up, nor awake my love, until he please." She values much the fellowship with which her beloved solaces her. She is jealously alarmed lest she should endanger the continuance of it; lest any sin on her part or on the part of her companions should cause the Beloved to withdraw himself in anger.

5 **Who is this that cometh up from the wilderness** Now it is a very striking fact that immediately after we read a verse so full of solicitous care concerning the maintenance of communion,

we immediately fall upon another verse in which the upward progress of that selfsame spouse is the theme of admiration; she who would not have her beloved disturbed is the selfsame bride who cometh up from the wilderness, leaning herself upon him; from which it is clear that there is a most intimate connection between communion with Christ and progress in grace, and therefore the more careful we are to maintain fellowship with our Lord, the more successful shall we be in going from strength to strength in all those holy graces which are landmarks on the road to glory.

The text says, "Who is this?" What made them inquire, "Who is this?" It was because they were so astonished to see her looking so happy and so little wearied. Nothing amazes worldlings more than genuine Christian joy. Holy peace in disturbing times is a puzzle to the ungodly. When they hear the righteous sing, "God is our refuge and strength, a very present help in trouble; therefore will not we fear, though the earth be removed, and though the mountains be carried into the midst of the sea" (Ps 46:1–2), they say one to another, "Where did these men learn that tune? They are men of like passions with ourselves, how is it they have learned thus to bear trial?" Therefore they inquire, "Who is this? Who is this?"

leaning upon her beloved? Note the title that is given to the companion of the spouse. "*Her beloved.*" Indeed, he of whom the song here speaks is beloved above all others. He was the Beloved of his Father or ever the earth was; he was declared to be the Lord's Beloved, in the waters of Jordan, and at other times, when out of the excellent glory there came the voice, "This is my beloved Son, in whom I am well pleased" (Matt 3:17). Beloved of his Father now, our Jesus sits forever glorious at God's right hand. Jesus is the Beloved of every angel, and of all the bright seraphic spirits that crowd around the throne of his august majesty, casting their crowns before his feet, and lifting up their ceaseless hymns. They are not merely servants who obey because they must, but reverent admirers who serve because they love. He is the Beloved of every being of pure heart and holy mind. The hosts triumphant, who have washed their robes and made them white in the blood of the Lamb, sing that word "Beloved" with an emphasis which our colder hearts as yet have failed to reach, but still is he Beloved of the militant band this side the Jordan.

Her posture then is that of "leaning." His relation to her is that of a divine supporter. What does this leaning mean? Why, first of all, there can be no leaning on another unless we believe in that other's presence and nearness. A man does not lean on a staff which is not in his hand, nor on a friend of whose presence he is not aware. The instincts which lead us to preserve our uprightness would not permit us to lean on a shadow or on a nothing.

One would imagine that there must have been of late years a society for the improvement of texts of Scripture, and if so I cannot congratulate that honorable company upon its success. This text has been a favorite object of the society's care, for I think I never heard it quoted correctly in my life. It is generally quoted, "Who is this that cometh up from the wilderness, leaning upon *the arm of* her beloved?" But it is not so in the text at all. Here is no distinct reference to an arm at all. There is an arm here undoubtedly, but there is a great deal more—there is a whole person; and the text speaks of leaning upon the whole person of "*her beloved.*" Observe, then, that the Christian leans upon Christ in his personality and completeness; not merely upon the arm of his strength, as that altered text would have it, but upon the whole Christ.

ILLUSTRATION

Plant Bulbs and Seeds, Not Cut Flowers

Preaching Themes: Character, Growth

We may strive after moral virtue if we will, but we shall be like those foolish children who pluck flowers and thrust them into their little gardens without roots; but if we strive after increasing faith in Jesus, we shall be as wise men, who plant choice bulbs and living seeds, from which shall in due time uprise the golden cups or the azure bells of lovely flowers, emblems of things that are lovely and of good repute. To live near to Christ is the one thing needful; to keep up that nearness, and never to suffer our fellowship to be interrupted, should be our one great business here below; and all other things, this being sought after in the first place, will be added to us.

---

6 **Set me as a seal upon thine heart, as a seal upon thine arm**
I think I can perhaps explain this text best by a reference to the high priest of old. You know that when he put on his holy garments—those robes of glory and beauty—he wore the breastplate of cunning work in which four rows of precious stones were set. If you will turn to Exodus 39:14, you read, "And the stones were according to the names of the children of Israel, twelve, according to their names, like the engravings of a signet, everyone with his name, according to the twelve tribes." How suggestive of this prayer! "Set me as a seal or as an engraved signet, as a precious stone that has been carved—set my name upon your breast." Let it be always glittering there.

But beside this breastplate, there was the ephod, and we are told that "they made shoulderpieces for it, to couple it together: by the two edges was it coupled together" (Exod 39:4). Then in the sixth verse we read, "And they wrought onyx stones inclosed in ouches of gold, graven, as signets are graven, with the names of the children of Israel; and he put them on the shoulders of the ephod, that they should be stones for a memorial to the children of Israel; as the Lord commanded Moses." So that it was set as a signet upon his shoulder, or upon his arm, as well as upon his heart. I think these were to indicate that the high priest loved the people, for he bore them on his heart, and that he served the people as a consequence of that love; therefore he bore them upon his shoulders.

And I think the prayer of the spouse is just this—she would know once for all that Christ's heart is entirely hers, that he loves her with the intensity and the very vitality of his being, that his inmost heart, the life-spring of his soul, belongs to her. And she would also know that that love moves his arm. She longs to see herself as supported, sustained, strengthened, defended, preserved, and kept by that same strong arm which put Orion in its place in the sky, and holds the Pleiades that they should give their light forever more. She longs that she may know the love of his heart, and that she may experience the power of his arm.

For love is strong as death She pleads that he would show her his love, because of *the strength of it*. "Thy love is strong as death." Some expositors think that this means the church's love; others say, "No, it means the love of Christ to his church." I am not careful to determine which it means, for they are extremely like each other. Christ's love to his church is the magnificent image; the affection which his people bear to him is the beautiful miniature. They are not alike in degree and measure, for the church never loves Christ so much as Christ loves her, but they are as much alike as the father in his strength is to the babe in weakness; there is the same image and superscription. The love of the church to Christ is the child of Christ's love to the church, and consequently there is something of the same attribute in both, and while it is true that Christ's love to us is so strong that he did defy and endure death for us, it is true also that the love of the church to him is as strong as death.

ILLUSTRATION

The Strong Love of a Mother

Preaching Themes: Sacrifice, Love, Death, Character

What a mighty instinct of love glows in the mother's heart! You recollect that famous story of the mother whose child was taken from her by a Jesuit missionary to be trained separate and apart from its parents. How she swam through rivers, and passed through what seemed to be impenetrable forests, guided only by the midnight star, till she arrived at the place where her offspring was—braving death in a thousand shapes. From wild beasts and venomous serpents, from floods and jungles, from fierce men and relentless persecutors, might she but reach her child.

Have there not been instances where, in the stormy blasts of winter, a mother has wrapped her garments about her infant, and, exposing herself to the fury of the elements, has sacrificed her own life that the little one might live? Love has indeed often proved itself to be strong as death.

Jealousy is cruel as the grave Krummacher,[1] in a sermon upon this passage, following the translation of Luther, quotes it as though it ran thus: "Jealousy is firm as hell." And I believe that such is the proper translation, at least quite as correct as the present one.

"Jealousy is firm as hell." Those of you who have Bibles with the margins in them (and the margins are generally like fine gold) will perceive the words in the corner: "Hebrew *hard*." "Jealousy is hard as the grave," which is just the idea of firmness—it is as firm as the grave. *Sheol*, I believe the word is here for "grave"—otherwise we translate it "Hades"—the place of separate souls, without reference to good or evil—or as Luther translates it, "hell." "Jealousy is hard as hell." The idea is just this: that the love of Christ in the form of jealousy is as hard and as sternly relentless as is the grave and hell.

Our Lord Jesus Christ, we know, has a love for us that passes all understanding. And, however it may seem to grate upon the ear, it is equally true that he has a jealousy over his people,

1. Friedrich Wilhelm Krummacher (1796–1868), a German Reformed pastor. —ed.

which watches them with incessant care. I need not prove to you that the love of Jesus Christ for us is as strong as death; he verified that when he tasted death in all its bitterness—forsaken, not only by men, but, worst of all, forsaken of his God. "*Eli, Eli, lama sabachthani*," was the concentration of all griefs. Such was his cry upon the accursed tree. Death never made him flinch. He faced and felt its agonies extremely, and loved us then as he loved us before, and as he loves us still with infinite tenacity.

The fact that his love is strong as death admits of no question. But here is the point I am coming to: his jealousy is cruel, or hard, as the grave. He is never cruel towards his people, but he is very hard on foe or rival that would come between his people and himself—yes, hard as the grave.

The coals thereof are coals of fire, Which hath a most vehement flame If the love of Christ is strong as death; if it be such that it can never be moved from its object, yet the question arises, may not the love itself die out? Even should it abide the same in its purpose, yet may not its intensity be diminished? "No," says the Shulamite, "it is an attribute of Christ's love that 'the coals thereof are coals of fire, which hath a most vehement flame.' " More forcible is the language of the original: "The coals thereof are the coals of God"—a Hebrew idiom to express the most glowing of all flames. "The coals of God!" As though it were no earthly flame, but something far superior to the most vehement affection among men.

Some who look carefully at it think there is an allusion in this sentence to the fire which always burned at the altar and which never went out. You remember there were coals of fire which were always kept burning under the Levitical dispensation. The flame was originally kindled by fire from heaven, and it was the business of the priest perpetually to feed it with the sacred fuel. You will remember, too, that one of the cherubim flew and took a live coal from off this very altar, and said to Isaiah, "Lo, this hath touched thy lips" (Isa 6:7).

Now, the love of Christ is like the coals upon the altar which never went out. But the spouse has brought out a fuller idea than this. She seems to say, "Its vehemence never decreases; it is always burning to its utmost intensity." Nebuchadnezzar's furnace was heated seven times hotter, but no doubt it grew cool; Christ's love is like the furnace, but it is always at the sevenfold heat, and it always has within itself its own fuel. It is not like fire merely, but like coals of fire, always having that within itself which supports it.

ILLUSTRATION

Idols and Christ's Jealousy

Preaching Themes: Idolatry, Jealousy

I recollect the story of a Christian woman who had made a great idol of her child. He was her only son, and she lost him. Nothing then could console her, till at length one day she went into a Quakers' meeting. She sat there a long time, and not a word was spoken. Presently one of the members rose up and simply said, "Verily I perceive thy children are idols." Not another word was uttered during the whole of the meeting. That word, however, was sent by the providence of God, and fastened like a nail in a right place. It had done its work; the mother's heart was comforted; she saw the reason of her loss, and submitted her soul to the discipline.

Now it is not children only of which we make idols. There are twenty other things. Twenty, did I say? Why, the world swarms with idols! Man is such an idolator that, if he cannot idolize anything else, he will idolize himself, and set himself up, and bow down and worship himself. But the Lord Jesus will never tolerate idolatry in any heart which belongs to him.

---

7 **Many waters cannot quench love, Neither can the floods drown it** The argument seems to me to run thus: "Yes, but if Christ's love does not die out of itself—if it has such intensity that it never would fail by itself, yet may not you and I put it out?" No, says the text, "Many waters cannot quench love, neither can the floods drown it." Christ has endured many waters already—the waters of bodily affliction, the waters of soul travail, the waters of spiritual desertion. Christ was in this world like Noah's ark; the depths came up from beneath; hell troubled him; the great water-floods came from above; it pleased the Father to bruise him. The cataracts leaped on him from either side; he was betrayed by his friends; he was hunted by his foes. But the many waters could no more destroy his love than it could drown the ark of gopher wood. Just as that ark mounted higher, and higher, and higher, the more the floods prevailed; so then that love of Christ seemed to rise higher, and higher, and higher, just in proportion to the floods of agony which sought to put it out.

If a man would give all the substance of his house for love, it would utterly be contemned Neither Christ's love to us nor our love to him can be purchased. Neither of these could be bartered for gold, or rubies, or diamonds, or the most precious crystal. If a man should offer to give all the substance of his house for either of these forms of love, it would utterly be condemned.

The love of our Lord Jesus Christ is altogether unpurchasable. It must be quite impossible to purchase the love of Christ, because *it is inconceivable that he ever could be mercenary*. It would be profane, surely, it would amount to blasphemy, and a very high degree of it, to suppose that the love of his heart could be bought with gold, or silver, or earthly stores. No, if he loves, it must be all free, like his own royal self.

The saints' love is not purchased by Christ's gifts. The love of saints to their Lord is not given to Christ because of his gifts to them. It is "Jesus Christ himself" who wins the love of our hearts! *If he had not given us himself, we should never have given to him ourselves*. All else that may be supposed to be of the substance of his house would not have won his people's hearts, until at last they learnt this truth, and the Spirit of God made them feel the force of it, "He loved me ... and gave himself for me" (Gal 2:20).

"My beloved is mine, and I am his" (Song 2:16) is now one of the sweetest stanzas in love's canticle. The spouse does not say, "His crown is mine, his throne is mine, his breastplate is mine, his crook is mine"; she delights in everything that Christ has as a King, and a Priest, and a Shepherd, but above all else that which wins and charms her heart is this: "He himself is mine, and I am his."

ILLUSTRATION

The Love of Damon and Pythias

Preaching Themes: Friendship, Love

Damon loved Pythias;[2] the two friends were so bound together that their names became household words, and their conduct towards one another grew into a proverb. Yet Damon never purchased the heart of Pythias, neither did Pythias think to pay a yearly stipend for the love of Damon. The introduction of the question of cost would have spoiled it all. The very thought of anything mercenary, anything like payment on the one side or receipt upon the other, would have been a death blow to their friendship.

No. If a man should give all the substance of his house even for human love, for the common love that exists between man and man, it would utterly be contemned.

---

2. Damon and Pythias (or sometimes Phintias) refers to a Greek legend where Pythias gets sentenced to death by Dionysius I, but requests to "get his affairs in order" before he is executed. Dionysius agrees as long as Pythias's friend Damon stays in prison in Pythias's stead. If Pythias does not return, Damon will be killed in his place. When Pythias returns to be executed, Dionysius is amazed and allows both men to live. —ed.

8–10 **What shall we do for our sister in the day when she shall be spoken for?** There are many who cannot say Ishi ["husband"], for Christ is not Ishi to them; Baali ["master"] is the only word they can use to God. What shall we do for them, those who know the Lord? What shall we do for these? We have a little sister; what shall we do for her against the day that she shall be spoken for unto the King? If she be a wall, we will build upon her with many prayers, precious as silver. If she be a door, we will enclose her with the cedar of our supplication; we will day and night pray for these poor souls who are not yet brought in, but many of whom must be brought in, that there may be one fold and one Shepherd.

APPLICATION

The Necessity of Leaning

There is no part of the pilgrimage of a saint in which he can afford to walk in any other way but in the way of leaning. He comes up at the first, and he comes up at the last, still leaning, still leaning upon Christ Jesus; yes, and leaning more and more heavily upon Christ the older he grows. The stronger the believer becomes, the more conscious he is of his personal weakness; and, therefore, the more fully does he cast himself upon his Lord and lean with greater force on him. It is a blessed thing to keep to this posture in all we do. It is good preaching when you lean on the Beloved as you preach and feel, "he will help me, he will give me thoughts and words, he will bless the message, he will fill the hungry with good things, and make the Sabbath to be a delight to his people." It is blessed praying when you can lean on the Beloved; you feel then that you cannot be denied; you have come into the King's court, and brought your advocate with you, and you lay your prayer at the foot of the throne, the Prince himself putting his own sign manual and seal and stamp of love upon your desires. This is the sweet way to endure and suffer with content. Who would not suffer when Jesus makes the bed of our sickness, and stays us up and gives us tokens of his love? This is the divine method of working. Believe me, no sacred work can long be continued with energy except in this spirit, for flesh flags, and even the spirit languishes except there be the constant leaning upon the Beloved.

As for you, men of business, you with your families and with your shops, and with your fields, and your enterprises, you will find it poor living unless you evermore lean on your Beloved in all things. If you can bring your daily cares, your domestic troubles, your family sicknesses, your personal infirmities, your losses and your crosses—if you can bring all things to Jesus, it will be easy and happy living. Even the furnace itself, when the coals glow most, is cool and comfortable as a royal chamber spread for banqueting with the king, when the soul reclines on the bosom of divine love. You saints, strive after more of this. We are such lovers of caring for ourselves, we so want to set up on our own account; we pine to run alone while our legs are too weak; we aspire to stand alone when the only result can be a fall. Oh, to give up this willfulness, which is our weakness, and like a babe to lie in the mother's bosom, conscious that our strength is not in ourselves, but in that dear bosom which upbears us!

I would encourage the heir of heaven who is in trouble to lean. I can encourage you from experience. The Lord has laid on me many burdens in connection with much serving in his church, and I sometimes grow very weary. But whenever I bring myself, or rather the Holy Spirit brings me to this pass, that I am clear that I cannot do anything of myself, and do not mean to try, but will just be God's obedient servant and ready instrument, and will leave every care with him, then it is that peace returns, thought becomes free and vigorous, and the soul once more having cast aside its burden, runs without weariness and walks without fainting. I am sure, my dear fellow servants, life will break you down unless you learn the habit of leaning on Jesus. Do not be afraid to lean too much. There was never yet a saint blamed for possessing too much faith; there was never such a thing known as a child of God who was scolded by the Divine Father for having placed too implicit reliance upon his promise. The Lord has said, "As thy day … thy strength shall be" (Deut 33:25). He has promised, "I will never leave thee, nor forsake thee" (Heb 13:5). He has told you that the birds of the air neither sow nor reap, nor gather into barns, and yet are fed. He has assured you that the lilies of the field toil not, neither do they spin, and yet your heavenly Father makes them more beautiful than Solomon in all his glory. Why do you not cast your care on him who cares for ravens and for flowers of the field? Why are you not assured that he will also care for you?

Strength in Weakness

I do believe that as long as we have a grain of self-sufficiency, we never trust in the All-sufficient. While there is anything of self left we prefer to feed on it, and only when at last the moldy bread becomes too sour for eating, and even the husks that the swine eat are such as cannot fill our belly, it is only then that we humbly ask for the bread of heaven to satisfy us.

My soul, learn to hate every thought of self-sufficiency. Do you not find yourselves tempted at times, especially if you have had a happy week, and have been free from trials, to think, "Now, really I am better than a great many. I think I am now growing to be an old, experienced saint. I have now escaped the power of ordinary temptations, and have become so advanced in grace that there is no likelihood of my sinning in those directions wherein new converts show their weakness"? There is your weak point. Set a double guard where you think you are strongest. Just when you are most afraid, and say to yourself, "O that I might be kept from such a sin—I know that is my besetment, and I am afraid I shall be led into it," you are less likely to sin there than anywhere. Your weakness is your strength, your strength is your weakness. Be nothing, for only so can you be anything. Be poor in spirit, for only so can you be rich towards God. The spouse leaned because she was weak. Is not this good argument for you? For me? Are not we also weak? Come then, let us lean wholly upon him who is not weak, but to whom all power belongs to bear all his people safely through.

Facing Persecution

Although you and I are not born in an age in which we are likely to attain to the distinguished honor of wearing the ruby crown of martyrdom, their example may excite our emulation. Have you been subjected to a little jeering and sneering in the workshop, or to a little harsh treatment at home? Maybe you begin to falter and flag. Remind yourself, then. What part have you in that love which is strong as death if it cannot bear this? If any of you have been sorely tempted to do an unholy thing to get you out of your pecuniary embarrassments, ask yourselves, where is the love which is strong in death, and will you dare to stoop? If you do not maintain your integrity, you have not a drop of martyr's blood in you. If you have not the Spirit of Christ, you are none of his.

When I see professors turn pale at a laugh of the thoughtless, or look terrified when some article in a newspaper or a magazine thrusts hard at their principles, I wonder how they would have behaved themselves in the grand old times of Luther, or had they belonged to the school of which Calvin was the great exponent. Or might it have been their fortune to encounter the struggles, political and social, with which such bold reformers as Wickliffe [Wycliffe] and Hugh Latimer[3] were mixed up? Let not worthy sons of valiant sires pander to craven fears. Rather let that love which is as strong as death brace your nerves and replenish you with a divine inspiration. Doubtless we shall have an opportunity of testing this love, though not at the ignominious stake perhaps, nor yet in the desolate prison. The average trials and troubles of life, the peculiar contingencies of each individual's career, the special besetments and temptations that pertain to a child of God—all these make it momentous to live; to live as become godliness.

And what do you think? Can it be child's play to die? To finish one's course, to know that alterations and emendations cannot be made. Our flesh creeps at the prospect of the grave, but our soul trembles at the outlook and the judgment. Our faith must be firm and our fellowship unwavering. Then our love will be tenacious; yes, as strong as death. You should not lose your confidence when you lose your health. The animal spirits may sink, but you are not dependent upon anything so contingent as they are on the atmosphere. The spirit that sustains you is divine. With decay comes depression; they are both the fruit of disease or of infirmity. Faith can survive—love can triumph over both.

3. Hugh Latimer (c. 1485–1555) was an English Protestant Reformer who worked as a fellow at Clare College and as the bishop of Worcester. Later in his life he was the Church of England's chaplain to King Edward VI before he became a martyr at the hands of Mary Tudor.

SONG OF SOLOMON 8:11–14

11 Solomon had a vineyard at Baal-hamon;
He let out the vineyard unto keepers;
Every one for the fruit thereof was to bring a thousand *pieces*
of silver.
12 My vineyard, which *is* mine, *is* before me:
Thou, O Solomon, *must have* a thousand,
And those that keep the fruit thereof two hundred.
13 Thou that dwellest in the gardens,
The companions hearken to thy voice:
Cause me to hear *it*.
14 Make haste, my beloved,
And be thou like to a roe or to a young hart
Upon the mountains of spices.

EXPOSITION

11 **Solomon had a vineyard at Baal-hamon** We have no difficulty in understanding that this vineyard is Christ's church. She is not compared to a grove of trees—even of fruit-bearing trees—because there are many trees which are valuable, not only for their fruit, but also for their timber; and should they bring forth no fruit, they would still be of some value. Not so is it with the members of Christ's church; they are like the vine, for the vine, if it bringeth forth no fruit, is fit for nothing, it cumbereth the ground. The Lord said to the prophet Ezekiel, "What is the vine tree more than any tree, or than a branch which is among the trees of the forest? Shall wood be taken thereof to do any work? Or will men take a pin of it to hang any vessel thereon? Behold, it is cast into the fire for fuel: the fire devoureth both the ends of it, and the midst of it is burned.

Is it meet for any work?" (Ezek 15:2–4). No, if it is fruitless, it is useless. It must bear fruit, or it is of no value whatsoever. Hence the church is always compared to a vineyard, because, if she does not bring forth fruit to the Lord Jesus Christ, she is less useful even than an ordinary mercantile and commercial community. That mercantile community, or body corporate, instituted for wise purposes, may further some useful design; but the church is of no use whatever unless she brings forth the fruits of holiness and of gratitude to her Lord, her Divine Husbandman. Better that she be not called a church at all than that she should pretend to be the church of Christ, and yet bring forth no fruit to his praise.

he let out the vineyard unto keepers; every one for the fruit thereof was to bring a thousand pieces of silver Every one of us whom the Lord has brought to himself, has a part of his vineyard to keep for him. We do not sing, with Wesley—

A charge to keep I have,
A God to glorify,
A never-dying soul to *save*,
And *fit* it for the sky[1]

—because we do not believe anything of the kind. We leave the work of saving our souls in higher hands than our own. But after our souls are saved, then we have a charge to keep, and that charge is to publish the name and fame of Jesus to the utmost of our power, to seek to bring others under the sound of the gospel, and to tell them what they must do to be saved.

12 **My vineyard, which is mine** The Master here, then, *claims a special property in his church*. Twice does he mention that claim: "*My* vineyard, which is *mine*," as if he meant to assert his rights, and to maintain them against all comers; being ready to defend them in Heaven's High Court of Chancery, or before all the hosts of his enemies who might seek to snatch

1. These lines are from the Charles Wesley hymn "A Charge to Keep I Have." —ed.

his inheritance from him. "Whatever is not mine," says the Divine Lover, "my church is. She is so mine that, if I gave up Lebanon, if I should renounce Bashan, and give up all the rest of my possessions, I must retain Zion, my vineyard, my best-beloved." We know that the church is Christ's by special bonds—not simply by creation. It is true that the Lord Jesus has created all his people, but then he does not claim them merely upon that ground, because all men are his by creation; no, the very devils in hell are his in that sense. And, therefore, he does not claim his church simply by the right of being her Creator. Nor does he claim her merely by the prerogatives of providence; for, in that sense, the cattle on a thousand hills are his, and the lions of the forest, and the young ravens which cry unto him, for he supplies their needs. All things are his by providence, from the stars of heaven down to the midge in the summer's air, or the worm that conceals itself in the grass at eventide. But our Lord Jesus claims his church by a far higher title than that of creation or providence. Nor is the church his merely by right of conquest. It is true that he hath fought for his people, and that they may be considered as the spoils that he hath taken in war; he hath rescued his people from the hand of him that was stronger than they; all of them, as he shall take them with him into heaven, may be looked upon as signs and wonders, trophies of what his strong arm hath done in delivering them from their mighty and malignant foes. But, beloved, Christ claims his church by a better title even than this.

First, he claims the church as his own by his Father's gift. You know that the church is the property of all the three Persons of the holy and blessed Trinity. She is the Father's property by election; she is the Son's property by donation, passing from the hand of the Father to that of the Mediator; and, then, the Church is the Spirit's by his indwelling and inhabitation; so that all three of the Divine Persons have a right to the church for some special office which they exercise towards her.

Next, Christ's church is his by purchase. The good Shepherd laid down his life for his sheep. Christ loved his church, and gave himself for it. He bought his own people with his blood. He purchased, not the world's wide wilderness, but the "spot enclosed by grace," the vineyard which his own right hand hath planted. Dear, then, to the heart of Jesus is every vine, and every cluster of grapes, in this vineyard, because he bought the whole of it with his blood.

More than this, the church is Christ's by one other tie, which, perhaps, makes it dearer still to him. She is his bride, his spouse.

is before me The church is "before" Christ in the sense that he so loves her that he never has her out of his presence. The vineyard is so dear to the Husbandman that he never leaves it. He may sometimes hide himself among the vines; but he is always close at hand, watching how they progress, and delighting himself with their fragrance and fruitfulness. The Bridegroom is never absent from his spouse, for he loves her too much to be separated from her.

The expression, "My vineyard, which is mine, is before me," may also mean that Jesus is always caring for it, as well as always loving it. There is never a moment when Christ ceases to care for his vineyard. He himself said, "I the Lord do keep it; I will water it every moment: lest any hurt it, I will keep it night and day" (Isa 27:3). What! Water it every moment? Keep it night and day? Yes, he will never neglect it. His word to his church is, "Lo, I am with you alway" (Matt 28:20)—not merely for half a day, or for an hour in the day, leaving his ministers to care for them at other times—but, "Lo, I am with you alway, even unto the end of the world." Jesus still walks among the golden candlesticks; he does not light the candles and then leave them to burn by themselves but he walks among them, and so keeps them from going out.

Thou, O Solomon, must have a thousand, And those that keep the fruit thereof two hundred Whatever others have, our Lord must have Solomon's portion, "and those that keep the fruit thereof two hundred." So, then, in the first place, the fruit of the vineyard belongs to Christ. But, in the second place, both Christ and his church agree to reward the keepers of the vineyard and to let them have their two hundred.

First, then, *all the fruit of the vineyard belongs to Christ, and he must have it*. Dwell on that word "*must*," and let each one of you feel the blessed necessity. The vineyard is Christ's, he purchased it with his own life's blood; so the fruit is all his, and he must have it all, none of it must be given to anyone else.

"And those that keep the fruit thereof two hundred" means that *the keepers of the vineyard are to receive a reward*. Christ's ministers are to receive the love, and regard, and esteem of his people for his sake. Joseph Irons put this thought very prettily; I forget his exact words, but they are to the effect that Christ's ministers really do get their two hundred. They have one hundred while they are preaching, in their own enjoyment of the sweetness of the mystery which they open up to others; and then they have another hundred in the success of their ministry—in the joy of seeing sinners saved, harlots reclaimed, and drunkards converted.

ILLUSTRATION

Paying Preachers

Preaching Themes: Church Leadership, Giving, Poverty

I was once traveling through Hertfordshire, and stayed the night at a certain place, and the minister said to me, "Will you preach here this evening, sir?" "Yes," I replied, "I should like an opportunity of talking to your people if you will give them notice." I went into the minister's house, and I found that they only gave him thirteen shillings a week, and I saw that his coat was threadbare. When I went into the pulpit, I thought, "I will just give these people something"; and I *did*, too, I can assure you. After that, I gave *him* something, and they gave him something, and we just managed to contribute together enough to get him a new suit of livery as he called it; and I do not think that brother has been quite as low down in the depths of poverty as he was then. There are scores of places in the country where ministers are treated as that poor man was, but it ought not to be so. The minister of Christ must have some regard, some esteem, some honor in his church; but, after all, our Lord Jesus Christ must have his thousand.

---

13 **Thou that dwellest in the gardens** The Song is almost ended: the bride and Bridegroom have come to their last stanzas, and they are about to part for a while. They utter their adieux, and the Bridegroom says to his beloved, "Thou that dwellest in the gardens, the companions hearken to thy voice: cause me to hear it." In other words—when I am far away from thee, fill thou this garden with my name, and let thy heart commune with me. She promptly replies, and it is her last word till he cometh, "Make haste, my beloved, and be thou like to a roe or to a young hart upon the mountains of spices." These farewell words of the Well-beloved are very precious to his chosen bride. Last words are always noticed: the last words of those who loved us dearly are much valued; the last words of one who loved us to the death are worthy of a deathless memory. The last words of the Lord in this canticle remind me of the commission which the Master gave to his disciples or ever he was taken up; when he said to them, "Go ye into all the world, and preach the gospel to every creature" (Mark 16:15). Then, scattering benedictions with both his hands, he ascended into the glory, and "a cloud received him out of their sight" (Acts 1:9).

The bridegroom, speaking of his bride, says, "Thou that dwellest in the gardens." The Hebrew is in the feminine, and hence we are bound to regard it as the word of the Bridegroom to his bride. It is the mystical word of the church's Lord to his elect one. He calls her "inhabitress of the gardens"—that is the word. So then, dear friends, we who make up the church of God are here addressed this morning under that term, "Thou that inhabitest the gardens."

The companions hearken to thy voice She was in the gardens, but she was not quiet there, and why should she be? God gives us tongues on purpose that they should be used. As he made birds to sing, and stars to shine, and rivers to flow, so has he made men and women to converse with one another to his glory. Our tongue is the glory of our frame, and there would be no glory in its being forever dumb.

Cause me to hear it It is beautiful to hear the Beloved say in effect, "I am going away from you, and you see me no more; but I shall see you: do not forget me. Though you will not hear my voice with your bodily ears, I shall hear your voices: therefore, speak to me. Unseen I shall feed among the lilies; unperceived I shall walk the garden in the cool of the day: when you are talking to others do not forget me. Sometimes turn aside, and when you have shut the door, and no eye can see, nor ear can hear, then let me hear thy voice: it has music in it to my heart, for I died to give you life. Let me hear the voice of your prayer, and praise, and love."

14 **Make haste, my beloved** The Song of Songs describes the love of Jesus Christ to his people, and it ends with an intense desire on the part of the church that the Lord Jesus should come back to her. The last word of the lover to the beloved one is, "Speed thy return; make haste and come back." Is it not somewhat singular that, as the last verse of the book of love has this note in it, so the last verses of the whole book of God, which I may also call the book of love, have that same thought in them? At the twentieth verse of the last chapter of the Revelation, we read, "He which testifieth these things saith, Surely I come quickly. Amen. Even so, come, Lord Jesus" (Rev 22:20). The song of love and the book of love end in almost the selfsame way, with a strong desire for Christ's speedy return.

ILLUSTRATION

If You Aren't Warm, You Aren't Near the Fire

Preaching Themes: Commitment, Truth

If you read the Bible, especially if you read the New Testament, and study the life of Christ, and yet you only admire it, and say to yourself, "Jesus Christ was a wonderful being," you do not know him yet; you have but a very indistinct idea of him. If, after reading that life, you sit down, and dissect it, and say to yourself, coolly, calmly, deliberately, "So far as is practicable, I will try and imitate Christ," you do not yet know him, you have not come near to the real Christ as yet. If any man should say, "I am near the fire," and yet he is not warm, I should question the truth of his words; and though he might say, "I can see the fire; I can tell you the appearance of the coals; I can describe the lambent flames that play about the stove," yet if he were not warmed at all, I should still think that he was mistaken, or that there was some medium that interposed between him and the fire at which he said he was looking.

And be thou like to a roe or to a young hart Upon the mountains of spices She cries to him to come from the place where he now is, which she calls "the mountains of spices."

Readers of Solomon's Song know that there are four mountains spoken of in the Song. The first set of mountains is mentioned in the seventeenth verse of the second chapter of the Song, where we read of *the mountains of division:* "Until the day break, and the shadows flee away, turn, my beloved, and be thou like a roe or a young hart upon the mountains of Bether" (Song 2:17), or the mountains of division, the divided crags, or the mountains that divide. This was Christ's first coming. There were mountains of division; our sins and God's justice, like great mountains, divided us.

But there were other mountains beside those, which you read of a little further on in the Song; these were *the mountains of the leopards*, the dens of the lions. Turn to the fourth chapter, at the eighth verse: "Come with me from Lebanon, my spouse, with me from Lebanon: look from the top of Amana, from the top of Shenir and Hermon, from the lions' dens, from the mountains of the leopards" (Song 4:8). Our Well-beloved came to us, over the mountains of the leopards and the dens of the lions, more than conqueror through the greatness of his love. Do you not see him as he comes from Edom, with dyed garments from Bozrah, traveling in the greatness of his strength, speaking in righteousness, mighty to save? In spite of all opposition, he finished the work of our redemption.

So Jesus came to us, over the mountains of separation, and over the mountains of the leopards. But there is a third mountain mentioned in this wonderful poetical book, and that is *the mountain of myrrh*. In the sixth chapter at the second verse, it says, "My beloved is gone down into his garden, to the beds of spices, to feed in the gardens, and to gather lilies" (Song 6:2). It is called a garden, but in the sixth verse of the fourth chapter it is called a mountain: "Until the day break, and the shadows flee away, I will get me to the mountain of myrrh, and to the hill of frankincense" (Song 4:6).

The "mountain of myrrh" is the third that is mentioned in the Song; but our text refers to "*the mountains of spices.*" I am not stretching this passage or drawing a lesson where there is none; the mountains of spices are those places where Jesus dwells at this very moment at the right hand of God. It is from there that we now call him with the spouse when she said, "Make haste, my beloved, and be thou like to a roe or to a young hart upon the mountains of spices."

What are these spices? Are they not Christ's infinite merits, which perfume heaven and earth? The foul corruption of our sins is not perceptible, because of the mountains of spices. One single sin would be vile enough to pollute a universe; what, then, were all our sins put together? Behold this wondrous sanitary power of divine grace; these mountains of spices more than nullify the foulness of our sins. Christ's merit is perpetually before the eye of his Father, so that no longer does he perceive our sins.

What shall I say next of these mountains of spices? Are they not our Lord's perpetual and prevailing prayers? He intercedes for his people before the throne of God. He is that great angel from whose swinging censer there goes up continually the incense of intercession. The prayers of saints are presented by him to his Father with all his own merit added to them. These are the mountains of spices, Christ's infinite merits, and his ceaseless prayers, his undying supplications to the great Father on behalf of all his people.

ILLUSTRATION

"Him Hath God Exalted"

Preaching Themes: Courage, Depression, Discouragement, Encouragement, Glory

Many years ago, after the Surrey Music Hall accident, I well-nigh lost my reason through distress of heart. I was broken down in spirit, and thought that, perhaps, I might never preach again. I was but a young man, and it was a great sorrow that crushed me into the dust through that terrible accident. But one passage of Scripture brought me recovery in a moment. I was alone, and as I was thinking, this text came to my mind, "Him hath God exalted with his right hand to be a Prince and a Saviour" (Acts 5:31), and I said to myself, "Is that so? Is Jesus Christ exalted? Then I do not care if I die in a ditch. If Christ is exalted to be a Prince and a Savior, that is enough for me."

I distinctly recollect remembering what is recorded of some of Napoleon's soldiers, who were well-nigh cut to pieces, lying dying, bleeding, suffering, agonizing on the battlefield. But when the Emperor rode by, every man lifted himself up as best he could, some resting on the only arm that was left, just to look at him once more, and shout, "*Vive l'Empereur*!" The Emperor had come along, he was all right, and that was enough for his faithful followers.

I think that I felt just like that; whatever happened to me, it was true of Christ, "Him hath God exalted."

APPLICATION

We Are Made to Work

Even for a perfect man unbroken leisure would not be a blessing. It is essential even to an unfallen creature that he should have work to do—fit work and honorable, seeing it is done by a creature for the great Benefactor who had created him. If we did not have our daily tasks to fulfill, rest would corrode into rust, and recreation would soon gender corruption.

You and I are set in the garden of the church because there is work for us to do which will be beneficial to others and to ourselves also. Some have to take the broad axe and hew down mighty trees of error. Others of a feebler sort can with a child's hand train the tendril of a climbing plant or drop into its place a tiny seed. One may plant and another may water. One may sow and another gather fruit. One may cut up weeds and another prune vines.

God has work in his church for us all to do, and he has left us here that we may do it. Our Lord Jesus would not keep a single saint out of heaven if there were not a reason for his being here in the lowlands, to trim these gardens of herbs and watch these beds of spices. Would he deny his well-beloved the palm branch and the crown if it were not better for us to be holding the pruning hook and the spade? A schoolbook with which to teach the little children may be for a while more to our true advantage than a golden harp. To turn over the pages of Scripture with which to instruct the people of God may be more profitable to us than to hear the song of seraphim. I say, the Master's love to his own which prompts him to pray, "I will that they also whom you have given me be with me where I am, that they may behold my glory," would long ago have drawn all the blood-bought up to himself above, had it not been the fact that it is in infinite wisdom seen to be better that they should abide in the flesh. You are the lights of the world; you are the salt of the earth (Matt 5:13, 14). Shall the light and the salt be at once withdrawn? You are to be as a dew from the Lord in this dry and thirsty land; would you be at once exhaled?

Brothers, have you found out what you have to do in these gardens? Sisters, have you found out the plants for which you are to care? If not, arouse yourselves and let not a moment pass till you have discovered your duty and your place. Speak unto him who is the Lord of all true servants, and say to him, "Show me what you would have me to do. Point out, I pray you, the place wherein I may serve you." Would you have it said of you that you were a wicked and slothful servant? Shall it be told that you dwelt in the gardens, and allowed the grass to grow up to your ankles, and suffered the thorns and the thistles to multiply until your land became as the sluggard's vineyard, pointed at as a disgrace and a warning to all that passed by? "O thou that dwellest in the gardens!" (Song 8:13). The title sets forth employment constant and engrossing.

Don't Worry About Another Person's Vineyard

There are a great many people who seem to forget that they have a vineyard of their own to keep. Or else, if they remember it, they cannot say, "My vineyard, which is mine, is before me," for they go about gazing on other people's vineyards instead of keeping their eyes fixed upon their own. They say, "Look at so-and-so's vineyard. I don't think he trims his vines in the new style." I usually notice that those persons who have such wonderful plans of their own, and who are always finding fault with other people's plans, never do anything except find fault.

I like the deacons and elders of the church, and the teachers in the Sunday school, to have no other plan than this: to do all the good they can, and to do it in the name of the Lord Jesus. When they are doing that, let other people not interfere with them, but themselves do all the good that they can. It is always well when a man has his work before him, knows what he is going to do, and then goes straight at it.

There are far too many people gadding about to see what others are doing, and to find out their plans and methods of working. Let me tell you, the best way to succeed is to have no plan but this: "Whatsoever thy hand findeth to do, do it with thy might" (Eccl 9:10).

When I see the members of a church laying down a multiplicity of rules, I know that they are getting themselves into a multiplicity of troubles. If they will but leave rules and regulations to come up when they are needed, they will find them when they want them. Let every man who has the Spirit of God within him set about the work which he is called to do. Let him attend to the portion of the vineyard which is before him, and try to get his thousand pieces of silver out of his own portion, and not out of another's. There is always a set of grumblers about who think they could preach better, and manage Sunday schools better, than anybody else. They are the people who generally do nothing at all.

I pray that this church, and every member of it, may ever be able to say, in the words of our text, "'*My* vineyard, which is *mine*, is before me.' I am not responsible for my brother, but I am responsible for myself."

Longing for the Lord's Return

We sometimes need certain incentives to stir up our souls to cry for our Lord's return. One reason that ought to make the believer long for Christ's coming is that *it will end this conflict*. Our lot is cast in a wretched time, when many things are said and done that grieve and vex God's Holy Spirit, and all who are in sympathy with him. Sometimes, it is false doctrine that is proclaimed; and if you preach the truth, they smite you on the mouth, and then you say to yourself, "Would God the Lord would come!" At other times, it is sheer blasphemy that is uttered, when men say, "The Lord delays his coming," or when they talk as if he were not Lord, as if his gospel were no gospel, and his salvation were worn out. Then we say, "Make no tarrying, O our God! Come, Lord, and tarry not!" We grow almost impatient then for his coming.

And, dear friend, when you see the oppression of the poor, when you hear the cry of the needy, when you know that many of them are ground down to bitter poverty, and yet are struggling hard to earn a bare pittance, you say, "Lord, will this state of things always exist? Shall not these wrongs be righted? Oh, that he would come, who will judge the people righteously, and vindicate the cause of the poor and the oppressed!"

Then we look even on the professing church, and we see how lukewarm it is, how honeycombed it is with heresy and worldliness, and how often the church that ought to honor Christ insults him, and he is wounded in the house of his friends. We say, "Will not this evil soon be at an end? Will not the conflict speedily be over?" Oh, how have I stood, in the midst of the battle, when the deadly shafts have flown about me on the right hand and on the left, and, wounded full sore, I have cried, "Will not the King himself soon come, and shall I not ere long hear the sound of those blessed feet, whose every step means victory, and whose presence is eternal life?" "Come, Lord! Make haste, my Beloved! Come to the rescue of thy weak and feeble servants; come, come, come, we beseech thee!" Put yourself into this great fight for the faith; and if you have to bear the brunt of the battle, you will soon be as eager as I am that Jesus should make haste, and come to your relief. You also will cry, "Make haste, my Beloved," when you think what wonders he will work at his coming.

WE PREACH CHRIST AND HIM CRUCIFIED

JONAH 1

JONAH 1:1–3

[1] Now the word of the Lord came unto Jonah the son of Amittai, saying, [2] Arise, go to Nineveh, that great city, and cry against it; for their wickedness is come up before me. [3] But Jonah rose up to flee unto Tarshish from the presence of the Lord, and went down to Joppa; and he found a ship going to Tarshish: so he paid the fare thereof, and went down into it, to go with them unto Tarshish from the presence of the Lord.

EXPOSITION

1 **Now the word of the Lord came unto Jonah the son of Amittai, saying** Observe the misconduct of the prophet Jonah. He had a plain command from the Lord, and he knew it to be a command. But he felt that the commission given to him would not be pleasant and honoring to himself, and therefore he declined to comply with it. We see, from his action, how some, who really know God, may act as if they knew him not.

2 **Arise, go to Nineveh, that great city, and cry against it; for their wickedness is come up before me** The book of Jonah should be exceedingly comfortable to those who are despairing because of the wickedness of their times. Nineveh was a city as great in its wickedness as in its power. If any of us with little faith had been told to go round about her, and "tell the towers thereof, and mark well her bulwarks" (Ps 48:12–13)—if we had been commanded to go through her streets and behold her both in the blaze of the sun and in the light of the moon as her inhabitants indulged in vice, we should have said, "Alas!

alas! The city is wholly given into idolatry, and it is wrapped about with a wall of sin, as stupendous as its wall of stone."

Suppose that the problem had been given to us to solve: How shall this city be moved to repentance? How shall its vice be forsaken, and the God of Israel worshiped by all its inhabitants from the highest to the lowest? If we had not been paralyzed with despair, which is the most probable, we should nevertheless have sat down carefully to consider our plans. We should have parceled it out into missionary districts; we should have needed at least several hundreds, if not thousands, of able ministers. At once, expenses would have to be incurred, and we should have considered ourselves bound to contemplate the erection of innumerable structures in which the word of God might be preached. Our machinery would necessarily become cumbrous; we should find that we, unless we had the full resources of an empire, could not even begin the work. But what does the Lord say concerning this? Putting aside the judgments of reason, and all the plans and schemes that flesh and blood so naturally do follow, he raises up one man.

3 **But Jonah rose up to flee unto Tarshish** Why did Jonah wish to run away? Because he did not like the Ninevites? I think that there was something of that on his mind. He was a stern old Jew, and he loved his race, and he felt no desire to see anything done for the Gentiles or for the heathen outside the Abrahamic covenant; and therefore, he had no passion for a mission to Nineveh.

Was it not, possibly, because Jonah knew that God was merciful? "Now," said he to himself, "if I have to go through Nineveh and say, 'Yet forty days, and Nineveh shall be overthrown,' and, if these people repent, it will not be overthrown. And then they will say, 'Pretty prophet, that Jonah! He is a man that cries "Wolf" when there is no wolf,' and I shall lose my reputation."

But still there was a higher and a better motive, though even that was a bad one—for anything is bad, however true and excellent in itself, that leads a man to run contrary to God's mind. It was this: He thought that the character of God himself would suffer. For if he went down to Nineveh and proclaimed, "Yet forty days, and Nineveh shall be overthrown," then the people might repent, and Jehovah would allow them to live. And then, after a while, the people would say, "Who is Jehovah? His word does not stand fast. He does not carry out his judgments. He lays his hand on the hilt of his sword, and then pushes it back into the scabbard." Thus, the Lord himself, by his mercy, would lose his name for truth and immutability. Jonah would have preferred the destruction of Nineveh to the least dishonor to the name of the Lord.

from the presence of the Lord When we read that he fled from the presence of God, we do not suppose that Jonah thought that he could get away from God as to his omnipresence, but he wanted to escape serving in the divine presence. He wished to avoid being employed by God in his special service as a prophet. He thought that the Lord might call him and send him on errands if he went to Nineveh, for Assyria had some measure of evident relationship to the Lord and his people. But if he could travel as far as Tarshish, he would be out of the world altogether, and would no more have to speak in the name of the Lord. He imagined that there could be no relationship between Tarshish and Israel, and he would not be expected to do any further prophetic work; or, if he did, he would not suffer in repute, for the report would not reach Jerusalem. If he did not want to get away from the toilsome and self-denying duty of prophecy, he did, at least, wish to avoid an expedition to the heathen of Nineveh—an expedition he foresaw would not be for his own honor.

ILLUSTRATION

Attend to the Work

Preaching Theme: Work

We must not wish to leave our post, no, not even to go to heaven. We ought not to be sighing to be gone. Employers do not like a man who is always looking for

Saturday night. Let him attend to the work of Tuesday, and Thursday, and Friday, and the week will end quite soon enough. One does not like to see a fellow standing about, stretching his arms upward, and sighing, "The week is very long; I wish it was Saturday." You like a man who means to do a fair day's work for a fair day's wage, and who does not watch until you turn your back that he may slacken his labor. We must not be crying, "Oh that I had wings like a dove!" (Ps 55:6). What should we do with them if we had them? Such heavy mortals as some of us are had better keep nearer the ground.

---

he found a ship going to Tarshish Learn from this that providence alone is not a sufficient guide for our actions. Jonah may have said, "It was very singular that there was a ship there going to Tarshish, just when I reached the port. I gather from this that God was not so very disinclined for me to go to Tarshish." Precepts, not providences, are to guide believers. When Christian men quote a providence against a precept—which is to set God against God—they act most strangely. There are devil's providences as well as divine providences, and there are tempting providences as well as assisting providences, so learn to judge between the one and the other.

When he tempted Jonah to go to Tarshish, the evil one knew that there was a ship at Joppa waiting for a fair wind to sail for Tarshish; therefore, he whispered into Jonah's ear, "Go to Tarshish," because he knew that he would not be thwarted in following out the base suggestion. Our tempter has a complete acquaintance with what is going on in the world, and therefore he can plot and scheme so that his suggestion shall be supported by events which are transpiring. He is not omniscient, but his army of spies keeps him well posted up. He can therefore fit his temptations to our surroundings.

The way of sin may well be easy, since evil men will help you that way. If anything wrong is to be done, the sons of Belial will lend a willing hand. Thus, an evil device may well succeed, since all the world pulls that way. Only set up a calf, and the tribes will haste to cry, "These be thy gods, O Israel" (Exod 32:4). Sin is soon made popular. All men will praise the evil way which yields them pleasure. In the rush along the downward road the eager crowd will carry you off your feet and bear you with them down to destruction without your needing to exert yourself, and therefore it is generally easy to go wrong. It is swimming with the stream, flying with the wind.

so he paid the fare thereof What did Jonah lose? Jonah had to pay as part of his fare *the presence and comfortable enjoyment of God's love*. He went down into the bottom of the vessel and hid himself from sight. I think I see him, that Jonah, who a few days after, having walked with all the boldness of a lion through the streets of Nineveh, crying, "Yet forty days, and Nineveh shall be overthrown!"; that Jonah, who confronted Nineveh's haughty monarch and was not afraid to tell him that in forty days his city would be overthrown; that Jonah goes sneaking down among the goods at the bottom of the hold, for fear anybody should see him, and there hides his coward, craven head. Poor Jonah, you have lost the hallowed fellowship of your God, you have lost his presence, and consequently your courage has all oozed out of you; this is a dear price that you have paid for shunning Nineveh.

In the next place, Jonah *lost all peace of mind*. When he was in Nineveh, crying, "Yet forty days, and Nineveh shall be overthrown" (Jonah 3:4), he was not afraid of the edge of the sword, nor of the tyrant's rage. He felt that he was doing God's work, and he knew that when on God's errands he was perfectly safe. His heart beat gently, like that of a man in a happy, tranquil frame of mind, wearing the herb called heart's-ease in his bosom. But now, down there, in the hold of the vessel, his heart is palpitating, he does not know what may happen, and until sleep happily comes in to ease the distress of his mind, he is like a poor hunted stag, panting with alarm.

These were two great things to lose—God's presence, and his own peace of mind—but these were not all his damage and injury. He was now *brought into great peril*—he must be thrown into the sea. In all likelihood he will meet with a watery grave. Had he gone to Nineveh, that would not have occurred. He would have been under the care of God's special providence there, but now the winds and waves threaten him.

ILLUSTRATION

We All Must Pay the Fare

Preaching Themes: Creation, Death and Dying, Weakness

As a general rule, wherever we go, whatever we do, we must "pay the fare thereof." Expenditure is connected with every act, work, and operation. The sun does not constantly flood this world, and all its sister spheres, with light and heat without some kind of consumption within itself, nor does the earth yield her fruits of harvest except at the cost of the matter of which it is composed. By the force of wind and frost, the very "mountain falling cometh to nought, and the rock is removed out of his place" (Job 14:18). The rivers do not reach the sea without wearing away their banks and cutting channels in the earth through which their floods may flow. The raindrops, the generous gifts of heaven, have first been loaned from the treasury of the great deep; the air itself is constantly in process of consumption, and if it were not that a fresh supply is daily being produced, even the atmosphere would become exhausted. All the processes of nature involve a constant expenditure of power. Ponderous as is the engine of creation, and little as it shows the fretting power of age, it is certain that in the whole of its machinery, from its most stupendous wheel down to its smallest valve, it is daily and necessarily experiencing an appointed amount of wear and tear.

It is assuredly so with regard to the lesser world of man. The body cannot move a limb or contract a muscle without expense. The lifting of my hand, the pointing of my finger, the motion of my tongue, the stirring of my brain in thought, all cost something, and make a draft on the inner store of strength. You cannot so much as gaze on the world around you without some wear of that marvelous optical instrument by which outward sights are brought to the inward mind. Friction operates on flesh, and bone, and sinew, and a higher friction acts on mind, and intellect, and passion, for even these grow weak with strain and age.

APPLICATION

We Cannot Avoid Duty Without Expense

Jonah's duty was to go to Nineveh and preach the word. He preferred not to go; he therefore shirked the work, went down to Joppa and paid his fare to go to Tarshish. I hope we are not in the habit of doing the same, but yet there are occasions when even God's servants shrink from duty, and seem willing to forget that where God calls, they are bound to go.

Possibly this remark may apply to some minister who may come under the word. He is called to bear his protest against a certain sin, and he thinks to himself, "If I so speak, some of those who hear me will never come again. I may lose rich subscribers. I will not say a word on that point." Or he has it laid on him to cry against the monstrous evils in the state church, but he puts his finger to his lips and remains silent, inwardly calculating, "I had better hold my peace on that subject, for I may risk my popularity." Such a minister should reflect that it is a very expensive thing to try to fly to Tarshish when you ought to go to Nineveh, for a man cannot avoid duty without expense.

I have known good people who will say, "I know so-and-so is what I ought to do, but still you see the path is very difficult, and I do not feel called upon to make so great a sacrifice." Well, friend, if you do not make the sacrifice when God demands it of you, he has other ways of taking away your treasured goods. In the long run you will find it far more expensive to shun the work and will of God than at once to give yourself to it. You will be a loser by your prudence; you shall find that the scriptural rule holds good, "He that would lose his life shall save it, but he that would save his life shall lose it" (Matt 16:25). If you are willing to be a loser for Christ you shall be a gainer, but if you insist upon being held harmless, and try at all hazards to make provision for the flesh, then you shall find that before long you will have to pay the fare thereof to your own grievous hurt and injury.

Those Like Nineveh

Let each man among us look to his life, and who is there here that need not blush? Some of us have been moral. We have by the training of our youth and by the restraints of grace been kept from the immoralities of others, but even we are compelled to lay our mouths in the dust. While looking into our heart, we discover it to be a nest of unclean birds, full of all manner of evil and loathsome things. We have been as vicious in our hearts as the worst of men have been in their acts.

But there are too many who cannot even plead that they have been moral, though this would be but a poor excuse for the lack of love to God. Look to your lives. Who among us has been free from murmuring against God? Who is it that has loved his neighbor as himself? Who is it that has never been angry without a cause? Who has never cursed God in his heart, even if he has not done so with his lips? Who among us have always scrupulously kept our eye from lust and our heart from covetousness? Have we not all sinned? If our iniquities could now be revealed; if on every man's brow were written his sin, which of you would not put his hand upon his forehead to hide his iniquity from his fellows? It will be of essential service to many of you if you will read over your lives. Turn, I beseech you, to the of your memory, and let the black, blotted, misspelled now be read again.

Do not think that the preacher understands how to flatter his congregation. It has become fashionable in these times to look upon our hearers as all being good and excellent; would not this be a lie and a falsehood before Almighty God? Are there not here those that can indulge secretly in vices which we must not mention? Are there not those who do that to their fellows in trade which they would despise in others? What! Are none of you covetous? Do none of you overreach or defraud your neighbors? Do none of you practice the common frauds and tricks in trade? Are none of you liars, and none deceivers, none slanderers who bear false witness against your neighbors? Am I so happy as to have a spotless congregation here? I cannot flatter myself that such can be the truth.

No, our iniquities are great, and our sins are hideous. Oh, that we were all ready to confess, each man for himself, the iniquities which we have done! Surely, if the Spirit of God shall but shine into our hearts, and show us the evil of our ways, we shall find ourselves in a sorrowful condition indeed, and shall be ready to cry out before God, even as Nineveh did of old.

JONAH 1:4–7

4 But the LORD sent out a great wind into the sea, and there was a
mighty tempest in the sea, so that the ship was like to be broken.
5 Then the mariners were afraid, and cried every man unto his god,
and cast forth the wares that were in the ship into the sea, to light-
en it of them. But Jonah was gone down into the sides of the ship;
and he lay, and was fast asleep. 6 So the shipmaster came to him,
and said unto him, What meanest thou, O sleeper? arise, call upon
thy God, if so be that God will think upon us, that we perish not.
7 And they said every one to his fellow, Come, and let us cast
lots, that we may know for whose cause this evil is upon us. So
they cast lots, and the lot fell upon Jonah.

EXPOSITION

4 **But the LORD sent out a great wind into the sea, and there was a mighty tempest in the sea, so that the ship was like to be broken** Learn from this that "Omnipotence has servants everywhere."[1] The Lord is never short of sheriff's officers to arrest his fugitives, and on that occasion he "sent out a great wind into the sea." "The wind bloweth where it listeth" (John 3:8). That is true, but it is also true that the wind bloweth where God listeth, and he knew how to send that great wind to that particular ship. No doubt many ships were on the Mediterranean at that time, but possibly unto none of them was the storm sent except unto the one which carried Jonah, the son of Amittai. We say, "Every bullet has its billet," and this great wind was sent to pursue the fugitive prophet.

1. A quotation from Thomas T. Lynch's hymn "Say Not My Soul." —ed.

ILLUSTRATION

The Little Diamond

Preaching Themes: Providence of God, Salvation

The great wheels of providence are continually revolving in fulfillment of God's purposes concerning his own people. For them, winds blow and tempests rise. It is a wonderful thing that the whole machinery of nature should be made subservient to the divine purpose of the salvation of his redeemed.

I was in a diamond-cutting factory at Amsterdam, and I noticed that there were huge wheels revolving, and a great deal of power being developed and expended. But when I came to look at the little diamond—in some cases a very small one indeed—upon which that power was being brought to bear, it seemed very remarkable that all that power should be concentrated upon such a little yet very precious object. In a similar style, all the wheels of providence and nature, great as they are, are brought to bear, by divine skill and love, upon a thing which appears to many people to be of trifling value, but which is to Christ of priceless worth—namely, a human soul.

5 **Then the mariners were afraid, and cried every man unto his god** If there is ever a special time for prayer, it is a time of need. Nature seems then to compel men to utter prayer of such a sort as it is, for it is but nature's prayer at the best.

and cast forth the wares that were in the ship into the sea, to lighten it of them Life is precious, and a man will give up everything else in order to save it. Satan spoke the truth when he said, "Skin for skin, yea, all that a man hath, will he give for his life" (Job 2:4). From the action of these mariners, we may learn that sometimes we may lighten our ship for the safety of our souls. When we have less to carry, probably we shall sail more safely. Losses and crosses may turn out to be our greatest gains. Let the ill-gotten ingots go to the bottom of the sea; and lo, the ship rights herself at once!

ILLUSTRATION

Death in the Body

Preaching Themes: Death and Dying, Evangelism

We are told by anatomists that there is no part of the body which is dead. Even the teeth and bones are alive. Life abhors alliance with death; and if a dead substance once gets into the body, all the efforts of nature are directed to the one point where the foreign body is found, to drive it out. Often ulcers and running sores, and such like things, are but the effects of nature seeking to expel the dead substance from the body.

Now, there is nothing in Christ's real church that is dead. If ever dead substances get into the church, they will not lie there still and quiet, but the church shall be aware of it in her every nerve and pore, and she shall soon begin to exert her strength and vitality to expel the foreign substance from her living body. Would that this energy could be spared for other works, for the saving of souls for Jesus!

But Jonah was gone down into the sides of the ship Here is this common-looking Jew—Jonah, named, according to the general rule that names go by contraries, "a dove," for, at any rate, on this occasion he looked more like the raven that would not come back to the ark. And for this one man—this altogether unamiable prophet—the sea must be tossed in tempest, and a whole ship full of people must have their lives put in jeopardy.

This truth is a very far-reaching one. You cannot well exaggerate it. The vast universe is but a platform for the display of God's grace, and all material things that now exist will be set aside when the great drama of grace is completed. The material universe is but scaffolding for the church of Christ. It is but the temporary structure upon which the wonderful mystery of redeeming love is being carried on to perfection. See, then, that, as the great wind was raised to follow Jonah, and to lead to his return to the path of duty, so all things work together for the good of God's people, and all things that exist are being bowed and bent toward God's one solemn eternal purpose—the salvation of his own.

and he lay, and was fast asleep Why was Jonah asleep? I suppose that it was partly the reaction after the excitement through which his mind had passed in rebelling against God. He had wearied himself with seeking his own evil way; so now, after the disobedience to God of which he had been guilty, his spirit sinks, and he sleeps. Besides, it is according to the nature of sin to give, not physical sleep, I grant you, but to give spiritual slumber. There is no opiate like the commission of an evil deed. A man who has done wrong is so much less able to repent of the wrong, so much the less likely to do so. Jonah's conscience had become hardened by his willful rejection of his Lord's commands, and therefore he could sleep when he ought to have been aroused and alarmed.

Besides, he wished to get rid of the very thought of God. He was trying to flee from God's presence. I suppose he could not bear his own thoughts; they must have been dreadful to him. So, being in a pet against his God, and altogether in a wrong spirit, he hunts about for a snug corner of the ship, stretches himself out, and there falls asleep, and sleeps on right through the storm.

Out of the whole company on board that ship, Jonah was the only man who knew how to pray to the one living and true God. All the mariners "cried every man unto his god." But those were idle prayers because they were offered to idols; they could not prevail because they were presented to dumb, dead deities. But here was a man who could pray—and who could pray aright, too—yet he was asleep.

6 **So the shipmaster came to him, and said unto him** It is hard when sinners have to rebuke saints, and when an uncircumcised Gentile can address a prophet of God in language like this.

ILLUSTRATION

Running from a Methodist Minister

Preaching Theme: Conversion, Providence of God

I have heard of one in the backwoods of America who was unloading his furniture, and while doing so up rode a Methodist minister. "Confound you," said he, "I have moved half-a-dozen times to get away from you Methodist fellows; I am never comfortable where you are. I will put the things on the cart again and find a spot where I shall be free from you." On they went to another clearing, but when they reached it the first thing that happened, before the man took up his lodging, was the appearance of a Methodist minister. "Where shall I go to get away from you Methodist preachers?" "There is nowhere I know of," said the minister, "that you can go, for I am afraid if you go to hell you will find some of them there, for preachers have been lost. The very best thing you can do is to yield at once, and let me hold a service tonight in your camp."

That was sound advice, and so some of you will be pestered and worried as long as you live if you will not come to Christ. Omnipotence has servants everywhere, and these are all charged to warn you of your peril.

What meanest thou, O sleeper? arise, call upon thy God, if so be that God will think upon us, that we perish not Of all the men in the ship, Jonah was the person who ought most to have been awake; but nevertheless, he was not only asleep, but *fast* asleep. All the creaking of the cordage, the dashing of the waves, the howling of the winds, the straining of the timbers, and the shouting of the mariners did not arouse him; he was fast locked in the arms of sleep.

See here, in Jonah's heavy slumber, the effect of sin. No noxious drug can give such deadly sleep as sin. The body never knows so dread a sleep when under the influence of opiates as the soul does when sin has cast it into a slumber. If men could be awake to the evils, to the danger, to the desperate punishment of sin, sin would not be half so deadly as it is; but when it puts its sweet cup of nightshade to the lip, that cup soon blinds the eye and "steeps the senses in forgetfulness," and man does not know what or where he is.

Nor is sin the only cradle in which evil rocks the soul. The world too, casts men into slumber. I do not know that Jonah ever slept so soundly anywhere as when he had gotten into the midst of busy mariners who were going to Tarshish. It is comparatively easy for us to keep awake in the midst of God's church; it is easy for us to maintain our steadfastness and integrity when we meet with those who rejoice in his name. But the world is an enchanted ground, and happy is that Christian who is able to survive the deadening influence of business, the soporific influence which creeps over the minds of men whose merchandise increases, whose houses are filled with the riches of nations. What downy pillows does the world sew to all armholes! What beds of ease she spreads for those whom she entraps!

See also the slumbering effects of the flesh. It was to spare himself a little toil, it was to avoid personal dishonor, that Jonah fled. Pleasures and comforts, if sought as ends, are desperate drains upon the vigor of the spirit. When the body is indulged, then the soul lies cleaving to the dust. It is not possible for us to pamper the flesh without at the same time starving the soul. If we sacrifice unto our own lusts, we are quite certain to get the sacrifices by robbing God's altar. The body shall not have pleasure in sin, except the soul shall soon be in a state of misery and decay.

See also, in our text, one of the devices of Satan. He seeks to lull God's prophets into slumber, for he knows that dumb dogs that are given to sleep will never do any very great injury to his cause. The wakeful watchman he always fears, for then he cannot take the city by surprise; but if he can cast God's watchman into slumber, then he is well content, and thinks it almost as well to have a Christian asleep as to have him dead. He would certainly sooner see him in hell, but next to that he is most glad to see him rocked in the cradle of presumption, fast asleep.

7 **And they said every one to his fellow, Come, and let us cast lots, that we may know for whose cause this evil is upon us. So they cast lots, and the lot fell upon Jonah** We do not commend the action of these men in casting lots, but we admire the providence by which "the lot fell upon Jonah." Solomon says, "The lot is cast into the lap" (Prov 16:33), but he did not say that it was right that lots should be cast into the lap; and he very properly added, "but the whole disposing thereof is of the Lord."

APPLICATION

The Responsibility of the Church

Let us remember that, as Jonah was the only man in the ship whose prayer could be of any avail, so *the children of God are the only ones who can do any real spiritual service to the perishing world.* All the cries of the shipmaster and his crew were addressed to the gods of their various countries, who had ears which could not hear, and hands which could afford no aid. Jonah was the only man who worshiped the Lord that made the sea and the dry land; hence, his prayers alone could save the ship.

Now, the salvation of the world under God lies with the *church.* Christ has finished the atonement; it is for the church to finish the ingathering. Christ has paid the purchase price and completed redemption by blood. It is for the church to seek the Holy Spirit, and fully to redeem the world by power. Suppose, then, that you who fear God say, "This is no case of mine; I am not my brother's keeper." Suppose that you waste opportunities, and throw precious time to the dogs, then the world must go down to its awful doom; but, mark you, its blood shall be upon your skirts. This generation, under God, must have salvation given to it through our ministry, through our evangelists, through our Sunday schools, through our missionaries, through our preaching and teaching; and if we do it not, the world will not stay from perishing while we are staying from laboring.

Jonah worshiped no false god; he worshiped only the living and true God. He was a professed and avowed believer in Jehovah. He was not ashamed to say—even when his conduct had laid him open to blame, and when there was nobody to support him—"I am a Hebrew; and I fear the Lord, the God of heaven, which hath made the sea and the dry land." Yet, though he was a believer in God, he was in the sides of the ship, fast asleep.

O Christian man—a real Christian man, too—if you are in a similar condition, how is it that you can be slumbering under such circumstances? Should not the privileges and the honor, which your being a believer has brought to you by divine grace, forbid that you should be a slumberer, inactive, careless, indifferent? I may be addressing dozens of Jonahs, those who are really God's people, but who are not acting as if they were chosen of the Most High but are forgetful of their election, their redemption, their sanctification, the life they have begun to live here below, and the eternal glory that awaits them hereafter.

Do Not Delay!

If you are out of Christ, do not pretend to be happy! Do not accept any happiness till you find it in him. To some of you, I would speak very pointedly. Are you sick? Do you feel that your life is very precarious? You are like Jonah when the ship was like to be broken. Do not delay. Has some relative been taken away, and does there seem some likelihood that you may have the same disease? Oh, do not sleep, but awake! Are you getting old? Are the gray hairs getting thick around your brow? Oh, do not delay! For unsaved young people, it is wrong to sleep, for he that sleeps when he is young sleeps during a siege. But he that slumbers when he is old sleeps during the attack, when the enemy is actually at the breach and storming the walls. Do any of you work in dangerous trades? Do you have to earn your bread where an accident might easily happen, as it has often happened to others? Oh, be prepared to meet your God!

But, having begun this list, I might continue it almost indefinitely; but I will end it in a sentence or so. *Are you a mortal man? Can* you die? *Will* you die? May you die *now?* May you drop dead in the street? May you go to sleep and never wake up again on earth? May your very food or drink become the vehicle of death to you? May there be death in the air you breathe? May it be so? Will you one day, at any rate, have to be carried to your long home, like others, and lie asleep in the grave? Will you give account to God for the things done in the body? Will you have to stand before the great white throne, to make one of that innumerable throng, and to be there put into the balance to be weighed for eternity? If so, do not sleep, I beseech you, as do others; but bestir yourself. May God's Holy Spirit bestir you to make your calling and election sure! Lay hold on Jesus Christ with the grip of an earnest, humble faith, and surrender yourself, henceforth, to the service of him who has bought you with his precious blood. God grant to all of us the grace to awake, and arise, that Christ may give us life and light, for his dear name's sake!

JONAH 1:8–17

8 Then said they unto him, Tell us, we pray thee, for whose cause
this evil is upon us; What is thine occupation? and whence comest
thou? what is thy country? and of what people art thou? 9 And he
said unto them, I am an Hebrew; and I fear the LORD, the God of
heaven, which hath made the sea and the dry land. 10 Then were
the men exceedingly afraid, and said unto him, Why hast thou
done this? For the men knew that he fled from the presence of
the LORD, because he had told them. 11 Then said they unto him,
What shall we do unto thee, that the sea may be calm unto us?
for the sea wrought, and was tempestuous. 12 And he said unto
them, Take me up, and cast me forth into the sea; so shall the sea
be calm unto you: for I know that for my sake this great tempest
is upon you. 13 Nevertheless the men rowed hard to bring it to the
land; but they could not: for the sea wrought, and was tempestuous against them. 14 Wherefore they cried unto the LORD, and
said, We beseech thee, O LORD, we beseech thee, let us not perish
for this man's life, and lay not upon us innocent blood: for thou,
O LORD, hast done as it pleased thee. 15 So they took up Jonah, and
cast him forth into the sea: and the sea ceased from her raging.
16 Then the men feared the LORD exceedingly, and offered a sacrifice unto the LORD, and made vows.

17 Now the LORD had prepared a great fish to swallow up Jonah.
And Jonah was in the belly of the fish three days and three nights.

EXPOSITION

8 **Then said they unto him, Tell us, we pray thee, for whose cause this evil is upon us; What is thine occupation? and whence comest thou? what is thy country? and of what people art thou?** I do not know whether these men had traded

with those who then lived in these islands, but they had a very English custom of not judging a man before they had heard him speak. It would be well if we all practiced it more—so that, before we condemn men, we were willing to hear their side of the question. Considering that there was such a storm raging, the questions put to Jonah were remarkably calm. They were very comprehensive and went to the very root of the matter.

9 **And he said unto them, I am a Hebrew** That let them know whence he came, and what his country was.

and I fear the LORD, the God of heaven, which hath made the sea and the dry land That, I suppose, must be regarded as his occupation. What a blessed occupation it is—to be occupied with the fear of the Lord! So you see that, though Jonah was not properly following his occupation while he was on board that ship, yet he did not hesitate to avow, "I am a Hebrew; and I fear the LORD, the God of heaven, which hath made the sea and the dry land." The child of God, even when he gets where he ought not to be, if you test him and try him, will stand to his colors. He will confess that he is, after all, a servant of the living God.

10 **Then were the men exceedingly afraid, and said unto him, Why hast thou done this?** Jonah had to go through this catechism, question after question, and this was the hardest of them all: "Why hast thou done this?" Could you, dear friend, submit every action of your life to this test? "Why hast thou done this?" I am afraid that there are some actions which we have performed for which we could not give a reason, or the reasons for which we should not like to give to our fellow men, much less to our God.

For the men knew that he fled from the presence of the LORD, because he had told them His Master had said to him, "Jonah, go to Nineveh," but Jonah was a strong-willed, headstrong fellow. Though a true servant of God and a prophet, yet he fled from the presence of the Lord. To Nineveh, he resolved within himself, he would not go. He could foresee no honor to himself out of the journey, no increase of his own reputation, no deference that would come to him among those proud Assyrians, so, in direct defiance of the divine command, he set off to Joppa, to take a ship and to flee from God's presence. Into the ship he got, paid the fare, and went sailing down the sea to go to Tarshish; but all this while he never thought of God.

11 **Then said they unto him, What shall we do unto thee, that the sea may be calm unto us?** Here is another question; the catechism is not yet finished, and this is one of the most difficult of all.

12 **And he said unto them, Take me up, and cast me forth into the sea; so shall the sea be calm unto you** Notwithstanding all his faults, Jonah was an eminent type of Christ. We know that from our Lord's own words, for he was as long in the belly of the whale as Christ was in the heart of the earth.

13 **Nevertheless the men rowed hard to bring it to the land** These mariners manifested most commendable humanity. They were not willing, even though it were to preserve their own lives, to cast overboard an innocent man; therefore they first used their best endeavors; and when these failed they made a solemn appeal to God, entreating him not to lay upon them innocent blood: and then, since necessity has no law, Jonah as a last resource was given up to the boisterous element, but not until every effort had been made to save him.

We should be very careful of human life, doing nothing which even indirectly may destroy or injure it. And if we should be jealous over life, how much more anxious should we be concerning men's souls! And how watchful lest we should do anything by which the least of the human family may have his eternal interests endangered by our example or teaching! God give us, like these mariners, to row hard that, if possible, we may bring the ship to land, laboring that none around us may be left to perish.

but they could not: for the sea wrought, and was tempestuous against them Their safety lay in the sacrifice, not in the labor. They rowed hard to bring the ship to land, but their efforts were of no avail. If they would cast Jonah overboard, then they would be safe.

ILLUSTRATION

Mining for Coal Where There Is None

Preaching Themes: Good Works, Justification

Some years ago, certain persons engaged in a speculation to sink a coal mine in a part of England where coal was never found. Prospectuses were issued, directors obtained, and shareholders duped; and the workmen began to sink their shaft. Now it was absolutely certain—any geologist could have told them so—that they would not find coal, let them dig to doomsday.

Suppose you and I had gone there and seen them digging, and had laughed at them, or told them it was all of no avail, wiseacres might have replied, "You ought not to discourage coal mining. You ought not to discourage men who are working so very hard." I would say, "I would not discourage coal mining in any place where there is coal to be had. But for these poor souls to throw away their sweat and their money for that which is not coal, I *will* discourage them in that insane enterprise, and think I do them good service." When we see men struggling after eternal life through their own efforts, we know eternal life is not to be had there.

---

14 **Wherefore they cried unto the Lord, and said, We beseech thee, O Lord, we beseech thee, let us not perish for this man's life, and lay not upon us innocent blood: for thou, O Lord, hast done as it pleased thee** If ever you have to cast a brother out of the church—if ever you have to relinquish the friendship of any man—do it as these men did with Jonah;

patiently, and carefully. Investigate the matter, and do not act until you are driven to it after consulting the Lord.

15 **So they took up Jonah and cast him forth into the sea: and the sea ceased from her raging** Here is Jonah; leave out the fact that he was sinful, and he becomes an eminent type of Christ. "Take me up and cast me into the sea, and the sea shall become calm under me." Substitution saves the mariners: substitution saves sinners. This is the essential oil of gospel truth. Jesus Christ saith to his people, "I am cast into the sea; there in that depth I sleep for a while, like Jonah, to rise again on the third day: but my being cast into the sea makes a deep calm to you." How very simple this process was. They take Jonah—he himself desires it—he is thrown overboard, and the deeps swallow him up. Ah, poor Jonah, what a fall! what a terrible descent! what a frightful end to his prophetical career! Down he goes. Did not I see huge jaws opening amid the billows? Was he not devoured by some terrible monster? Poor fellow, he must have our pity! But how strange it is! Why, the wind has ceased—it has dropped dead! And the waves seem to be playing now where they were battling fiercely a moment ago! No, the sea is glassy; we do not need the oars any longer; up with the sails, we shall soon be safe in port. An odd thing this, the drowning of one becomes the safety of all; mariners, let us sacrifice to Jonah's God.

It is a strange and marvelous thing! It is that which sets angels singing and makes the redeemed spirits wonder on forever, that Jesus came down into this ship of our common humanity to deliver it from tempest. The vessel had been tossed about on all sides by the waves of divine wrath. Men had been tugging and toiling at the oar; year after year philosopher and teacher had been seeking to establish peace with God; victims had been offered and rivers of blood had flowed, and even the firstborn of man's body had been offered up; but the deep was still tempestuous. But Jesus came, and they took him and cast him overboard. Out of the city they dragged him: "Away with him, away with him, it is not fit that he should live." Out of all comfort they had cast him long ago: now from society they cast him too. From pity they cast him; from all sympathy they cast him; and at last, from life itself they hurl him, while God stands there to help them to cast him into a sea of woes. As he, Jesus, dies, there is a calm. Deep was the peace which fell upon the earth that dreadful day, and joyous is that calm which yet shall come as the result of the casting out of that representative man who suffered the just for the unjust to bring us to God.

16 **Then the men feared the Lord exceedingly, and offered a sacrifice unto the Lord, and made vows** Jonah had been the means of causing a greater change than he expected. His conduct and punishment had been a warning to those thoughtless sailors. They could not but believe in the God who had thus followed up his fugitive servant.

17 **Now the Lord had prepared a great fish** He prepared a storm, he prepared a fish, and we afterwards read that he prepared a gourd, and he prepared a worm. In the great things of life, and in the little things, God is ever present. The swimming of a great fish in the sea is, surely, not a thing that is subject to law. If ever there is free agency in this world, it must certainly be in the wanderings of such a huge creature that follows its own instincts and ploughs its way through the great wastes of the wide and open sea. Yes, that is true, yet there is a divine predestination concerning all its movements. Over every motion of the fin of every minnow predestination presides. There is no distinction of little or great in God's sight; he that wings an angel guides a sparrow.

to swallow up Jonah I do not suppose there was ever any other fish of the sort. Naturalists cannot find such a whale, they say, nor need they look for it, for the Scripture says, "The Lord prepared a fish." He knew how to make it to hold Jonah exactly, and the fish accommodated its passenger, and brought him right enough to shore. Providence makes special preparation for every tried saint. If you are God's servant, and are called to very peculiar trial, some singular providence, the like of which you have never read of, shall certainly happen to you to illustrate in your case the divine goodness and faithfulness. Oh, if we had more faith!

And Jonah was in the belly of the fish three days and three nights So round about the truant prophet was the preventing grace of Jehovah.

APPLICATION

Struggling to Obtain Eternal Life

Our Savior selected Jonah as one of his peculiar types: "There shall no sign be given," said he, "to the men of this generation but the sign of the prophet Jonas" (Matt 16:4). We believe, therefore, that we are not erring if we translate the details of the history of Jonah into spiritual illustrations of man's experience and action with regard to Christ and his gospel. We have before us a picture of what most men do before they will resort to God's remedy; that remedy is here most fairly imaged in the deliverance of the whole ship's company by the sacrifice of one on their behalf.

Sinners, when they are tossed upon the sea of conviction, make desperate efforts to save themselves. The men rowed hard to bring the ship to land. The Hebrew is they "digged" hard, sending the oars deep into the water with much exertion and small success. The tempest so tossed the sea about that they could not row in good and orderly manner. But they desperately tugged at the oars, which the towering waves rendered useless by too deep a digging. Straining every sinew, they laboured by violence to get the ship in safety to the haven.

No word in any language can express the violence of earnest action with which awakened sinners strive and struggle to obtain eternal life. Truly, if the kingdom of God were in the power of him who wills and him who runs, they would possess it at once. Since they struggle, however, in an unlawful manner, the crown of victory will never be awarded them; they may kindle the fire and rejoice in its sparks, but thus saith the Lord: "This shall ye have of mine hand; Ye shall lie down in sorrow" (Isa 50:11).

God Has Prepared a Storm

You may have found, dear friend, that God has prepared a storm in your life. There was a tempest which checked you in your career of sin. You had determined to go to destruction, and you had "paid the fare thereof," but there came a great trial, something or other that stopped your ship, and threatened utterly to swallow it up. After that, there came delivering mercy; you who were cast into the sea were, nevertheless, not lost but saved. What you judged to be your destruction turned out to be for your salvation, for God had from of old prepared the means of saving you, and he sent you such a deliverance that you were compelled to say with Jonah, "Salvation is of the Lord." Since that time, I should not wonder if you have seen the hand of God in many very singular ways, possibly in much the same form as Jonah did, not literally, but spiritually. Especially if you have erred as Jonah did, if you have fallen into ill-humors as he did, you have probably had to bear the same kind of discipline and chastisement.

Self-Sacrifice

There is nothing for me to do to complete my salvation. It is all done. There is not one jot or tittle left to complete the covenant of my salvation; the covenant of effectual grace is all written out in the fair handwriting of my Savior with a pen dipped in his own blood, and it guarantees all spiritual blessings to me forever. The edifice has been built, and there is not needed a beam or a brick, or even a nail or a tin-tack to complete it. From its foundation to its top stone it is all of grace, and all perfect. My garment of salvation has been woven from the top throughout; there is not a rag of thread or stitch of mine needed to complete it. "It is finished," said the Savior, as he dipped it for the last time in the glorious carmine of his own blood, and made a rich royal robe for his people to wear forever. If there were one stone to be put to the walls of our salvation, one single trowel full of mortar to make the stones set firmly, it would be all undone, all in ruin. But the whole of it has been completed. Stone and mortar, from basement to summit, all has been completed by sovereign grace.

And what shall you and I do? Since Jesus has been cast overboard for us, let us now rest in perfect quiet; let us enjoy the peace "that passeth all understanding, which shall keep our hearts and minds through Christ Jesus" (Phil 4:7). And then, having been saved in such a way as this, let us now go to our work for God. Not to win life, not to win heaven—life and heaven are ours already—but loved by him, let us now love him with a perfect heart. The man who has not attained to rest in Jesus is incapable of virtue. A man who does anything for his own salvation acts from a selfish motive, does everything for himself, and has no virtue in him. But the man who is saved, who knows there is nothing for him to do, either to put himself into salvation or to keep himself in it, knowing that all is now finished, having no need to do anything for self, he does everything for God, and is holy in heart and life.

JONAH 2

JONAH
2:1–5

[1] Then Jonah prayed unto the LORD his God out of the fish's belly,
[2] And said,

I cried by reason of mine affliction unto the LORD, and he heard me;
Out of the belly of hell cried I, and thou heardest my voice.
[3] For thou hadst cast me into the deep, in the midst of the seas;
And the floods compassed me about:
All thy billows and thy waves passed over me.
[4] Then I said, I am cast out of thy sight;
Yet I will look again toward thy holy temple.
[5] The waters compassed me about, even to the soul:
The depth closed me round about,
The weeds were wrapped about my head.

EXPOSITION

1 **Then Jonah prayed** Jonah had not prayed when he went down to Joppa. He had taken the management of himself into his own hands and referred nothing to God as to that rash voyage. How could he pray in such a temper? He paid his fare to go to Tarshish; he did not pray God's blessing on that expenditure, I am quite sure. When the sea began to work, and was tempestuous, he was in the sides of the ship, but he did not pray; no, he went to sleep. His conscience had become stupid and seared as with a hot iron; there was no prayer in him, but a certain numbness of mind and lethargy of heart. And now he gets into the fish's belly, a very close, dead place, where one would think he would lie in a state of

coma, or in a sort of fainting fit, if it were possible for him to live at all; yet there he begins to pray.

Some of those who have least time for prayer pray most, and those who have most opportunity and everything congenial are too often found to be most slack in their petitions. Jonah's oratory was narrow, and this pressed the prayer out of him. He did not pray in the sides of the ship, where he had room enough and to spare, but he prayed where he could not get upon his knees or hear his own voice. Laid out in his living coffin, he began his pleadings. One would think it hard to make the belly of hell the gate of heaven, but Jonah did so. He prays, and one of the surest evidences of a living faith is prayer.

unto the Lord his God out of the fish's belly What a strange place for prayer! Surely this is the only prayer that ever went up to God out of a fish's belly. Jonah found himself alive—that was the surprising thing, that he was alive in the belly of a fish—and because he was alive, he began to pray. It is such a wonder that some people here should continue to live that they ought to begin to pray. If you live with death so near, and in so great peril, and yet you do not pray, what is to become of you?

This prayer of Jonah is very remarkable because it is not a prayer at all, in the sense in which we usually apply the word to petition and supplication. If you read the prayer through, you will see that it is almost all thanksgiving; and the best prayer in all the world is a prayer that is full of thankfulness. We praise the Lord for what he has done for us, and thus we do, in effect, ask him to perfect the work which he has begun. He has delivered us; so we bless his holy name, and by implication we beseech him still to deliver us.

Notice that it says here, "Then Jonah prayed *unto the Lord his God*." There is a mint of meaning here! If you go upstairs and pray to God as everybody's God, you have done what every Jack, Tom, and Harry may do. But to go to your closet and cry to the Lord as your own God is what none but an heir of grace can do. Oh to cry, "My Father and my Friend! My God in covenant, my God to whom I have spoken years ago, and from whom I have heard full many a time: You whom I love; you who love me, Jehovah, my God." This laying hold upon God as our own God is a business the outer-court worshiper knows nothing of. Have some of you got a God at all? "Oh," you say, "I know there is a God." Yes, I know there is a bank, but that does not make me rich. What is your God to me? I want to say "my God," or I cannot be happy. Have you a God to yourself, all to yourself; for if it be so, you will pray the prayer of faith when you draw near to him, and this will prove that whatever your condition may be, you are not cast out from the sight of the Most High.

2 **And said, I cried by reason of mine affliction unto the LORD** There is one thing about Jonah I want you particularly to notice: that as his faith made him pray, and made him pray to the Lord his God, *his faith made him deal familiarly with holy Scripture*. He had but a small Bible compared with ours, but he had laid much of it up in his memory. Evidently, he loved the book of Psalms, for his prayer is full of David's expressions. Kindly look at Jonah's prayer. I think I am right in saying that there are no less than seven extracts from the Psalms in that prayer and its preface. It was Jonah's own prayer, and no man compiled it for him, for he was far away from the haunts of men, yet his heart led him to his former readings, and his memory came to his aid with expressions most suitable, and forcible, borrowed from a former much tried servant of the Lord.

A deep experience is bound to resort to Scripture for its expression. Human compositions suffice for surface work, but when all God's waves and billows have gone over us, we quote a psalm. When our soul faints within us, we are not to be revived by human songs, but we turn to the grave sweet melodies of inspiration.

and he heard me You see that this is not praying, it is telling the Lord what he had done for his disobedient servant. Jonah had prayed, and the Lord had heard him, yet he was still in the fish's belly. Unbelief would have said, "You have lived so long,

Jonah; but you cannot expect to live to get out of this dreary, damp, fetid prison." Ah, but faith is out of prison even while she is in it. Faith begins to tell what God has done before the great work is actually accomplished.

Out of the belly of hell cried I, and thou heardest my voice He was like a man in the unseen world among the dead. He felt that he was condemned and cast away; yet God had heard him, and now he sings about it in the belly of the fish. No other fish that ever lived had a live man inside him singing praises unto God.

Let it never be forgotten that Jonah was a man of God. I often hear great fault found with him, and he richly deserves the condemnation; he was not at all an amiable person; but, for all that, he was a man of God. When he was in the very depths of the sea, when he appeared to be cut off from all hope, he prayed as none but a man of God could pray: "Out of the belly of hell cried I, and thou heardest my voice." It takes a real saint to cry out of such a place as Jonah was in—the living tomb of the belly of the fish. He was also a man of faith, else had he not been a man of prayer. But he did still believe in his God; it was even as the result of a mistake that was made by his faith, rather than by his unbelief, that he tried to run away. He had such regard for God's honor that he could not bear to exercise a ministry which he feared would raise a question about the truthfulness of God, and represent him to be changeable. So far as his idea of God went, he was faithful to it; his fault mainly lay in that imperfect idea of God which had taken possession of his mind.

3 **For thou hadst cast me into the deep, in the midst of the seas** The word Jonah used implies that God had violently cast him away into the deep. "Cast me not off," prayed David (Ps 51:11), but here is a man who says that God did cast him out like a thing flung overboard into the vasty deep.

One sharp part of Jonah's misery was that *God's hand was so evidently in his misery*. He sees it and trembles. Observe how he ascribes all to God: "*Thou* hadst cast me into the deep, in the midst of the seas; and the floods compassed me about; all *thy* billows and *thy* waves passed over me." We can bear a blow from an enemy, but a wound from our best friend is hard. If the Lord himself go forth against us, the war is one to tremble at. If the messenger of grief be commissioned by Jehovah himself, and we know it, mere carnal reason concludes that all is over finally, and that henceforth all we can do is to sit down and die. Faith does not think in this way, but this is after the manner of flesh and sense.

And the floods compassed me about "They rolled all over me, beneath me, above me, around me."

All thy billows and thy waves passed over me Jonah had evidently read his Bible; at least, he had read Psalm 42, for he quotes it here. It is a blessed thing to have the Bible in your mind and heart so that, wherever you may be, you do not need to turn to the book because you have the book inside you. Here is a man inside a fish with a book inside of him, and it was the book inside of him that brought him out from the fish again.

4 **Then I said, I am cast out of thy sight** Jonah had tried to get away from God, and God had pursued him with a tempest, and almost broken the ship to pieces in order to be at him. As the result of the tempest, he had been hurled into the sea, and in the sea a great fish had swallowed him, and he had been carried down until the floods compassed him about. Did not all his surroundings confirm his suspicion that he was a castaway? Could he expect ever again that the word of the Lord would come to Jonah the son of Amittai? Could he hope ever again to stand with the joyful multitude that kept holy day in the courts of the Lord's house, or to present his sacrifice of thanksgiving upon Jehovah's altar? No; if he judged by his feelings, he was shut up to the conclusion which he expressed. There remained nothing to him but bare life, and that in such a condition that one could hardly desire to have it continued. He reckoned with abundant show of reason that he must be cast out of God's sight. Yet it was not so, and therefore I invite

those of you who have begun to judge your God by what you feel, and by what you see, to revise your judgment, and in future to be very diffident as to your power to come to any just conclusion as to God's dealings with you. Thank God, you will be wrong if you despair. It is much better for you to show your faith by relying on your God than to display your folly by saying, "I am cast out."

As this verdict of sense seemed to be correct, Jonah must have felt that *it was assuredly deserved*. If the Lord had dealt with Jonah according to his sins, he would have been a castaway. He had hurried to Joppa and taken a passage in a ship to go to Tarshish, or anywhere else, to flee from the presence of God. Now, what was a fitter punishment for him than that he should be cast out from the sight of God? Had not this been his inquiry at Joppa, "Whither shall I go from thy Spirit?" Was not this his demand, "Whither shall I flee from thy presence?" (Ps 139:7). Now he has his answer—he is carried down until the depth closed him round about. His waywardness had come home to him. He had been paid in his own coin, and what could Jonah feel but that he was filled with his own ways? Had he died in the sea he could not have doubted the Lord's justice. If he had been driven away as an outcast, it had but been righteous retribution to a runaway who refused his Master's service. This must have made him doubly sorrowful; a guilty conscience is the sourest ingredient of all. When each wave howled in Jonah's ear, "You deserve it," he was in an evil plight indeed.

Thus, I have brought out somewhat the force of this verdict of sense—"I am cast out of thy sight"—but I want you further to notice that *it was not true*. There was ground for grief, but not for this despairing inference. The verdict was not sustained by sufficient evidence. It was a great deal more than Jonah should have said, "I am cast out of thy sight." What, alive in the sea, Jonah— alive in the deep! alive in the belly of a fish!—and say that you are cast out from God's sight! Surely if God was anywhere in the world, it was in that great fish. Where else could there have been surer proofs of his present power and Godhead than in keeping a man alive in a living charnel? There was a constant standing miracle for three days and nights; and where there is a miracle, there is God most visibly seen. If Jonah could have asked the seas and asked the deep places of the earth, they would have told him that the Lord was not far away. If he could have asked the fish itself, it would have owned that God was there. If those who go down to the sea in ships see the works of the Lord and his wonders in the deep, much more might he have seen them who went into the sea in a fish's belly.

Yet I will look again toward thy holy temple Jonah appears to be in a despairing condition—"I am cast out of thy sight"—and still he has hope, for he resolves, "Yet I will look again toward thy holy temple." Everything seems lost, and yet as long as a man can look to God nothing is lost. God cannot see him, so he thinks, yet he talks about looking toward God. This is singular, is it not? It is as if he said, "I am cast out of your sight, and yet you are the object of my sight." I do not know of a more gloomy sentence that human lips can speak than this: "I am cast out of thy sight." I do not know of a more hopeful resolution that the human heart can determine upon than this: "Yet I will look again toward thy holy temple."

According to the Hebrew, the word should be rendered "only" instead of "yet": "only I will look again toward thy holy temple." *Faith looks to God only.* Faith comes alone to her God and seeks no company to keep her in countenance. When we were first saved it was by faith only, and we must be saved in the same way still. In Jonah's case all props were knocked away. He had nothing to look to in the whale's belly at the bottom of the sea, but then and there he trusted God, and that was all. He could not think very clearly, or confess before men, neither could he be or do anything, for he was packed away in quarters too close for action. But he could look again toward the temple of God, and this alone he did. He could give the faith-look when all looking with the eyes was far out of the question.

How could he tell in which direction to look for the temple when all around him rolled the dark sea? His look was inward and spiritual, and he was content to do that, and that only. His state was looking, looking—only looking. Let it be ours to believe, to believe, and yet again to believe. Jonah looked again to the place where God revealed himself, and we look to the person of the Lord Jesus Christ, in whom dwells all the fullness of the Godhead bodily. He looked to the mercy-seat sprinkled with the blood of sacrifice, where the Lord was wont to pardon and bless all suppliant sinners, and we also look to Jesus as the great propitiation.

5 **The waters compassed me about, even to the soul** They seemed to get right into his spirit; his heart became waterlogged.

The depth closed me round about, The weeds were wrapped about my head Like his shroud—as if the waxed cloth of the grave were wrapped about his mouth, and ears, and eyes, and he was consigned to a living tomb. This narrative is a graphic description of the natural motion of the great fish which had swallowed Jonah. When the fish found this strange being inside him, the first thing that he did was to plunge as deep as ever he could into the waters. You will see that Jonah did go down very deep indeed. The next thing was for the fish to make for the weeds; as certain creatures eat weeds to cure them when they feel very ill, this fish went off to the weedy places to see if he could get a cure for this new complaint of a man inside him.

APPLICATION

Look Again to Jesus

Faith is described in other ways beside looking; it is taking, grasping, possessing, feeding. But faith first of all is looking; and so, whenever you fall into grievous trouble, it will be wise to resort to the beginning of your confidence and hold it fast to the end. If you cannot grasp, yet look. There are several grades of faith, and when you cannot reach the higher grade, it will be wise to enter fully into the lower one. Remember, the lowest form of faith will save, and even the smallest measure of faith is effectual for salvation, though not for consolation. Look! Look to Jesus! "There is life in a look."[1] There is heaven in a look. "Look unto me, and be ye saved, all the ends of the earth" (Isa 45:22). Look! If you cannot go forth to fight by faith, stand still and look by faith. If you cannot declare the glory of the Lord, still look. If you cannot tell what God *has* done for you, still keep yourself looking by faith to see what God *will* do for you. Do your first work, and as your first work was a simple look at the crucified one, look again to him.

Even if you forget all the rest of my text, remember those two words: "Look again." If any of you are in sore trouble, I will bid you go home with only these two words ringing in your ears: "Look again!" If you did look once, but have fallen into new darkness, look again. It is frequently a great benefit to overhaul the foundations and begin again at the beginnings. I did look to Christ three and thirty years ago or more; so did some of you. But the devil may say, "Your faith was fancy; your conversion was a delusion." Be it so, O Satan; we will not dispute with you, but we will begin again from this moment. It is such a mercy that faith does not need to grow old before it saves us: the faith born this moment saves the soul in its very birth.

Is it that your faith is not more than five minutes old? Have you only just begun to trust Christ? Well, your faith has saved you quite as effectually as the faith of a man who has believed in Christ for fifty years. We must believe anew each day; yesterday's believing will not do for today. Let us now look to Jesus Christ upon the cross, and trust him this morning as if we never trusted him before. "I will look again toward thy holy temple." It will do each man good to look anew to that cross which is the sole hope of his soul. There is nothing more sweetening to the spirit than to confess sin and accept mercy in the original style, and to go to Jesus anew just as we went at first. Let us do so at this moment.

---

1. A reference to John Parker's hymn "There Is Life in a Look at the Crucified One." —ed.

Never Cast Out

There is a text that Jonah could never have heard, which I commend to you against the time when you get to be where Jonah was. I do not suppose you ever will be buried alive in a fish literally, but you may spiritually sink as deep as the prophet did. What is that text? "Him that cometh to me I will in no wise cast out" (John 6:37). Jonah said, "I am cast out," but that was not true. Poor Jonah! The mariners cast him out, but God did not. He was cast out of the ship, but not out of the sight of God. The Lord of old was faithful, and it was his rule never to cast away his people; even as David said, "For the Lord will not cast off for ever: but though he cause grief, yet will he have compassion, according to the multitude of his mercies" (Lam 3:31–32).[2]

Mark the text I quoted from our Lord's own lips: "Him that cometh to me I will in no wise cast out." Never question this sacred word. He will never, never cast out a single person that trusts him. So that if ever you should be in a condition which seems to you quite as forlorn as that of this prophet in the midst of the sea, you may yet be sure that you are not cast off nor cast out. He who says he is cast out says more than can possibly be true, since the infallible promise is, "Him that cometh to me I will in no wise cast out." It is not for us to forge a lie against the God of the whole earth. He does not speak that which is false, but out of his mouth proceeded verity. Even if all things in earth and hell should swear that the Lord has cast away one of his own believing people, it will be our duty to disbelieve them all. For it is impossible that he should cast out any believer, in any way, for any reason or motive whatsoever.

---

2. When Spurgeon attributes this quote to David he may be misspeaking; several other places in his sermons he attributes Lamentations to Jeremiah. —ed.

JONAH 2:6–10

6 I went down to the bottoms of the mountains;
The earth with her bars was about me for ever:
Yet hast thou brought up my life from corruption, O Lord
my God.
7 When my soul fainted within me I remembered the Lord:
And my prayer came in unto thee, into thine holy temple.
8 They that observe lying vanities forsake their own mercy.
9 But I will sacrifice unto thee with the voice of thanksgiving;
I will pay that that I have vowed.
Salvation is of the Lord.
10 And the Lord spake unto the fish, and it vomited out Jonah
upon the dry land.

EXPOSITION

6 **I went down to the bottoms of the mountains** To the very roots and foundations of the mountains, where the big jagged rocks made huge buttresses for the hills above.

The whale, of course, was near the surface when it first sucked Jonah in, but it goes down, perhaps half-a-mile; it must go deeper yet, and so it stirs up the deep in its pain, for it has an indigestible morsel within, and it does not know what to do with it; it plunges down, down, down, till Jonah says he went to the bottoms of the mountains, and the weeds were wrapped about his head, and the earth with her bars was about him forever: yet even then, "underneath were the everlasting arms" (Deut 33:27), and therefore the whale comes up, and Jonah stands upon the dry land once more. So shall it be with you, beloved, for in your worst trials and times of difficulty, underneath you are the everlasting arms.

ILLUSTRATION

God Hears Prayer Everywhere

Preaching Themes: Prayer, Presence of God

God will hear prayer on the land, and on the sea, and even under the sea. I remember a brother, when in prayer, making use of that last expression. Somebody who was at the prayer meeting was rather astonished at it, and asked, "How would God hear prayer under the sea?" On inquiry, we found out that the man who uttered those words was a diver, and often went down to the bottom of the sea after wrecks, and he said that he had held communion with God while he had been at work in the depths of the ocean.

Our God is not the God of the hills only; but of the valleys also. He is God of both sea and land.

The earth with her bars was about me for ever Down went the fish, as deep as he could go. Of course, down went Jonah too, and he might well imagine that he was in a vast prison from which there was no way of escape.

Yet hast thou brought up my life from corruption, O Lord my God And, dear friend, God can bring you up, however low you may have gone. Though, in your own feelings, you feel as if you had gone so low that you could not go any lower, God can, in answer to prayer, bring you up again. O despairing one, take heart, and be comforted by this story of Jonah! God is dealing with you as he was with him. There may be a great fish, but there is a great God as well. There may be a deep sea, but there is an almighty God to bring you up out of it.

7 **When my soul fainted within me** Jonah was certainly in a very terrible condition in the belly of the fish, but the position itself was probably not so dark as his own reflections, for conscience would say to him, "Alas, Jonah! you came here by your own fault. You had to flee from the presence of God because in your pride and self-love you refused to go to Nineveh, that great city, and deliver your Master's message." It gives a sting to misery when a man feels that he himself is alone responsible for it. If it were unavoidable that I should suffer, then I could not repine, but if I have brought all this upon myself, by my own folly, then there is a double bitterness in the gall. Jonah would reflect that now he could not help himself in any way. It would answer no purpose to be self-willed now; he was in a place where petulance and obstinacy had no liberty. If he had tried to stretch out his arm, he could not; he was immured in a dungeon that imprisoned every sense as well as every limb, and the bolts of his cell his hand could not draw. He was cast into the deep in the midst of the seas, the waters compassed him about even to the soul, the weeds were wrapped about his head. His state was helpless, and, apart from God, it was hopeless.

I remembered the Lord It is a blessed memory that serves us faithfully in a fainting fit. Mostly, when the heart faints, the memory fails; but Jonah remembered the Lord when his soul fainted within him.

And my prayer came in unto thee, into thine holy temple Jonah was so comforted with the thoughts of God that he began to pray, and his prayer was not drowned in the water, nor choked in the fish's belly, neither was it held captive by the weeds that were about his head, but up it went like an electric flash, through waves, through clouds, beyond the stars, up to the throne of God, and down came the answer like a return message. Nothing can destroy or detain a real prayer; its flight to the throne is swift and certain.

Think of Jonah's prayer going right within the veil and reaching the ear and heart of God in his holy temple. He said that he was cast out of God's sight, yet his prayer went into God's temple. Oh, the prevalence of a bold believing prayer!

8 **They that observe lying vanities forsake their own mercy.** If you trust anywhere but in God, you will run away from your own mercy. God is the only really merciful One who can always help you. But if you trust in your own righteousness, if you trust in priestcraft, if you trust in any superstition, you are observing lying vanities, and forsaking your own mercy. God is the source of your mercy. Do not run away from him to anyone or anything else.

9 **But I will sacrifice unto thee with the voice of thanksgiving** "I long to do so. I cannot do it just now, but I would if I could; and I will do it when thou shalt grant me deliverance from my present peril."

Salvation is of the Lord That is one of the grandest utterances that any man ever made: "SALVATION!" Write it in capital letters. It is a very emphatic word in the Hebrew, and I might read it, "Mighty salvation is of Jehovah." This is real, old-fashioned Calvinistic doctrine spoken centuries before John Calvin was born. The whale could not endure it, and he turned Jonah out directly he said, "Salvation is of the Lord." The world does not like that doctrine, and there are many professing Christians who do not like it. They say, "Salvation is of man's free will, or salvation is of the works of the law, or salvation is of rites and ceremonies," and so on. But we say, with Jonah, "Salvation is of the Lord." He works it from beginning to end, and therefore he must have all the praise for it forever and ever.

ILLUSTRATION

A Sinner in His Castle

Preaching Themes: Good Works, Repentance, Salvation

The sinner in his natural estate reminds me of a man who has a strong and well-nigh impenetrable castle into which he has fled. There is the outer moat; there is a second moat; there are the high walls; and then afterwards there is the dungeon and keep, into which the sinner will retire. Now, the first moat that goes around the sinner's trusting place is his good works. He says, "I am as good as my neighbor. I am no sinner. 'I tithe mint and cumin.' A good, respectable gentleman I am indeed." Well, when God comes to work with him, to save him, he sends his army across the first moat; and as they go through it, they cry, "Salvation is of the Lord." And the moat is dried up, for if it is of the Lord, how can it be of good works?

But when that is done, he has a second entrenchment: ceremonies. "Well," he says, "I will not trust in my good works, but I have been baptized, I have been confirmed. Do I not take the sacrament? That shall be my trust." "Over the moat! Over the moat!" And the soldiers go over again, shouting, "Salvation is of the Lord." The second moat is dried up; it is all over with that.

Now they come to the first strong wall. The sinner, looking over it, says, "I can repent; I can believe whenever I like. I will save myself by repenting and believing." Up come the soldiers of God, his great army of conviction, and they batter this wall to the ground, crying, "'Salvation is of the Lord.' Your faith and your repentance must all be given to you, or else you will neither believe nor repent of sin."

And now the castle is taken; the man's hopes are all cut off. He feels that it is not of self. The castle of self is overcome, and the great banner upon which is written "Salvation is of the Lord" is displayed upon the battlements.

But is the battle over? Oh no, the sinner has retired to the keep, in the center of the castle; and now he changes his tactics. "I cannot save myself," says he; "therefore I will despair. There is no salvation for me." Now this second castle is as hard to take as the first, for the sinner sits down and says, "I can't be saved, I must perish." But God commands the soldiers to take this castle too, shouting, "Salvation is of the Lord." Though it is not of man, *it is of*

God. "He is able to save, even to the uttermost," though you cannot save yourself. This sword, you see, cuts two ways: it cuts pride down, and then it cleaves the skull of despair. If any man says he can save himself, it halves his pride at once; and if another man says he cannot be saved, it dashes his despair to the earth. For it affirms that he can be saved, seeing, "Salvation is of the Lord." That is the effect this doctrine has upon the sinner. May it have that effect on you!

---

10 **And the Lord spake unto the fish, and it vomited out Jonah upon the dry land** God has only to speak, and even sea monsters obey him. I know not how he spoke to the fish. I do not know how to talk to a fish, but God does. And as the Lord could speak to that fish, he can speak to any sinner. However far you may have gone from all that is good, he who spoke to that great fish, and made it disgorge the prophet Jonah, can speak to you. Then you will give up your sins as the whale gave up Jonah. God grant that it may be so this very hour!

APPLICATION

You Are Not a Hypocrite

Some of us have enjoyed for years a full assurance of our pardon and justification. We have walked in the light as God is in the light, and we have had fellowship with the Father and with the Son, and the blood of Jesus Christ his Son has cleansed us from all sin. We have often felt our hearts dance at the assurance that "there is therefore now no condemnation to them which are in Jesus Christ" (Rom 8:1). We have stood at the foot of the cross and seen the records of our sins nailed to the tree as the token of their full discharge. Yet, at this time, we may be suffering an interval of anxious questioning, and unbelief may be lowering over us. It is possible that our faith is staggered, and, therefore, our old sins have risen up against us and are threatening our peace. At such times, conscience will remind us of our shortcomings, which we cannot deny, and Satan will howl over the top of these shortcomings, "How can you be a child of God? If you were born from above, how could you have acted as you have done?" Then, if for a moment we look away from the cross, if we look within for marks of evidences, the horrible bog of our inward corruptions will be stirred, and there will pour into the soul such dark memories and black forebodings that we shall cry, "I am utterly lost, my hope is hypocrisy; what can I do? What shall I do?"

Let me assure you that, under such exercises, it is no wonder if the soul of the Christian faints within him. Let it be remembered, also, that soul-fainting is the worst form of fainting. Though Jonah in the whale's belly could not use his eyes, he did not need them, and if he could not use his arms or his feet, he did not require to do so. It did not matter if they all failed him, but for his soul to faint—this was horror indeed! So is it with us. Our other faculties may go to sleep if they will, but when our faith swoons, and our confidence staggers, things go very hard with us. Do not, however, when in such a state, write yourself down as a hypocrite, for many of the most valiant soldiers of the cross know by personal experience what this dark sensation means.

When You Are Faint, Remember the Lord

Jonah, when he was in sore trouble, tells us, "I remembered the LORD." What is there for a faint heart to remember in the Lord? Is there not everything? There is, first, his nature. Think of that. When I am faint with sorrow, let me remember that he is full of pity and compassion. He will not strike too heavily, nor will he forget to sustain. I will, therefore, look up to him and say, "My Father, do not break me in pieces. I am a poor weather-beaten bark that can scarcely escape the hungry waves; do not send your rough wind against me, but give me a little calm that I may reach the desired haven." By remembering that the Lord's mercies are great, we shall be saved from a fainting heart.

Then I will remember his power. If I am in such a strait that I cannot help myself, *he* can help me. I have exigences and sharp pinches, but there are no such things with him. There are no emergencies and times of severe pressure with God. With him all things are possible; therefore I will remember the Lord. If the difficulty is one that arises out of my ignorance, though I do not know which way to take, I will remember his wisdom. I know that he will guide me; I will remember that he cannot make a mistake, and committing my way unto him my soul shall take courage. Beloved, all the attributes of God sparkle with consolation to the eye of faith. There is nothing in the Most High to discourage the man who can say, "My Father, my God, in you I put my trust." None who have trusted in him have ever been confounded; therefore, if your soul sinks within you, remember the nature, and character, and attributes of God.

When you have remembered his nature, then remember his promises. What has he said concerning souls that faint? Think of these texts if you think of no other: "I will never leave thee, nor forsake thee" (Heb 13:5). "Thy shoes shall be iron and brass; and as thy days, so shall thy strength be" (Deut 33:25). "My grace is sufficient for thee: for my strength is made perfect in weakness" (2 Cor 12:9). "Trust in the Lord, and do good: so shalt thou dwell in the land, and verily thou shalt be fed" (Ps 37:3). "No good thing will he withhold from them that walk uprightly" (Ps 84:11). When we get upon this strain and begin to talk of the promises, we need hours in which to enlarge upon the exceeding great and precious words, but we mention only these; we let fall this handful for some poor Ruth to glean. When your soul is faint, catch at a promise, believe it, and say unto the Lord, "Do as you have said," and your spirit shall speedily revive.

Remember, next, his covenant. What a grand word that word "covenant" is to the man who understands it! God has entered into covenant with his Son, who represents us, his people. He has said, "As I have sworn that the waters of Noah should no more go over the earth; so have I sworn that I would not be wroth with thee, nor rebuke thee. For the mountains shall depart, and the hills be removed; but my kindness shall not depart from thee, neither shall the covenant of my peace be removed" (Isa 54:9–10). Truly, we may say with good old David, "Although my house be not so with God; yet he hath made with me an everlasting covenant, ordered in all things, and sure" (2 Sam 23:5). When everything else gives way, cling in the power of the Holy Spirit to covenant mercies and covenant engagements, and your spirit shall be at peace.

Again, when we remember the Lord, we should remember what he has been to us in past times. When any of us fall to doubting and fearing, we are indeed blameworthy, for the Lord has never given us any occasion for doubting him. He has helped us in sorer troubles than we are passing through at this time. We have tested his faithfulness, his power, and his goodness at a heavier rate than now, and though hardly tried, they have never failed us yet; they have borne the strain of many years, and show no signs of giving way; why, then, are we distrustful? Many saints have proved the Lord's faithfulness for fifty, sixty, or even seventy years; how can they be of doubtful mind after this? What! Has your God been true for seventy years, and can you not trust him a few more days? Has he brought you to seventy-five, and can you not trust him the few months more that you are to remain in the wilderness? Call to remembrance the days of old, the love of his heart, and the might of his arm, when he came to your rescue, and took you out of the deep waters, and set your feet upon a rock, and established your goings. He is the same God still; therefore, when your soul faints within you, remember the Lord, and you will be comforted.

Prayer

God the Holy Ghost writes our prayers, God the Son presents our prayers, and God the Father accepts our prayers, and with a Trinity to help us in it, what cannot prayer perform? I may be speaking to some who are under very severe trials—I feel persuaded I am—let me beg them to take this promise to themselves as their own; and I pray God the Holy Ghost to lay it home to their hearts and make it theirs—"I will never leave thee, nor forsake thee" (Heb 13:5). God will not fail you though you fail yourself. Though you faint, he faints not, neither is weary. Lift up your cry, and he will lift up his hand.

Imitate Jonah's example, and send up a prayer to heaven, for it will come up even to God's holy temple. Jonah had no prayer-book, and you need none. God the Holy Ghost can put more living prayer into half-a-dozen words of your own than you could get out of a ton weight of paper prayers. Jonah's prayer was not notable for its words. The fish's belly was not the place for picked phrases, nor for long-winded orations. We do not believe that he offered a long prayer either, but it came right up from his heart and flew straight up to heaven. It was shot by the strong bow of intense desire and agony of soul, and, therefore, it speeded its way to the throne of the Most High. If you would now pray, never mind your words—it is the soul of prayer that God accepts. If you would be saved, go to your chamber, and do not rise from your knees until the Lord has heard you. Yes, where you now are let your souls pour out themselves before God, and faith in Jesus will give you immediate salvation.

JONAH 3

JONAH 3:1–10

1 And the word of the LORD came unto Jonah the second time,
saying, 2 Arise, go unto Nineveh, that great city, and preach unto
it the preaching that I bid thee. 3 So Jonah arose, and went unto
Nineveh, according to the word of the LORD. Now Nineveh was
an exceeding great city of three days' journey. 4 And Jonah began
to enter into the city a day's journey, and he cried, and said, Yet
forty days, and Nineveh shall be overthrown. 5 So the people of
Nineveh believed God, and proclaimed a fast, and put on sackcloth, from the greatest of them even to the least of them. 6 For
word came unto the king of Nineveh, and he arose from his
throne, and he laid his robe from him, and covered him with
sackcloth, and sat in ashes. 7 And he caused it to be proclaimed
and published through Nineveh by the decree of the king and his
nobles, saying, Let neither man nor beast, herd nor flock, taste
any thing: let them not feed, nor drink water: 8 But let man and
beast be covered with sackcloth, and cry mightily unto God: yea,
let them turn every one from his evil way, and from the violence
that is in their hands. 9 Who can tell if God will turn and repent,
and turn away from his fierce anger, that we perish not? 10 And
God saw their works, that they turned from their evil way; and
God repented of the evil, that he had said that he would do unto
them; and he did it not.

EXPOSITION

1–2 **Arise, go unto Nineveh, that great city** The men of Nineveh were like those in the days of Noah. They were married and given in marriage; they ate and they drank; they built and they planted. The whole world was their granary, and the kingdoms of the earth their hunting-ground. They were rich and mighty above all people, for God had greatly increased their prosperity; and they had become the greatest nation upon the face of the earth. Locked in security they fell into great and abominable sins.

and preach unto it the preaching that I bid thee There is no preaching like that which God bids us. The preaching that comes out of our own heads will never go into other men's hearts. If we will keep to the preaching that the Lord bids us, we shall not fail in our ministry.

3 **Now Nineveh was an exceeding great city of three days' journey** For those times, Nineveh was "an exceeding great city," but it is far exceeded in size by this modern Nineveh of London.

How was one man to admonish and evangelize the whole of it? Preposterous! Might he not have been aided by at least one colleague? Even Moses had his Aaron. Why did not the Lord send forth a college of prophets, or an army of preachers, and bid them go and divide the vast city into districts, and hold services in all the large halls, and at the corners of the streets, or even visit from house to house? Must one man be pitted against hundreds of thousands? Would a single voice be heard amid the noise of a city which was full of tumult? The odds were great against the lone man. Was that why Jonah ran away? I think not, but it has been the cause of the flight of many others.

4 **And Jonah began to enter into the city a day's journey** A true Christian who lives near to God, and is filled with grace and is kept holy, may stand in the midst of sinners and do wonders. What a marvelous feat was that which Jonah did! There was the great city of Nineveh, having in it six score thousand souls that did not know their right hand from their left, and one man went against it—Jonah—and as he approached it he began to cry, "Yet forty days and Nineveh shall be overthrown." He entered the city—perhaps he stood aghast for a moment at the multitude of its population, at its richness and splendor, but again he lifted up his sharp shrill voice, "Yet forty days and Nineveh shall

be overthrown." On he went, and the crowd increased around him as he passed through each street, but they heard nothing but the solemn monotony, "Yet forty days and Nineveh shall be overthrown," and yet again, "Yet forty days and Nineveh shall be overthrown." And on he went, that solitary man, until he caused convulsion in the midst of myriads, and the king on his throne robed himself in sackcloth and proclaimed a fast, a day of mourning and of sadness. Yet on he went, "Yet forty days and Nineveh shall be overthrown," "Yet forty days and Nineveh shall be overthrown," until all the people bowed before him, and that one man was the conqueror of the myriad.

Believer, if you will go out and do the same, if you will go into the streets, the lanes, the byways, the houses, and into the privacies of men, and still with this continued cry against sin and iniquity, say to them, "Look unto the cross and live, look unto the cross and live." Though there were but one earnest man in London who would continue that monotony of "Look unto the cross and live," from end to end this city would shake, and the great leviathan metropolis would be made to tremble.

and he cried, and said, Yet forty days, and Nineveh shall be overthrown His message was short and sharp, there was not a word of mercy in it. There was nothing to distract the attention of the hearers from the one point and the one subject; and there is a great deal in that. We may sometimes say too much in a single sermon and give our hearers a field of wheat instead of a loaf of bread. But Jonah said what he was bidden to say, no more and no less: "Yet forty days, and Nineveh shall be overthrown."

Through the broad streets of that gigantic city, and through its lanes and alleys, in its public squares, the voice was heard, sharp and shrill, of that lone man—"Yet forty days and Nineveh shall be overthrown." No rod was turned into a serpent; no mountains were made to smoke; none were struck dead by the sudden hand of God; no paralytics and sick folk were healed; no signs were given to the men of Nineveh, but the declaration of that one man sent of God was sufficient to denounce and discover their sin. They felt that they had been guilty of sins that deserved to be denounced. He pronounced their punishment, and they felt that the punishment also was well deserved, and therefore, from the king on the throne to the meanest of the citizens, all the inhabitants of that great city humbled themselves, and Jonah's work was done and God repented and forgave the city.

5 **So the people of Nineveh believed God, and proclaimed a fast** The prayers offered at Nineveh, were they spiritual prayers? Did you ever hear of a church of God in Nineveh? I have not, neither do I believe the Ninevites were ever visited by converting grace, but they were by the preaching of Jonah convinced that they were in danger from the great Jehovah, and they proclaimed a fast, and humbled themselves, and God heard their prayer, and Nineveh for a while was preserved.

Many a time in the hour of sickness, and in the time of woe, God has heard the prayers of the unthankful and the evil. Do you think God gives nothing except to the good? Have you dwelled at the foot of Sinai and learned to judge according to the law of merit? What were you when you began to pray? Were you good and righteous? Has not God commanded you to do good to the evil? Will he command you to do what he will not do himself? Has he not said that he "sendeth rain on the just and upon the unjust" (Matt 5:45), and is it not so? Is he not daily blessing those who curse him, and doing good to those who despitefully use him? This is one of the glories of God's grace; and when there is nothing else good in the man, yet if there is a cry lifted up from his heart the Lord deigns full often to send relief from trouble.

Now, if God has heard the prayers even of men who have not sought him in the highest manner, and has given them temporary deliverances in answer to their cries, will he not much more hear you when you are humbling yourself in his sight, and desiring to be reconciled to him?

and put on sackcloth, from the greatest of them even to the least of them Note that the only message they had heard was a prophecy of impending judgment. God had sent his servant to warn them of the coming destruction. Since he had warned them that he meant to destroy them, they could infer that he might possibly intend pity toward them should they repent, but there was as yet, no verbal declaration of mercy or hope.

6 **For word came unto the king of Nineveh, and he arose from his throne, and he laid his robe from him, and covered him with sackcloth, and sat in ashes** I think I see the king of Nineveh sitting down with his nobles at a council of state, and one of them would say, "We have little hope of mercy, for if you will observe Jonah never offered us any. How terribly he spoke. There was not so much as a tear in his eye. I am persuaded that Jonah's God is very just and severe. He will by no means spare us; we shall be cut off." But the king's answer to his councilor was, "Who can tell? you only think so, but you cannot say it, let us yet hope, for "*Who can tell.*"

7–8 **let man and beast be covered with sackcloth, and cry mightily unto God: yea, let them turn every one from his evil way** I think the greatest confidence which the king of Nineveh would have would be derived from the following suggestion. "Oh," said he, "if God had meant to destroy us without giving us an opportunity of pardon, he would not have sent Jonah forty days beforehand. He would have given us no time at all. He would simply have given a blow and a word, but the blow would have been first. He would have overthrown the city in his wrath without a single message. What did he to Sodom? He sent no messenger there. The sun rose and the fire descended from God's terrible right hand. Not so Nineveh; it had its warning.

9 **Who can tell if God will turn and repent, and turn away from his fierce anger, that we perish not?** These people went to God with nothing better to sustain them than this: "Who can tell?" How much more guilty than these Ninevites are they who refuse to humble themselves before God, even when they have distinct injunctions from God, and explicit promises that whosoever shall confess and forsake his sins shall find mercy!

These men of Nineveh will rise up in judgment against the men of London, and the men of this generation, and condemn them, for they repented at the preaching of Jonah, and now men do not repent even at the testimony of Jesus Christ the Son of God. To despise the prophet Jonah, would have involved these people in certain destruction; of how much sorer punishment shall they be thought worthy who despise the Christ of God, and do despite unto the Spirit of grace!

ILLUSTRATION

Hung in Chains

Preaching Themes: Death and Dying, Mercy

It was an old and a horrible custom of past governments, when a man was executed for murder, to allow him to be hung in chains, so that as often as anyone passed by the gibbet [gallows-type structure] they might learn, as was thought, the severity of justice. I fear, however, that they more frequently learned the brutality and barbarism of the age. Now, as these were hung in chains as warnings, I would translate this horrible figure into one that shall glitter with joy and delight. God, in order that you may know his mercy, has been pleased to preserve instances thereof, that so often as you look upon them you may be led to say, if such and such a one was saved, why may not I?

---

10 **And God repented of the evil, that he had said that he would do unto them; and he did it not** There is no change in God, absolutely considered, but there is often an apparent change. That which he threatens, while men remain in sin, is not executed upon them when they repent and turn to him. He is always the same God. From the beginning, he has been "the Lord God, merciful and gracious, longsuffering, and abundant in goodness and truth, keeping mercy for

thousands, forgiving iniquity and transgression and sin." If he did not pardon sin, when men turn from it with sincere repentance, he would have changed his method of dealing with the penitent; but when he does forgive, it is according to his way from the beginning, for he has ever been a tender, and compassionate, and gracious God.

APPLICATION

God Uses the Weak

So skillful is God that with the weakest instrument he can produce the mightiest workmanship. That one man begins his journey. Already the inhabitants flock to listen to him. He proceeds—the crowd multiplies. As he stands at the corner of the alleys, and the lanes, every window is thrown up to listen, and the streets are thronged as he walks along. Still on he goes till the whole city has begun to shake with his terrible voice. And now the king himself bids him come into his presence, and the fearless prophet still propounds the threatening of God. Then comes the effect. All Nineveh is wrapped in sackcloth; the cry of man and beast go up in one terrible wailing to God. Jehovah is honored and Nineveh repents.

We see in this rich grounds for hope. What cannot God do? Do not think that he needs to wait for us. He can accomplish the greatest deeds by the meanest instrumentality. One man, if he willed it, would be sufficient to stir this giant city. One man, if God decreed it, might be the means of the conversion of a nation, nay, a continent should shake beneath the tramping of one man. There is no palace so high that this one man's voice should not reach it, and there is no den of infamy so deep that his cry should not be heard in it. All we need is that God should bare his arm, and who can withstand his might? Even though he may only grasp the jawbone of an ass—yet, is his arm mightier than Samson's?—and not only would it be heaps upon heaps, but city upon city, continent upon continent. With the meanest instrument would God slay his thousands and overcome his myriads.

Church of God, never fear. Remember the men that God has given you in the days of yore. Look back to Paul; remember Augustine;

think well of Luther, and of Calvin; talk of Whitfield, and of Wesley. Remember these were but separate individual men, and yet through them God did a work; the remembrance of it still rolls on and shall never cease while this earth endures.

More Hope than the Ninevites

The people of Nineveh lacked an encouragement that you and I have. They had never heard of the cross. Jonah's preaching was very powerful, but there was no Christ in it. There was nothing about the Messiah that was to come, no talking of the sprinkled blood, no mention of a great sin-atoning sacrifice—and therefore the men who were in the council of the king might have said, "Surely, we have never heard that any satisfaction has been offered to the injured justice of God. How therefore can he be just and yet the justifier of the ungodly? "Ah," said the king, "who can tell?" And on that slender "who can tell?" they ventured to cry for mercy.

Sinner, you are answered this day, that "God hath spared not his own Son, but freely delivered him up for us all, that whosoever believeth on him might not perish, but have everlasting life. For God so loved the world that he sent forth his only begotten Son, that whosoever believeth on him might not perish, but might be saved" (John 3:16). "For there is now no condemnation to them that are in Christ Jesus" (Rom 8:1).

It Is a Glorious Thing for God to Save

Sinner, remember that while it will be a happy thing for you to be saved, it will be a glorious thing for God to save you. Men do not object to do a thing that is expensive to them if it brings them some honor. They will not stoop to do a thing that involves shame and scorn, but if honor goes with a thing, they are ready enough to do it. Now soul, remember, if God shall save you, it will honor him. Why, will you not honor him if he will but blot out your sin? I thought when I was seeking mercy, if God would only save me, there was nothing I would not do for him. I would be cut in pieces rather than deny him. I would serve him all my life, and he might do what he would with me in heaven. And do you not sometimes feel that if God would only save you, you would sing loudest of them all in heaven?

Would you not love him; creep to the foot of his throne, and cast your crown before his feet, saying: "Lord, not unto me, not unto me, but unto thy name be all the glory"? God delights to save sinners because this puts jewels in his crown. He is glorified in his justice, but not as he is in his mercy. He appears in silken robes with a golden crown upon his head when he saves sinners. He wears an iron crown when he crushes them. Judgment is his strange work; he does that with his left hand, but his right-handed acts are those of mercy and of love. Hence, he puts the righteous always on the right hand that he may be ready to pardon and ready to deliver.

Oh, come then, soul, to Christ. You are not about to ask a thing which God is unwilling to give, or that which will slur his escutcheon, or blot his banner. You are asking for that which is as glorious to God as it is beneficial to yourself. Come, humble soul, and cry to Christ, and he will have mercy upon you.

JONAH 4

JONAH 4:1–11

[1] But it displeased Jonah exceedingly, and he was very angry. [2] And he prayed unto the LORD, and said, I pray thee, O
LORD, was not this my saying, when I was yet in my country?
Therefore I fled before unto Tarshish: for I knew that thou art
a gracious God, and merciful, slow to anger, and of great kindness, and repentest thee of the evil. [3] Therefore now, O LORD,
take, I beseech thee, my life from me; for it is better for me
to die than to live. [4] Then said the LORD, Doest thou well to be
angry? [5] So Jonah went out of the city, and sat on the east side
of the city, and there made him a booth, and sat under it in the
shadow, till he might see what would become of the city. [6] And
the LORD God prepared a gourd, and made it to come up over
Jonah, that it might be a shadow over his head, to deliver him
from his grief. So Jonah was exceeding glad of the gourd. [7] But
God prepared a worm when the morning rose the next day,
and it smote the gourd that it withered. [8] And it came to pass,
when the sun did arise, that God prepared a vehement east
wind; and the sun beat upon the head of Jonah, that he fainted, and wished in himself to die, and said, It is better for me
to die than to live. [9] And God said to Jonah, Doest thou well to
be angry for the gourd? And he said, I do well to be angry, even
unto death. [10] Then said the LORD, Thou hast had pity on the
gourd, for the which thou hast not laboured, neither madest it
grow; which came up in a night, and perished in a night: [11] And
should not I spare Nineveh, that great city, wherein are more
than sixscore thousand persons that cannot discern between
their right hand and their left hand; and also much cattle?

EXPOSITION

1 **But it displeased Jonah exceedingly, and he was very angry** A nice prophet this! Jonah was a man of a somewhat ugly disposition, yet I think he has been misunderstood. He was the true child of Elijah, the prophet of fire. Elijah was a rough, stern servant of the Lord, who felt that the indignities which had been done to Jehovah deserved instant and terrible punishment; and he seemed almost to wish to see that punishment inflicted, as he accused the people unto God, saying, "The children of Israel have forsaken thy covenant, thrown down thine altars, and slain thy prophets with the sword; and I, even I only, am left; and they seek my life, to take it away" (1 Kgs 19:10). He was bravely stern for God, and Jonah was cast in a similar mold. He seemed to feel, "I have been sent by God to tell these people that they will be destroyed for their sin. Now, if they are not destroyed, it will be thought that I have not preached the truth, and, what is far more serious, it will be thought that God does not keep his word." His whole thought was taken up with the honor of God, and his own honor as involved in that of the Lord.

There are many people nowadays who seem to think everything of man, and very little of God; and, consequently, they fall into grievous errors. Jonah, on the contrary, thought everything of God, and very little of men. He fell into an error by so doing, and there was a want of balance of judgment. Yet Jonah's error is so very seldom committed that I am half inclined to admire it in contrast with the error on the other side. He felt that it would be better for Nineveh to be destroyed than for God's truthfulness to be jeopardized even for a single moment. God would not have us push even concern for his honor too far. But we are such poor creatures that, very often, when we are within an inch of the right course, we fall into a snare of the enemy. It was so with Jonah when he was exceedingly displeased and very angry at what God had done in sparing the repentant people of Nineveh.

ILLUSTRATION

Jonah Was One of God's "Ironsides"

Preaching Themes: Character, War

Jonah was grandly stern amid a wicked generation; he was one of God's "Ironsides." He was the man for a fierce fight, and he would not hold back his hand from the use of the sword or do the work of the Lord half-heartedly. He was one who wished to make thorough work of anything he undertook, and to go to the very end of it. We need more of such men nowadays. He was not lacking in backbone, yet he was lacking in heart; in that respect we would not be like him. He was singularly strong where so many in these days are grievously weak. Perhaps he is all the more criticized and condemned because that virtue which he possessed is so rare today.

2 **I knew that thou art a gracious God, and merciful, slow to anger, and of great kindness, and repentest thee of the evil** This was as much as if he had said to the Lord, "I went and did your bidding, and told the Ninevites that they would be destroyed; but I knew in my heart that, if they repented, you would not carry out your threat, and now you are too gracious, too kind, to these wicked people." It is a strange thing, is it not, that Jonah was angry because his message was blessed to his hearers? As a good commentator says, "When Christ sees of the travail of his soul, he is satisfied; but when Jonah saw of the travail of his soul, he was dissatisfied."[1]

There are some men who leave off preaching because they do not succeed. But here was one who was ready to give up because he did succeed. It is strange that such a good man as Jonah should fall into such a foolish state of mind; but God still has a great many unwise children. You can, any of you, find

1. This may be a paraphrase of Matthew Henry's comments on Jonah 4:1–4. —ed.

one if you look in the right place; I mean, in a looking glass. We are all foolish at times; and it should be remembered that, although Jonah was foolish, and wrong in certain respects, there is this redeeming trait in his character. We might never have known the story of his folly if he had not written it himself. It shows what a true-hearted man the prophet was, that he just unveiled his real character in this book. Biographies of men are seldom truthful, because the writers cannot read the hearts of those whom they describe; and if they could read them, they would not like to print what they would see there. But here is a man, inspired of God to write his own biography, and he tells us of this sad piece of folly, and does not attempt in the least degree to mitigate the evil of it.

3 **Therefore now, O Lord, take, I beseech thee, my life from me; for it is better for me to die than to live** "For, if I live, the Ninevites will say, 'This man scared us needlessly. He is a prophet of evil, and he is a liar, too, for our great city is not destroyed. He frightened us into a kind of repentance for which there was no necessity, for his God does not carry out his threatenings,'" and so forth. And poor Jonah could not face such talk as that. But, brother, if you preach God's Word as he gives it to you, you have nothing to do with the consequences that come of it. God will justify his own truth; and even if it should seem that the worst rather than the best consequences ensue, it is for you still to go on in the name of him who sent you. Whenever you and I begin to try to manage God's kingdom for him, we find the divine scepter too heavy for our little hands to hold; our case would be like that of Phaeton trying to drive the horses in the chariot of the sun.[2] We cannot hold the reins of the universe. And poor Jonah, wanting to manage everything for God, makes a dreadful mess of it, and in his anger makes a very foolish request: "O Lord, take, I beseech thee, my life from me."

2. A Greek myth that describes Phaethon, the son of Helios (the sun god), driving Helios's chariot in a catastrophic manner. —ed.

4 **Then said the Lord, Doest thou well to be angry?** How kind of God to speak thus gently to his rebellious servant. Are any of you given to anger? Might not the Lord say to you, "Do you well to be angry, so soon, so often, so long, about such little things?"

5 **So Jonah went out of the city** When, no doubt, everybody would have been willing to entertain him, for all, even to the king, must have felt a deep respect for the messenger who had brought them to their knees before the Lord.

and sat on the east side of the city, and there made him a booth, and sat under it in the shadow, till he might see what would become of the city To see those forty days out, half hoping, perhaps, that there would come an earthquake to shake the city down, and then, under his little booth of boughs, he would not be hurt by the falling edifices. In as sulky and surly a spirit as he could be, he put himself to great inconveniences. The damps of the night fell on him, and the heat of the sun would soon wither up the branches. If, dear friends, like Jonah, you want to complain, you will soon have something to complain of. People who are resolved to fret generally make for themselves causes for fretfulness. Those who are angry with God show the littleness of their minds.

6 **And the Lord God prepared a gourd** Let me call your attention to Jonah's comfort, that is, the gourd which God prepared. *It was sent to him when he was in a very wrong spirit*, angry with God, and angry with his fellow men. He had hidden away from everybody in that bit of a shanty which he had put up for himself outside the city, as if he was a real Timon the man-hater.[3] Sick of everybody, and sick even of himself, he gets away into this little booth, and there, in discontent and discomfort, he sits watching to see the fate of the city lying below the hill. Yet God comforted him by preparing a gourd to be "a shadow over his head, to deliver him from his grief."

3. *Timon of Athens* is a play written by William Shakespeare, wherein a wealthy man named Timon spends his money on his "friends," becomes poor, and rejects human companionship to live in a cave. —ed.

You know that we are very apt to say of some people, "Well, really, they are of such a trying disposition, they fret about nothing at all, and they worry themselves when they have no cause for it; we have no patience with them." That is what you say, but that is not how God acts. He does have pity upon such people, and he has had patience with many of you when you have been of the number of such people.

and made it to come up over Jonah It was a gourd, a broad-leaved plant, very probably the castor-oil plant, which botanists call *Palma Christi* because of its resemblance to the human hand. In its native country it grows very rapidly, so that it would speedily afford a welcome shade from the heat. Whatever kind of gourd it was, God prepared the plant, and it was exactly the kind to shield Jonah from the burning heat of the sun. The Lord always knows how to send us just the very comfort that we most require.

that it might be a shadow over his head, to deliver him from his grief This gourd, like all our comforts, was sent to Jonah *with an exceedingly kind design*, and God made it to come up "that it might be a shadow over his head, to deliver him from his grief." One would not have thought of a gourd delivering a man like that from his grief. It is an unmanly thing for a prophet of Jehovah to have a grief from which a gourd can deliver him, but God knew his servant, and in condescension He sent this singular form of comfort with this motive: "to deliver him from his grief." I think that Jonah, when he wrote this verse, must have smiled to himself, and thought, "All through the ages, what a fool they will think I was!" yet he went on and honestly put it down.

So, often, when you and I have been comforted by some mere trifle, and we have been very grateful for it, yet, looking back upon it, we have thought to ourselves, "What poor creatures we were to have been comforted by so small a thing! How foolish it seems for us first to have been put out by so little a matter, and then to have been comforted by something equally little!"

So Jonah was exceeding glad of the gourd God has often sent us mercies that have made us exceeding glad, and we have been delivered from the pressure of heavy grief. But here is the sad note in the history of Jonah, as it has often been with us also: although he was exceeding glad, *he does not appear to have been exceeding grateful*. It is one thing to be glad of a mercy; it is another matter to be grateful for that mercy. Sometimes a man spends all his time in rejoicing over the comfort, which then becomes idolatry, whereas he ought to have expended it in blessing God for the comfort, and then it would have shown that he was in a right state of heart. I do not read that Jonah thanked God for this gourd; possibly, no worm would have devoured it if he had done so. Our comforts are always safest when they are enveloped in gratitude. Let us overlay the wood of our comfort with the gold plate of our gratitude; so shall it be preserved. An ordinary comfort protected with a sheet of gratitude shall become to us a double means of grace.

7 **But God prepared a worm when the morning rose the next day** Jonah's great comfort was destroyed by *a very little thing*. It was only a worm, but that was enough to destroy the gourd. It was also, probably, *an unseen thing* that wrought this havoc. Very likely Jonah did not see that worm. God prepared it, but the prophet did not discern it until he saw the destruction it had caused. And, my dear friends, some little unseen thing may yet come to you, and turn into grief all your present joy.

and it smote the gourd that it withered *It was a very foul thing*, a worm, a maggot, at the root of this gourd, and through this foul thing it withered and died. People often think that there is no worm which can eat into their comfort, but God can prepare one, as he did in the case of the prophet. He as much prepared the worm as he prepared the gourd; he as much destroyed the comfort as he first of all gave it to his sorrowing servant.

This worm, which God had prepared, *did its work very speedily*. The gourd was destroyed in a night; when Jonah fell asleep, there it was over his head, guarding him from the bright beams of the moon; but when he woke in the morning, it hung shriveled and worn out, affording no protection whatever from the fierce rays of the sun.

Further, when God prepared the worm to destroy Jonah's gourd, *the result of its work was very sad.* It left the poor man without that which had made him exceeding glad, and he was as angry and distressed as before he had been rejoicing. I want you, dear friends, just to pause here to learn this lesson. It is God who sends your trials; do not get into your head the notion that your sickness or anything else that grieves you is from the devil. He may have a finger in it, but he is himself always under the supremacy of God. When Job is vexed and plagued by Satan, the arch-enemy cannot touch him anywhere till God gives permission.

ILLUSTRATION

Biting at the Stick

Preaching Themes: Providence of God, Suffering

God stands evermore at the back of all that happens; therefore, do not begin kicking at the secondary agent. You know that, if you strike a dog with a stick, he bites at the stick; if he were a sensible dog, he would try to bite *you*. If you quarrel with anything that happens, your quarrel is virtually with God himself. It is no use to quarrel with the Lord's agent, for it is God, after all, who sends you the affliction, and "he doth not afflict willingly nor grieve the children of men" (Lam 3:33).

---

8 **And it came to pass, when the sun did arise, that God prepared a vehement east wind** Jonah could not escape the fury of the wind, especially when his gourd was withered. This wind came from the east, which, according to our old proverb, is "neither good for man nor beast." But it came from the east most vehemently, and, at the same time, after the protecting

gourd was gone, the fierce rays of the sun beat upon Jonah's head, where he seems to have been weakest, though he probably thought himself to be strongest just there.

So, dear friends, *God may send you troubles on the back of one another*. The gourd is gone; now the east wind comes. Troubles seldom come alone, they usually fly in flocks, like martins [type of bird]; and it will often happen that one will come upon the back of another, and you will say to yourself, "Why does this trial come just now when I am least able to bear it?"

Sometimes, also, *troubles come very fiercely*. It was "a vehement east wind." It came like the rush of scorching heat out of the open door of an oven. It was like the Sirocco, a sultry wind burning up everything in its track. This wind came with all its might upon poor Jonah, and just so may fierce and fiery trials come at any time upon the dearest servants of God.

When Jonah went away out of the city, he seemed to say, "There, I will get away from men; I will not have anything more to do with them, they have always worried and troubled me. I will get quite alone; there I shall sit and enjoy myself, for I cannot enjoy anybody else." But the troubles came even there; indeed, Jonah had built his booth "on the east side of the city," just where he would be likely to feel the full force of the wind blowing from that quarter. In going there, he had not gone out of the realm of withered gourds, and he had not gone beyond the reach of the vehement east wind. Neither have you, dear friend, though you say, "I thought, when I left my last trying situation, I should get into a comfortable place." Yes, I will tell you when you will get into a comfortable place, if you are a Christian, and that is when you pass out of this world altogether.

and the sun beat upon the head of Jonah, that he fainted, and wished in himself to die Jonah was soon up, and soon down. Yesterday, he "was exceeding glad of the gourd"; today, he is fainting because of the heat of the sun. If we allow our mercies to become too sweet to us, they will soon become, by their withdrawal, too bitter for us. When we feel too much affection for the creature, we shall soon find a great deal of affliction from the creature.

and said, It is better for me to die than to live It is a popular notion that trials sanctify those who have to endure them, but by themselves they do not. It is a sanctified trial that sanctifies the tried one, but trial itself, alone and by itself, might make men even worse than they are. Here, for instance, is Jonah. His gourd is gone, and the sun's fierce heat beats upon him and makes him faint, and even to the Lord himself he says that he does well to be angry, even unto death. The trial was not sanctified to him while he was in it, and it often happens that "nevertheless afterward" is the time in which trials benefit us: "No chastening for the present seemeth to be joyous, but grievous: nevertheless afterward it yieldeth the peaceable fruit of righteousness unto them which are exercised thereby" (Heb 12:11). You may have ten thousand trials, and yet be none the better for them unless you cry to God to sanctify every twig of the rod, and to make the fury of the east wind or the burning rays of the sun to be a blessing to you.

It seems that, at the time, *this trial only revealed Jonah's folly*, for it appeared to make him pray very foolishly and talk very foolishly. His trials were like the tossing of the troubled sea, whose waters cast up mire and dirt. This vehement east wind threw up great masses of black seaweed upon the shore of Jonah's character and made the great sea of his heart roll up the foul mass of corruption that otherwise might have been hidden and still.

9 **And God said to Jonah, Doest thou well to be angry for the gourd?** Unless the Lord had put Jonah through this process, he could not so well have argued with his servant. So the gourd must go, and the wind must come, and the sun must beat upon the fainting prophet, and Jonah in his angry temper must get to feel great grief over his poor gourd which had met with such an untimely death, and then God comes to him and says, "Are you troubled about your gourd? Do you have pity on a gourd, and should I not have pity on a great city with more

than a hundred and twenty thousand helpless children within its walls, and all those thousands of unsinning cattle? Should I not spare these, when you would have spared this tender plant, which sprang up in a night, and withered in a night?"

And he said, I do well to be angry, even unto death He had got into such a bad spirit that he could even brave it out with his God. Oh, that we might be preserved from such an evil temper! It is well for us that, "Like as a father pities his children, so the Lord pities them that fear him" (Ps 103:13). When a child is in a fever, and says a great many naughty things, his father puts it down to the sickness rather than to the child. So it was with God's poor fainting servant Jonah.

ILLUSTRATION

One Surviving Child

Preaching Themes: Comfort, Idolatry

There is many a mother who has had only one of her children spared to her, but what a comfort that one child has been! I have heard one good woman say, "My dear daughter is such a joy to me, she is everything I could wish." Or it may be that God has sent to you some other form of earthly comfort, which has been altogether invaluable to you; it has been a screen from the great heat of your trouble, "a shelter in the time of storm." Whenever you get such an invaluable blessing, praise God for it. Do not let your gourd become your god, but let your gourd lead you to your God. When our comforts become our idols, they work our ruin; but when they make us bless God for them, then they become messengers from God, which help toward our growth in grace.

---

10 **Then said the Lord, Thou hast had pity on the gourd, for the which thou hast not laboured, neither madest it grow; which came up in a night, and perished in a night** Do we wonder when we are suddenly deprived of our earthly comforts? Are they not fleeting things? When they came to us, did we receive a lease of them, or were we promised that they should last forever? Jonah sat under his withered gourd wringing his hands and complaining of God, but if you and I had been there we might have said "What ails you, man? Are you surprised that gourds wither?" "I murmur," said he, "because I have lost the shade which screened me from the sun." "But, man, is it not the nature of a gourd to die? It came up in a night, do you marvel that it perished in a night? A worm at the root of a gourd surely is no novelty. O prophet, do not be angry with your God; this is what you should look for from such a growth." If our tents are spoiled, we should remember that they are tents, and not fortresses; curtains, and not bulwarks. The thief can readily enough enter and spoil the habitation which is made of such frail material.

11 **And should not I spare Nineveh** "Nineveh, for which I have labored; Nineveh, which I made to grow; Nineveh, which has been many years in the building; Nineveh, which contains multitudes of immortal souls which will not perish in a night."

that great city, wherein are more than sixscore thousand persons that cannot discern between their right hand and their left hand This is always supposed to mean infants, and I judge that the supposition is a correct one. So, Nineveh had a population of over one hundred and twenty thousand who were under two years old, so it must have been an immense city. Who can tell the blessing that even infants bring to us? It may be that God spares London for the sake of the children in it. What a deal the Lord Jesus Christ made of children! He suffered the little children to come unto him, and forbade them not (Matt 19:14; Mark 10:14; Luke 18:16). Does God care for children? Yes, that he does; and so should his servants! They are the better part of the human race. There is more in them that is admirable than there is in us who are grown up. They are, in many respects, a blessing to the city, as these six-score thousand little ones were to Nineveh.

11 **and also much cattle?** Does God care for cattle? He does. And how that fact should teach his servants to be kind to all brute creatures! There is some truth in those lines of Coleridge—

> "He prayeth best, who loveth best
> All things, both great and small,"[4]

for everything that lives should be the object of our care for the sake of him who gave them life; and if he has given us to have dominion over all sheep and oxen, and the birds of the air, and so forth, let not our dominion be that of a tyrant, but that of a kind and gentle prince who seeks the good of that which is under his power.

Here ends the story of Jonah, which he tells himself. He did not add anything to it because nothing needs to be added. The Lord's question to him was altogether unanswerable, and Jonah felt it to be so. Let us hope that, during the rest of his life, he so lived as to rejoice in the sparing mercy of God. He had stood outside the door, like the elder brother who was angry, and would not go in, and who said to his father, "Lo, these many years do I serve thee, neither transgressed I at any time thy commandment: and yet thou never gavest me a kid, that I might make merry with my friends: but as soon as this thy son was come, which hath devoured thy living with harlots, thou hast killed for him the fatted calf." But after his father had said to him, "Son, thou art ever with me, and all that I have is thine" (Luke 15:29–31), I hope that he went in, and I trust that Jonah also went in and lived with the penitent Ninevites, and that all were happy together in the love of the God who had been so gracious to them.

---

4. These lines are from *The Rime of the Ancient Mariner*. —ed.

APPLICATION

Is Anger Acceptable?

Anger is not always or necessarily sinful, but it has such a tendency to run wild that whenever it displays itself, we should be quick to question its character, with this inquiry: "Do you well to be angry?" It may be that we can answer, "YES." Very frequently anger is the madman's firebrand, but sometimes it is Elijah's fire from heaven. We do well when we are angry with sin because of the wrong which it commits against our good and gracious God, or with ourselves because we remain so foolish after so much divine instruction, or with others when the sole cause of anger is the evil they do. He who is not angry at transgression becomes a partaker in it. Sin is a loathsome and hateful thing, and no renewed heart can patiently endure it. God himself is angry with the wicked every day, and it is written in his Word, "Ye that love the Lord, hate evil" (Ps 97:10).

Far more frequently it is to be feared that our anger is not commendable or even justifiable, and then we must answer, "NO." Why should we be fretful with children, passionate with servants, and wrathful with companions? Is such anger honorable to our Christian profession, or glorifying to God? Is it not the old evil heart seeking to gain dominion, and should we not resist it with all the might of our newborn nature? Many professing Christians give way to temper as though it were useless to attempt resistance. But let the believer remember that he must be a conqueror in every point, or else he cannot be crowned. If we cannot control our tempers, what has grace done for us? Someone told Mr. Jay[5] that grace was often grafted on a crab-stump. "Yes," said he, "but the fruit will not be crabs." We must not make natural infirmity an excuse for sin, but we must fly to the cross and pray the Lord to crucify our tempers and renew us in gentleness and meekness after his own image.

God's Wisdom and Our Wisdom

I do not believe that any of us would have proposed to make a gourd grow up to cover the head of the angry prophet. We should much

5. Preacher William Jay, a mentor of Spurgeon's. —ed.

more likely have called a committee meeting, and we should have agreed that, if the discontented brother liked to go and live in a booth, he had better work the experiment out. It would probably be for his good and make him come back and live in the city properly, like other people! Though he was left to feel the cold by night, and the heat by day, it was entirely his own choice. And if a person chooses such a residence, it is not for us to interfere!

That is how men talk, and men are so exceedingly wise, you know; but that is not how God talks, and he is infinitely wiser than any of his creatures. His wisdom is sweetly loving, but ours sometimes curdles into hardness. What do you think, brothers and sisters, has not God sent us many comforts when we did not deserve them? When, on the contrary, we had made a rod for our own back, and might well have reckoned upon being made to smart? Yet God has sent us comforts which have relieved us of the sorrow which we foolishly brought upon ourselves and made us stay the fretfulness which was our own voluntary choice. God has been wonderfully tender with us, even as a mother is with her sick child. Have you not found it so, brothers and sisters? Well, now, look back upon your past life, and think that all the comforts which came to you when you deserved to be left without them, came from God, and for them all let his name be blessed.

Reason for Suffering

Sometimes, God puts us through an unusual experience in order that we may the better understand him; and sometimes that we may the better know ourselves. Men who are of a hard nature must have hard usage, diamond must cut diamond, that at last the purpose of the great Owner of the jewels may be accomplished.

Then, dear heart, with your sore afflictions, *God is preparing you to be a comforter to others*. You distressed and troubled one, God is training you that you may be a very Barnabas, the son of consolation, to the sons and daughters of affliction in times to come. I would suggest to some of you here who have to bear double trouble that God may be preparing you for double usefulness, or he may be working out of you some unusual form of evil which might not be driven out of you unless his Holy Spirit had used these mysterious methods with you to teach you more fully his mind.

Suffering Alone Does Not Make Us Holy

Unless the Spirit of God comes upon us in power, we shall not grow holy through our trials. Even if we were washed in a sea of fire, we should not lose an atom of our sin by suffering. No, the very flames of hell shall never purify a soul or purge away a single sin; he that is filthy shall even there be filthy still. There is nothing in suffering, any more than there is in joy, in and of itself, to make a man holy. That is the work of God, and of God alone, yet God overrules both our joy and our grief to accomplish his own divine purpose by his Spirit. It is God who sends the wind; so, once again, I want you to pause, and bow your heads before him who sends all your trouble. Do not be angry with God for what he does to you, but feel that it must be right even though it should tear everything away from you, though it should leave you a widow and houseless, though it should strip you, and though it should even slay you. God is God still; and the deeper your trouble, the greater are your possibilities of adoration; for, when you are brought to the very lowest, it is that, *in extremis*, you can raise the song *in excelsis*, out of the deepest depths you can praise the Lord to the very highest. When we glorify God out of the fires of fiercest tribulation, there is probably more true adoration of him in that melody than in the loftiest songs of cherubim and seraphim when they enjoy God, and sing out his praises in his presence above.

Sources

Song of Solomon 1:1–7

"Better than Wine (Song 1:2)," in *The Metropolitan Tabernacle Pulpit Sermons*, 42:157–67. London: Passmore & Alabaster, 1896.

"Christ's Estimate of the People (Song 4:10–11)," in *The New Park Street Pulpit Sermons*, 5:457–64. London: Passmore & Alabaster, 1859.

"The Church's Love to Her Loving Lord (Song 1:7)," in *The Metropolitan Tabernacle Pulpit Sermons*, 11:349–60. London: Passmore & Alabaster, 1865.

"Expositions by C. H. Spurgeon: Genesis 45:1–13; Song of Solomon 1:1–7; 3:1–5," in *The Metropolitan Tabernacle Pulpit Sermons*, 43:226–28. London: Passmore & Alabaster, 1897.

"Expositions by C. H. Spurgeon: Jonah 3; 4:1–2; and Romans 5." *The Metropolitan Tabernacle Pulpit Sermons*, 43:560–64. London: Passmore & Alabaster, 1897.

"Expositions by C. H. Spurgeon: Psalm 22:1–22; and Song of Solomon 1:1–7; 2:1–7." *The Metropolitan Tabernacle Pulpit Sermons*, 59:466–68. London: Passmore & Alabaster, 1913.

"Exposition by C. H. Spurgeon: Solomon's Song 1." *The Metropolitan Tabernacle Pulpit Sermons*, 42:285–88. London: Passmore & Alabaster, 1896.

"The Good Shepherdess" (Song 1:7–8). *The Metropolitan Tabernacle Pulpit Sermons*, 19:313–24. London: Passmore & Alabaster, 1873.

"The Memory of Christ's Love" (Song 1:4). *The Metropolitan Tabernacle Pulpit Sermons*, 39:62–69. London: Passmore & Alabaster, 1893.

"A Refreshing Canticle" (Song 1:4). *The Metropolitan Tabernacle Pulpit Sermons*, 48:409–20. London: Passmore & Alabaster, 1902.

"Rejoicing and Remembering" (Song 1:4). *The Metropolitan Tabernacle Pulpit Sermons*, 42:181–89. London: Passmore & Alabaster, 1896.

"Self-Humbling and Self-Searching" (Song 1:6). *The Metropolitan Tabernacle Pulpit Sermons*, 17:266–76. London: Passmore & Alabaster, 1871.

"The Unkept Vineyard; Or, Personal Work Neglected" (Song 1:6). *The Metropolitan Tabernacle Pulpit Sermons*, 32:693–700. London: Passmore & Alabaster, 1886.

Song of Solomon 1:8–17

"Exposition by C. H. Spurgeon: Solomon's Song 1." *The Metropolitan Tabernacle Pulpit Sermons*, 42:285–88. London: Passmore & Alabaster, 1896.

"A Bundle of Myrrh" (Song 1:13). *The Metropolitan Tabernacle Pulpit Sermons*, 10:133–44. London: Passmore & Alabaster, 1864.

"Fragrant Graces." *The Metropolitan Tabernacle Pulpit Sermons*, 61:476–80. London: Passmore & Alabaster, 1915.

"The Good Shepherdess" (Song 1:7–8). *The Metropolitan Tabernacle Pulpit Sermons*, 19:313–24. London: Passmore & Alabaster, 1873.

Song of Solomon 2:1–7

"The Apple Tree in the Wood" (Song 2:3). *The Metropolitan Tabernacle Pulpit Sermons*, 19:373–84. London: Passmore & Alabaster, 1873.

"The Best of the Best" (Song 2:1). *The Metropolitan Tabernacle Pulpit Sermons*, 42:313–23. London: Passmore & Alabaster, 1896.

"Expositions by C. H. Spurgeon: Psalm 116:10–19; Sol. Song 2:1–7." *The Metropolitan Tabernacle Pulpit Sermons*, 62:562–64. London: Passmore & Alabaster, 1916.

"Expositions by C. H. Spurgeon: Solomon's Song 2:1–7; 3:1–5." *The Metropolitan Tabernacle Pulpit Sermons*, 63:94–96. London: Passmore & Alabaster, 1917.

"Exposition by C. H. Spurgeon: Solomon's Song 2; and 3:1–5." *The Metropolitan Tabernacle Pulpit Sermons*, 42:479–80. London: Passmore & Alabaster, 1896.

"Heavenly Love-Sickness!" (Song 5:8). *The Metropolitan Tabernacle Pulpit Sermons*, 9:625–36. London: Passmore & Alabaster, 1863.

"The Lily among Thorns" (Song 2:2). *The Metropolitan Tabernacle Pulpit Sermons*, 26:133–44. London: Passmore & Alabaster, 1880.

"The Roes and the Hinds" (Song 2:7). *The Metropolitan Tabernacle Pulpit Sermons*, 25:145–46. London: Passmore & Alabaster, 1879.

"The Rose and the Lily" (Song 2:1). *The Metropolitan Tabernacle Pulpit Sermons*, 13:673–84. London: Passmore & Alabaster, 1867.

"Under the Apple Tree" (Song 2:3). *The Metropolitan Tabernacle Pulpit Sermons*, 57:217–25. London: Passmore & Alabaster, 1911.

"Underneath" (Deut 33:27). *The Metropolitan Tabernacle Pulpit Sermons*, 24:265–76. London: Passmore & Alabaster, 1878.

Song of Solomon 2:8–17

"The Believer's Glad Prospects" (Song 2:17). *The Metropolitan Tabernacle Pulpit Sermons*, 58:485–86. London: Passmore & Alabaster, 1912.

"The Best of All Is, God Is with Us" (1 Chron 22:18). *The Metropolitan Tabernacle Pulpit Sermons*, 42:301–9. London: Passmore & Alabaster, 1896.

"Darkness before the Dawn" (Song 2:17). *The Metropolitan Tabernacle Pulpit Sermons*, 42:373–81. London: Passmore & Alabaster, 1896.

"Exposition by C. H. Spurgeon: Solomon's Song 2, and 3:1–5." *The Metropolitan Tabernacle Pulpit Sermons*, 42:479–80. London: Passmore & Alabaster, 1896.

"The Interest of Christ and His People in Each Other" (Song 2:16). *The Metropolitan Tabernacle Pulpit Sermons*, 7:215. London: Passmore & Alabaster, 1861.

"Loved and Loving" (Song 2:16). *The Metropolitan Tabernacle Pulpit Sermons*, 27:698–700. London: Passmore & Alabaster, 1881.

"Over the Mountains" (Song 2:16–17). *The Metropolitan Tabernacle Pulpit Sermons*, 58:293–96. London: Passmore & Alabaster, 1912.

"A Sermon for Spring" (Song 2:10–13). *The Metropolitan Tabernacle Pulpit Sermons*, 8:109–20. London: Passmore & Alabaster, 1862.

"A Song among the Lilies" (Song 2:16). *The Metropolitan Tabernacle Pulpit Sermons*, 20:481–92. London: Passmore & Alabaster, 1874.

"The Tender Grapes" (Song 2:13). *The Metropolitan Tabernacle Pulpit Sermons*, 42:409–19. London: Passmore & Alabaster, 1896.

Song of Solomon 3:1–5

"The Disconsolate Lover" (Song 3:1–4). *The Metropolitan Tabernacle Pulpit Sermons*, 61:529–38. London: Passmore & Alabaster, 1915.

"Expositions by C. H. Spurgeon: Genesis 45:1–13; and Song of Solomon 1:1–7; and 3:1–5." *The Metropolitan Tabernacle Pulpit Sermons*, 43:226–28. London: Passmore & Alabaster, 1897.

"Expositions by C. H. Spurgeon: Solomon's Song 2:1–7; 3:1–5." *The Metropolitan Tabernacle Pulpit Sermons*, 63:94–96. London: Passmore & Alabaster, 1917.

"Love's Vigilance Rewarded" (Song 3:4). *The Metropolitan Tabernacle Pulpit Sermons*, 42:469–78. London: Passmore & Alabaster, 1896.

"The Real Presence, the Great Want of the Church" (Song 3:4–5). *The Metropolitan Tabernacle Pulpit Sermons*, 18:85–96. London: Passmore & Alabaster, 1872.

Song of Solomon 3:6–11

"The Royal Pair in Their Glorious Chariot" (Song 3:6–11). *The Metropolitan Tabernacle Pulpit Sermons*, 8:661–71. London: Passmore & Alabaster, 1862.

"Paved with Love" (Song 3:10). *The Metropolitan Tabernacle Pulpit Sermons*, 19:541–52. London: Passmore & Alabaster, 1873.

Song of Solomon 4:1–16

"Christ's Estimate of His People" (Song 4:10–11). *The New Park Street Pulpit Sermons*, 5:457–64. London: Passmore & Alabaster, 1859.

"Come, My Beloved!" (Song 8:14). *The Metropolitan Tabernacle Pulpit Sermons*, 40:217–25. London: Passmore & Alabaster, 1894.

"Exposition by C. H. Spurgeon: Solomon's Song 4." *The Metropolitan Tabernacle Pulpit Sermons*, 56:513–16. London: Passmore & Alabaster, 1910.

"Fragrant Spices from the Mountains of Myrrh," in *The Sword and the Trowel* (1865): 62–67.

"Grace for Communion." *The Metropolitan Tabernacle Pulpit Sermons*, 33:37–40. London: Passmore & Alabaster, 1887.

"The Lord's Own View of His Church and People (Song 4:12)," in *The Metropolitan Tabernacle Pulpit Sermons*, 33:206–16. London: Passmore & Alabaster, 1887.

"'My Garden'—'His Garden' (Song 4:16)," in *The Metropolitan Tabernacle Pulpit Sermons*, 42:349–57. London: Passmore & Alabaster, 1896.

"Nearness to God (Eph 2:13)," in *The Metropolitan Tabernacle Pulpit Sermons*, 15:37–48. London: Passmore & Alabaster, 1869.

"A Secret and Yet No Secret (Song 4:12, 15)," in *The Metropolitan Tabernacle Pulpit Sermons*, 8:49–60. London: Passmore & Alabaster, 1862.

Song of Solomon 5:1–8

"Asleep and Yet Awake—A Riddle (Song 5:2)," in *The Metropolitan Tabernacle Pulpit Sermons*, 26:553–64. London: Passmore & Alabaster, 1880.

"Heavenly Love-Sickness (Song 5:8)," in *The Metropolitan Tabernacle Pulpit Sermons*, 9:625–36. London: Passmore & Alabaster, 1863.

"The King Feasting in His Garden (Song 5:1)," in *The Metropolitan Tabernacle Pulpit Sermons*, 16:133–44. London: Passmore & Alabaster, 1870.

"Morning, August 22 (Song 5:8)," in *Morning and Evening: Daily Readings*. London: Passmore & Alabaster, 1896.

"Nearer and Dearer (Song 5:2–8)," in *The Metropolitan Tabernacle Pulpit Sermons*, 14:61–72. London: Passmore & Alabaster, 1868.

Song of Solomon 5:9–16

"The Best Beloved, (Song 5:16)," in *The Metropolitan Tabernacle Pulpit Sermons*, 24:661–72. London: Passmore & Alabaster, 1878.

"Christ's Perfection and Precedence (Song 5:10)," in *The Metropolitan Tabernacle Pulpit Sermons*, 42:385–94. London: Passmore & Alabaster, 1896.

"Evening, October 28 (Song 5:11)," in *Morning and Evening: Daily Readings*. London: Passmore & Alabaster, 1896.

"The Immutability of Christ (Heb 13:8)," in *The New Park Street Pulpit Sermons*, 4:41–48. London; Glasgow: Passmore & Alabaster, 1858.

"The Incomparable Bridegroom and His Bride (Song 5:9)," in *The Metropolitan Tabernacle Pulpit Sermons*, 42:277–85. London: Passmore & Alabaster, 1896.

"Lessons from Christ's Baptism (Matt 3:16–17)," in *The Metropolitan Tabernacle Pulpit Sermons*, 58:181–90. London: Passmore & Alabaster, 1912.

"Spices, Flowers, Lilies, and Myrrh (Song 5:13)," in *The Metropolitan Tabernacle Pulpit Sermons*, 42:397–408. London: Passmore & Alabaster, 1896.

Song of Solomon 6:1–13

"The Chariots of Ammi-Nadib (Song 6:12)," in *The Metropolitan Tabernacle Pulpit Sermons*, 20:61–72. London: Passmore & Alabaster, 1874.

"The Church as She Should Be (Song 6:4)," in *The Metropolitan Tabernacle Pulpit Sermons*, 17:193–204. London: Passmore & Alabaster, 1871.
"Come, My Beloved! (Song 8:14)," in *The Metropolitan Tabernacle Pulpit Sermons*, 40:217–25. London: Passmore & Alabaster, 1894.
"Fragrant Spices from the Mountains of Myrrh," in *The Sword and the Trowel* (1865): 62–67.
"Heavenly Love-Sickness (Song 5:8)," in *The Metropolitan Tabernacle Pulpit Sermons*, 9:625–36. London: Passmore & Alabaster, 1863.
"Inward Conflicts (Song 6:13)," in *The Metropolitan Tabernacle Pulpit Sermons*, 10:561–72. London: Passmore & Alabaster, 1864.
"Overcoming Christ (Song 6:5)," in *The Metropolitan Tabernacle Pulpit Sermons*, 42:481–90. London: Passmore & Alabaster, 1896.
"'Return, Return, O Shulamite; Return, Return!' (Song 6:13)," in *The Metropolitan Tabernacle Pulpit Sermons*, 30:433–44. London: Passmore & Alabaster, 1884.
"The Secret of Health (Ps 42:11)," in *The Metropolitan Tabernacle Pulpit Sermons*, 21:181–92. London: Passmore & Alabaster, 1875.
"A Song among the Lilies (Song 2:16)," in *The Metropolitan Tabernacle Pulpit Sermons*, 20:481–92. London: Passmore & Alabaster, 1874.

Song of Solomon 7:1–13

"A Call for Revival (Song 7:11–13)," in *The Metropolitan Tabernacle Pulpit Sermons*, 18:457–68. London: Passmore & Alabaster, 1872.
"Fragrant Spices from the Mountains of Myrrh," in *The Sword and Trowel* (1865): 62–67.
"Good Works in Good Company (Song 7:11–13)," in *The Metropolitan Tabernacle Pulpit Sermons*, 10:705–16. London: Passmore & Alabaster, 1864.
"A Gross Indignity (Matt 27:30)," in *The Metropolitan Tabernacle Pulpit Sermons*, 60:205–13. London: Passmore & Alabaster, 1914.
"Growth in Grace (2 Pet 3:18)," in *The Metropolitan Tabernacle Pulpit Sermons*, 46:529–40. London: Passmore & Alabaster, 1900.
"The Palm Tree," in *The Sword and the Trowel* (1877): 50–55.
"Shoes for Pilgrims and Warriors (Eph 6:15)," in *The Metropolitan Tabernacle Pulpit Sermons*, 55:217–26. London: Passmore & Alabaster, 1909.
"The Shortest of the Seven Cries (John 19:28)," in *The Metropolitan Tabernacle Pulpit Sermons*, 24:217–28. London: Passmore & Alabaster, 1878.

Song of Solomon 8:1–10

"Fragrant Spices from the Mountains of Myrrh," in *The Sword and the Trowel* (1865): 62–67.
"God's Work in Man (Hos 2:16–17)," in *The Metropolitan Tabernacle Pulpit Sermons*, 45:313–24. London: Passmore & Alabaster, 1899.
"Leaning on Our Beloved (Song 8:5)," in *The Metropolitan Tabernacle Pulpit Sermons*, 15:349–60. London: Passmore & Alabaster, 1869.

"Love and Jealousy (Song 8:6)," in *The Metropolitan Tabernacle Pulpit Sermons*, 62:277–88. London: Passmore & Alabaster, 1916.

"The Redeemer's Prayer (John 17:24)," in *The New Park Street Pulpit Sermons*, 4:185–92. London: Passmore & Alabaster, 1858.

"The Shortest of the Seven Cries (John 19:28)," in *The Metropolitan Tabernacle Pulpit Sermons*, 24:217–28. London: Passmore & Alabaster, 1878.

"The Shulamite's Choice Prayer (Song 8:6–7)," in *The Metropolitan Tabernacle Pulpit Sermons*, 7:129–34. London: Passmore & Alabaster, 1861.

"Unpurchasable Love (Song 8:7)," in *The Metropolitan Tabernacle Pulpit Sermons*, 42:241–51. London: Passmore & Alabaster, 1896.

Song of Solomon 8:11–14

"The Bridegroom's Parting Word (Song 8:13)," in *The Metropolitan Tabernacle Pulpit Sermons*, 29:217–28. London: Passmore & Alabaster, 1883.

"Christ's Love for His Vineyard (Song 8:12)," in *The Metropolitan Tabernacle Pulpit Sermons*, 48:301–12. London: Passmore & Alabaster, 1902.

"Come, My Beloved! (Song 8:14)," in *The Metropolitan Tabernacle Pulpit Sermons*, 40:217–25. London: Passmore & Alabaster, 1894.

Jonah 1:1–3

"Exposition by C. H. Spurgeon: Jonah 1," in *The Metropolitan Tabernacle Pulpit Sermons*, 51:106–8. London: Passmore & Alabaster, 1905.

"Runaway Jonah, and the Convenient Ship (Jonah 1:3)," in *The Metropolitan Tabernacle Pulpit Sermons*, 36:589–602. London: Passmore & Alabaster, 1890.

"Travelling Expenses on the Two Great Roads (Jonah 1:3)," in *The Metropolitan Tabernacle Pulpit Sermons*, 11:181–92. London: Passmore & Alabaster, 1865.

"Who Can Tell? (Jonah 3:9)," in *The New Park Street Pulpit Sermons*, 5:401–8. London: Passmore & Alabaster, 1859.

Jonah 1:4–7

"Exposition by C. H. Spurgeon (Jonah 1)," in *The Metropolitan Tabernacle Pulpit Sermons*, 51:106–8. London: Passmore & Alabaster, 1905.

"Sleepers Aroused (Jonah 1:5)," in *The Metropolitan Tabernacle Pulpit Sermons*, 50:469–79. London: Passmore & Alabaster, 1904.

"The Voice behind Thee (Isaiah 30:21)," in *The Metropolitan Tabernacle Pulpit Sermons*, 28:421–32. London: Passmore & Alabaster, 1882.

"What Meanest Thou, O Sleeper? (Jonah 1:5–6)," in *The Metropolitan Tabernacle Pulpit Sermons*, 8:505–18. London: Passmore & Alabaster, 1862.

Jonah 1:8–17

"Exposition by C. H. Spurgeon (Jonah 1)," in *The Metropolitan Tabernacle Pulpit Sermons*, 51:106–8. London: Passmore & Alabaster, 1905.

"The Fainting Soul Revived (Jonah 2:7)," in *The Metropolitan Tabernacle Pulpit Sermons*, 62:205–14. London: Passmore & Alabaster, 1916.
"Jonah's Object-Lessons (Jonah 4:6–8)," in *The Metropolitan Tabernacle Pulpit Sermons*, 43:73–82. London: Passmore & Alabaster, 1897.
"Labour in Vain (Jonah 1:12–13)," in *The Metropolitan Tabernacle Pulpit Sermons*, 10:241–52. London: Passmore & Alabaster, 1864.
"The Valley of the Shadow of Death (Psalm 23:4)," in *The Metropolitan Tabernacle Pulpit Sermons*, 27:229–40. London: Passmore & Alabaster, 1881.

Jonah 2:1–5

"Exposition by C. H. Spurgeon (Jonah 2)," in *The Metropolitan Tabernacle Pulpit Sermons*, 54:346–48. London: Passmore & Alabaster, 1908.
"The Fainting Soul Revived (Jonah 2:7)," in *The Metropolitan Tabernacle Pulpit Sermons*, 62:205–14. London: Passmore & Alabaster, 1916.
"Jonah's Object-Lessons (Jonah 4:6–8)," in *The Metropolitan Tabernacle Pulpit Sermons*, 43:74–82. London: Passmore & Alabaster, 1897.
"Jonah's Resolve, or 'Look Again!' (Jonah 2:4)," in *The Metropolitan Tabernacle Pulpit Sermons*, 30:662–70. London: Passmore & Alabaster, 1884.

Jonah 2:6–10

"David's Prayer in the Cave (Psalm 142)," in *The Metropolitan Tabernacle Pulpit Sermons*, 38:541–49. London: Passmore & Alabaster, 1892.
"Exposition by C. H. Spurgeon (Jonah 2)," in *The Metropolitan Tabernacle Pulpit Sermons*, 54:346–48. London: Passmore & Alabaster, 1908.
"The Fainting Soul Revived (Jonah 2:7)," in *The Metropolitan Tabernacle Pulpit Sermons*, 62:205–14. London: Passmore & Alabaster, 1916.
"A Plain Talk upon an Encouraging Topic (Jonah 2:7)," in *The Metropolitan Tabernacle Pulpit Sermons*, 54:337–46. London: Passmore & Alabaster, 1908.
"Present Privilege and Future Favour (Deuteronomy 33:27)," in *The Metropolitan Tabernacle Pulpit Sermons*, 11: 205–16. London: Passmore & Alabaster, 1865.
"Salvation of the Lord (Jonah 2:9)," in *The New Park Street Pulpit Sermons*, 3:194–99. London: Passmore & Alabaster, 1857.

Jonah 3:1–10

"Exposition by C. H. Spurgeon (Jonah 3; 4:1–2; Romans 5)," in *The Metropolitan Tabernacle Pulpit Sermons*, 43:560–62. London: Passmore & Alabaster, 1897.
"Prayer Certified of Success (Luke 11:9–10)," in *The Metropolitan Tabernacle Pulpit Sermons*, 19:25–36. London: Passmore & Alabaster, 1873.
"The Queen of Sheba, (Matt 12:42)," in *The Metropolitan Tabernacle Pulpit Sermons*, 59:193–203. London: Passmore & Alabaster, 1913.

"Runaway Jonah, and the Convenient Ship (Jonah 1:3)," in *The Metropolitan Tabernacle Pulpit Sermons*, 36:589–602. London: Passmore & Alabaster, 1890.

"War! War! War! (1 Samuel 18:17)," in *The New Park Street Pulpit Sermons*, 5:203–8. London: Passmore & Alabaster, 1859.

"Who Can Tell?," in *The New Park Street Pulpit Sermons*, 5:401–8. London: Passmore & Alabaster, 1859.

Jonah 4:1–11

"Exposition by C. H. Spurgeon (Jonah 3; 4:1–2; Romans 5)," in *The Metropolitan Tabernacle Pulpit Sermons*, 43:560–62. London: Passmore & Alabaster, 1897.

"Exposition by C. H. Spurgeon (Jonah 4)," in *The Metropolitan Tabernacle Pulpit Sermons*, 43:82–84. London: Passmore & Alabaster, 1897.

"Jonah's Object-Lessons (Jonah 4:6–8)," in *The Metropolitan Tabernacle Pulpit Sermons*, 43:73–82. London: Passmore & Alabaster, 1897.

"Morning, July 13," in *Morning and Evening: Daily Readings*. London: Passmore & Alabaster, 1896.

"Sudden Sorrow (Jeremiah 4:20, 30)," in *The Metropolitan Tabernacle Pulpit Sermons*, 23:385–96. London: Passmore & Alabaster, 1877.

Scripture Index

Old Testament

New Testament

Index of Illustrations by Theme